Gus Grissom

The Lost Astronaut

Virgil I. "Gus" Grissom, one of America's original seven Mercury astronauts, gave his life for the American space program in the Apollo 1 fire on January 27, 1967.

INDIANA BIOGRAPHY SERIES

Gus Grissom

The Lost Astronaut

RAY E. BOOMHOWER

GENERAL EDITORS

RAY E. BOOMHOWER, KATHLEEN M. BREEN, AND PAULA J. CORPUZ

INDIANA HISTORICAL SOCIETY PRESS

INDIANAPOLIS 2004

© 2004 Indiana Historical Society. All rights reserved.
Reprinted 2005, 2006
This book is a publication of the
Indiana Historical Society Press
450 West Ohio Street
Indianapolis, Indiana 46202-3269 USA
www.indianahistory.org
Telephone orders 1-800-447-1830
Fax orders 317-234-0562
Orders online @ shop.indianahistory.org

Portions of this book previously appeared in the spring 1996 issue of
Traces of Indiana and Midwestern History.

Library of Congress Cataloging-in-Publication Data

Boomhower, Ray E., 1959–
  Gus Grissom : the lost astronaut / Ray E. Boomhower.
    p. cm. — (Indiana biography series)
  Includes bibliographical references.
  ISBN 0-87195-176-2 (hardcover : alk. paper)
    1. Grissom, Virgil I. 2. Astronauts—United States—Biography. I. Title.
  II. Series.

TL789.85.G7B66 2004
629.45'0092—dc22
  [B]   2004047577

Printed in Canada

This one is for my father, Walter R. Boomhower, with gratitude for that trip to Spring Mill State Park that helped introduce me to Gus Grissom and the American space program.

"We choose to go to the moon in this decade and do the other things, not because they are easy, but because they are hard, because that goal will serve to organize and measure the best of our energies and skills, because that challenge is one that we are willing to accept, one we are unwilling to postpone, and one which we intend to win."

—*John F. Kennedy, September 12, 1962, Rice University, Houston, Texas*

"If we die, we want people to accept it. We're in a risky business, and we hope that if anything happens to us it will not delay the program. The conquest of space is worth the risk of life."

—*Virgil I. "Gus" Grissom*

TABLE OF CONTENTS

THERE SEEMS TO BE SOMETHING ABOUT THE AMERICAN SPACE program that attracts members of the Boomhower family. My experience writing a biography of Gus Grissom is not the first time my family has been associated with the men who rode American rockets into space. On March 16, 1966, astronauts Neil A. Armstrong and David R. Scott blasted off from Cape Kennedy in Florida for their *Gemini 8* mission, which involved docking with an Agena target vehicle already in orbit around the Earth. Approximately six and a half hours after liftoff, the astronauts successfully docked with the Agena. Shortly after docking, however, the Gemini spacecraft experienced a violent roll (later blamed on a stuck thruster) that could only be controlled by activating the reentry control system. Such a maneuver necessitated an emergency landing at a secondary recovery area in the Pacific Ocean southeast of the island of Okinawa.

Just three hours after their splashdown, the astronauts and their capsule were safely aboard the USS *Leonard F. Mason*, a destroyer originally commissioned in 1945 and whose homeport was in Yokosuka, Japan. Serving onboard the *Mason* that day was my uncle, Cliff Boomhower Sr., a chief petty officer in charge of the ship's ASROC antisubmarine warfare weapon. "I believe the ship was off of Okinawa when we got word of the coming splashdown," according to my uncle. "The *Mason* was old and never had been pushed passed twenty-seven knots. But this day the engines were pushed at full speed with turns for thirty knots." Cliff recalled how the ship vibrated as it made its way to the astronauts' location and remembered the "surprise of Scott and Armstrong as they stepped out of the capsule [and] onto the deck of the *Mason*."

The excitement experienced by my uncle in helping rescue two American heroes (as all astronauts were in those days) is matched by the thrill I felt in talking and dealing with the many people who had a hand in making this book possible. Gus Grissom's family and friends were more than eager to talk about the astronaut and shared my belief that his story is one worth telling to a new generation that knows little about his illustrious career. Grissom's wife Betty spoke to me for several hours in her Houston home, sharing stories of her life with Gus and her two sons as an air force wife and as a "celebrity" in the heady early days of the American space program. Norman Grissom, surrounded by mementoes of his famous brother's career at the *Mitchell Tribune* office, reminisced about growing up in the small southern Indiana town and the excitement and tragedy of Gus's spaceflights.

Three of Gus's friends offered me rare insights into the astronaut's life. Grissom's childhood friend Bill Head drove me around Mitchell recounting tales of his youth and subsequent years with Gus, a man Head and his children considered to be a member of the family. I learned more about the men and machines who pushed the country into space through the good graces of longtime National Aeronautics and Space Administration engineer Sam Beddingfield, who seemed to have as much work packed into his retirement as he did in his career working on the Mercury, Gemini, Apollo, and Space Shuttle programs. Former Indianapolis 500 champion Jim Rathmann shared stories of flying and driving with Gus from his Chevrolet dealership in Melbourne, Florida, particularly the pranks the astronauts enjoyed playing on one another. All of these men offered this author a fuller picture of Gus's life and character.

Any biographer or historian is dependent upon the paper trail left by his subject, and the men and women who guard those documents in archives and repositories around the world. For their cheerful and willing assistance to my endeavors, I thank Shelly Henley Kelly, archivist for NASA's Johnson Space Center History and Oral History Collection at the University of Houston–Clear Lake, and Elaine Liston, archivist at the John F. Kennedy Space Center. Both of these women offered useful information and helpful guidance in conducting my research for this book.

At the Indiana Historical Society, Susan Darnell tirelessly transcribed my hours of interviews with those who knew Gus. In the William Henry Smith Memorial Library, Susan Sutton cheerfully dealt with my frequent requests for illustrations. The IHS Press staff, particularly senior editor Paula Corpuz and assistant editor Kathleen Breen, made sure that I would not make a fool of myself with sloppy writing or shoddy grammar. The goal of any editor should be to assist the author in achieving his task of communicating more effectively with the reader. Paula and Kathy reached that goal with this book. Any errors you might find between these covers are mine and mine alone.

Of course, the person to thank for all of this is my father, Walter R. Boomhower, who introduced me, as it were, to Gus with that trip to Spring Mill State Park so many years ago. Thanks Dad! Also, as with every one of my other books, my wife Megan McKee served as my inspiration. She's simply the best friend this writer has ever had.

1

The Hero

I WANTED TO BE AN ASTRONAUT, A STAR VOYAGER. AS DID MANY who grew up during the hectic 1960s, I became captivated by the adventures of the American space program. Dreaming of traveling among the stars, I often sat in the Mary Phillips Elementary School's library in Mishawaka listening to an album containing the sounds of National Aeronautics and Space Administration missions, and even constructed models of the gigantic Saturn 5 rocket for my school's science fair (I remain disappointed to this day at capturing only an honorable mention award for my display). On the evening of July 20, 1969, I strained to stay awake in order to watch on television as Neil Armstrong became the first person to walk on the moon and to hear him utter the now famous words: "That's one small step for [a] man, one giant leap for mankind." Space fever still gripped me a few years later when my family took a vacation to Spring Mill State Park, which is located near Mitchell, Indiana. What impressed me on that trip was not

Indiana governor Edgar D. Whitcomb speaks at the dedication of the Grissom Memorial at Spring Mill State Park in 1971. Behind Whitcomb are (left to right) Dennis and Cecile Grissom, the astronaut's parents, and their daughter, Wilma Beavers.

the park's Pioneer Village, with its restored log cabins and working gristmill, or the blind fish swimming in Donaldson's Cave, but rather a simple, low-slung structure near the park's entrance: the Virgil I. "Gus" Grissom Memorial.

Formally dedicated by Indiana governor Edgar D. Whitcomb in 1971, the memorial pays tribute to the Mitchell-born Grissom, one of the nation's seven original astronauts, the second American to go into space, the first

2

person to travel into space twice, and one of the first in NASA's space effort—along with *Apollo 1* crewmates Edward White and Roger Chaffee—to die, when a fire swept through the spacecraft during a test at Cape Kennedy early on the evening of January 27, 1967. To a space nut like me, the Grissom memorial was heaven. My two brothers and I eagerly explored the interior of Grissom's *Gemini 3* two-man capsule, which the astronaut had named after the title character in the Broadway musical *The Unsinkable Molly Brown*, about a woman who helped save a number of her shipmates on the ill-fated RMS *Titanic*. Naming the capsule after that character, Grissom reasoned, might help avert a calamity such as the one that befell him when his *Liberty Bell 7* Mercury capsule sank at the conclusion of his 1961 spaceflight. Also impressive to my young eyes was the memorial's Universe Room, which included a six-foot-in-diameter illuminated globe that rotated as a tape of Grissom and his ground-control cohorts during his Gemini flight played in the background. To this Hoosier, Gus Grissom has always been a full-blooded American hero.

To some, however, Grissom is not now remembered as such. Both Tom Wolfe's best-selling *The Right Stuff*, published in 1979, and the movie of the same name based on that book have implied that Grissom panicked—had, in test-pilot parlance, "screwed the pooch"—at the end of his approximately fifteen-minute Mercury spaceflight. Whether Grissom accidentally brushed against the plunger that triggered the hatch's firing or purposefully pushed it, the book and movie blamed him for causing the hatch to blow off the capsule, which allowed the craft to take on water and sink like a stone to the bottom of the Atlantic Ocean. Grissom's explanation of "I was lying there, flat on my back—and it just blew," was met, according to Wolfe, by a healthy amount of skepticism from space-agency officials and Grissom's test-pilot brethren. "The damned things had been wrung inside out, but never, so far as anyone could recall, had a single hatch ever 'just blown,'" Wolfe noted.[1] Both author Wolfe and film director Philip Kaufman found their hero in Chuck Yeager, World War II fighter ace and the first man to break the sound barrier; Grissom became the goat.

Wolfe's assertions about Grissom's panicky behavior after the Mercury flight and the depiction of Grissom in the movie as a bit of an oaf were met with anger and dismay by Mitchell residents, who had turned out by the thousands to cheer their local hero at a special Memorial Day parade following his Gemini flight in 1965. "The Gus Grissom that Mitchell knows is not the Gus Grissom that's depicted in the movie," said Bill Jenkins, who owned the theater where the movie played in Mitchell. "They just wanted to make a movie and they needed a little excitement, so they picked on Gus, probably because he's dead and the others are still alive." Don Caudell, who worked for years to build the rocket-shaped memorial honoring Grissom that now stands on the site of the astronaut's former elementary school, spoke for many

4

Grissom during his heyday as one of the country's astronaut heroes.

residents of the town when he said he worked so hard on behalf of the project not because of Grissom's tragic death, but rather because of his achievements. "He came from the ground up and, by his own efforts, he got to a place where people hadn't been before," Caudell said of the astronaut. "That's what made him special."[2]

Bill Head, another Mitchell resident, sees the rise of his childhood friend to worldwide renown as a success story comparable to that of another notable southern Indiana native son: Abraham Lincoln. Living in Mitchell during the height of the Great Depression, Head noted that he and Grissom's future seemed "damned dim. What did we have to look forward to?" The shocking thing to Head is not that both Grissom and Lincoln were raised in small-town Indiana, but that they "got out" and made something of themselves in the larger world outside of the Hoosier State. "He was in the right place at the right time with the right background," Head said of his friend. What's more, once Grissom became famous, said Head, he never forgot where he had come from. When early press accounts about the reaction to Grissom being named an astronaut were datelined Bedford, Grissom, Head pointed out, made sure that subsequent reports used Mitchell instead. "He put Mitchell on the map," he said. Head's description of his friend is in stark contrast to the portrayal in Wolfe's book of Grissom as one in a long line from the Midwest and elsewhere who "prostrated themselves daily in thanksgiving" at having escaped "the gray little town they came from."[3]

Others in the southern Indiana area were so inspired by Grissom's example that they too went on to careers in the American space program. Bedford, Indiana, native Charles D. Walker, a Purdue University graduate, NASA's first industrial payload specialist, and a veteran of three Space Shuttle missions, noted that he did not believe he could have accomplished what he has done in his life if it were not for Grissom. "He was my hero," said Walker. "He was somebody from home." Although born in Portsmouth, Virginia, Kenneth D. Bowersox graduated from Bedford High School in 1974 and considers the Lawrence County community to be his hometown. Growing up in the area with the memory of Grissom still fresh in the mind of many helped reinforce the Space Shuttle veteran's belief that he could accomplish whatever he wanted to do in his life. "I never thought I couldn't be an astronaut," said Bowersox. "It didn't hurt having Charlie Walker and Gus Grissom as examples that it really is possible to go and be an astronaut no matter what size community or high school you went to."[4]

Grissom also had his defenders among his fellow astronauts and NASA engineers, who claimed that the Korean War pilot, veteran of one hundred combat missions, had nothing to do with the hatch mishap. Wolfe's insinuations of panic on Grissom's part were way off base according to Gordon Cooper, one of the country's original seven astronauts. "He [Grissom] did not screw up and lose his spacecraft," Cooper said. "Later tests showed the hatch could

INDIANAPOLIS STAR

Brothers Jim and Tim Phipps walk past the stone rocket memorial in Grissom's hometown of Mitchell, Indiana. The memorial sits on the site of the astronaut's former elementary school.

malfunction, just as Gus said it did." Sam Beddingfield, a NASA engineer responsible for the pyrotechnics and recovery system on the Mercury capsule and a friend of Grissom's who believed in the astronaut's courage and poise, thoroughly investigated the incident and discovered ways in which the hatch could have blown in the manner described by Grissom.[5] Lead recovery helicopter pilot for the *Liberty Bell 7* flight, Jim Lewis, said years after the capsule's sinking that in his mind Grissom remained a great pilot. "When people say that Grissom panicked and blew the hatch," said Lewis, "I say he was a smart man. He was a test pilot. Nobody is going to look outside and see water at their eyeballs and open the door."[6] Even the actor who played the unlucky astronaut in the movie *The Right Stuff*, Fred Ward, expressed doubt about Grissom blowing the hatch on purpose. Ward learned that all the astronauts who did blow their hatches suffered a bruised hand, and Grissom's hand remained unmarked after his flight. "I think NASA sort of pointed the finger at him to take the blame off themselves for losing the capsule," the actor said. "I don't think he was responsible at all."[7]

Although the hatch incident still haunts Grissom's reputation today, it failed to harm his career with NASA. While the Mercury program continued to send men into space, Grissom moved on to work on the space agency's next project: Gemini. His influence on the design of the two-man spacecraft was so strong that his fellow astronauts dubbed it the Gusmobile. "Gus really had a big hand in everything, from the way the cockpit was laid out to what instruments went where," said John Young, Grissom's crewmate on *Gemini 3*, the first manned flight of the new craft. Fellow astronauts might have complained about the cramped crew compartment (modeled after Grissom's short height), but many shared Pete Conrad's sentiment when he compared Gemini's flight characteristics to that of "a high-performance fighter."[8]

NASA officials must have been pleased with Grissom's work on Gemini as he was selected as commander of the first Apollo flight, which became the ill-fated *Apollo 1*. If all had gone well with that assignment, the Mitchell-born flier was in line for another milestone—becoming the first man to walk on the moon. Donald K. "Deke" Slayton, one of the original seven astronauts who later picked crews as head of the astronaut office, said he and Robert Gilruth, director of the Manned Spacecraft Center in Houston, had agreed before the *Apollo 1* tragedy that if possible a Mercury astronaut would have first crack at walking on the moon. "And at that time Gus was the one guy from the original seven who had the experience to press on through to the [moon] landing," said Slayton. If Grissom had lived he, and not Armstrong, might have been the one remembered in history books for being the first human to stand on another world.[9]

Even without the historic distinction that would have come with being the first to plant a footprint on the moon's surface, Grissom and his life (particularly the continuing mystery of *Liberty Bell 7*'s hatch) have inspired the imagination of dreamers, deep-sea explorers, actor-scientists, and others. The film *Star Trek III: The Search for Spock*, released in 1984, featured an Oberth class Starfleet science vessel named in honor of the lost astronaut, the USS *Grissom*. In May 1999, Curt Newport, a veteran deep-sea explorer, found Grissom's spacecraft lying three miles down on the bottom of the Atlantic Ocean about three hundred miles southeast from where it was launched. Unable to raise the capsule due to the loss of the submersible craft *Magellan*, Newport returned to the site in July and successfully hoisted the *Liberty Bell 7* (minus its hatch) off the ocean floor, thirty-eight years after it became the only American manned space-craft to be lost following a successful mission. The operation ended nearly fifteen years of research and planning by Newport, whose expedition was financed and filmed by the Discovery Channel. Although the Kansas Cosmosphere and Space Center restored the capsule and sent it on a nation-wide tour, it failed to find a definitive answer to the blown-hatch mystery. For the hit CBS television series *CSI: Crime Scene Investigation*, which premiered in 2000, the lead char-acter from the show, forensic scientist Gil Grissom, had been set to be named Gil Scheinbaum. The actor playing the role, William L. Petersen, however, was such a fan of the astronaut that he had the name of his character changed to Grissom.[10]

The astronaut is also still revered in the Hoosier State. To commemorate the end of the twentieth century, the

NASA

Grissom prepares to enter his Liberty Bell 7 *spacecraft for his suborbital Mercury mission on July 21, 1961.*

Indianapolis Star in December 1999 announced an effort to name the ten greatest Hoosiers of the past century. Approximately 6,000 readers cast their opinion in what the *Star* called "one of the largest reader participation projects in the newspaper's history." When all the ballots were counted, Grissom, the son of a railroad worker, ranked fifth in the voting, placing behind such legendary figures as businessman Eli Lilly, poet James Whitcomb Riley, war correspondent Ernie Pyle, and composer Cole Porter, and ahead of such great names as songwriter Hoagy Carmichael, comedian Red

Skelton, businesswoman Madam C. J. Walker, basketball star Larry Bird, and former Indianapolis Motor Speedway owner Tony Hulman.[11]

Grissom's appeal continues into the twenty-first century. In September 2003, the astronaut's widow Betty, joined by sons, Scott and Mark, attended ceremonies in Mitchell dedicating Gus's home as a museum. "Gus Grissom was a pioneer in spaceflight, and we hope that by restoring his boyhood home, we hope it can show kids growing up here that they can come from middle-class America and accomplish something," said Mark Hartzell, chairman of Virgil I. Grissom Memorial Inc. The astronaut also continues to serve as an inspiration for those who hope to explore further into space. "He's one of the people that decided to take a chance and try this thing called spaceflight, and he died trying," said Adam Butt, a Purdue University student who dreamed of traveling to Mars. "It's the kind of mentality, that pioneer mentality, that I really attach to." If Butt ever makes it to Mars, he could visit hills bearing the astronaut's name. In late January 2004 NASA announced it had named the hills surrounding its Mars Exploration Rover *Spirit*'s landing site in Gusev Crater for the *Apollo 1* crew—Grissom Hill, Chaffee Hill, and White Hill. "Through recorded history, explorers have had both the honor and responsibility of naming significant landmarks," said NASA administrator Sean O'Keefe. "Gus, Ed, and Roger's contributions, as much as their sacrifice, helped make our giant leap for mankind possible. Today,

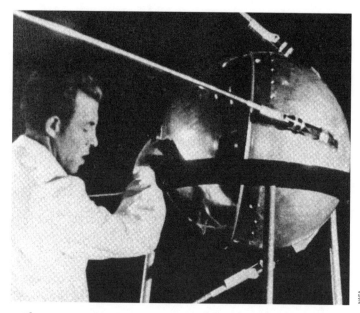

NASA

The Soviet Union's Sputnik *is shown here on a rigging truck in the assembly shop in the fall of 1957 as a technician puts finishing touches on the Earth-orbiting satellite.*

as America strides towards our next giant leap, NASA and the Mars Exploration Rover team created a fitting tribute to these brave explorers and their legacy."[12]

The wildly differing viewpoints of Grissom as a man and as a pilot over the years can be seen in part as a reflection of the times. Upon his selection as an astronaut in 1959, the United States was engaged in a seemingly desperate struggle for survival with the Soviet Union—a country that had beaten America into space two years before with its *Sputnik* (a "traveling companion" or "fellow traveler") satellite. The Russian success, followed shortly by launching a dog into orbit, shocked the American public, which, as historian William Manchester noted, seemed to believe that this country held a monopoly on technological advances.[13] "Until that time," said Sherman Adams, a key adviser to President Dwight Eisenhower, "nobody in Washington had really given much consideration to the possible importance of an invasion of space as psychological propaganda or even as a scientific achievement."[14] But the launch of *Sputnik* meant that the Soviet Union had developed an intercontinental ballistic missile that could threaten American cities with nuclear annihilation.

The Eisenhower administration attempted to downplay the Russian achievement, but both the public—and the Democratic opposition in Congress—clamored for action. "Control of space means control of the world, far more totally than any control that has ever or could ever be achieved by weapons, or troops of occupation," warned then–U.S. Senate majority leader Lyndon B. Johnson. "Whoever gains that ultimate position gains control, total control, over the earth, for the purposes of tyranny or for the service of freedom."[15] When asked for his comment on *Sputnik*, Adams, in a remark quoted widely in the media, claimed that the administration was not interested in gaining a high score in an outer-space basketball game. Adams later noted that he was only trying to follow the president's wish for calm, but did note that his comment "seemed to be

*America's Vanguard rocket explodes on the launchpad
on December 6, 1957.*

an overemphasis on the de-emphasis."[16]

When the United States attempted to match the Communists' achievements, it floundered badly. In July 1955 the White House had announced plans to launch a small Earth-orbiting satellite in observation of the International Geophysical Year (established by the International Council of Scientific Unions as July 1, 1957, to December 31, 1958, a time of high solar activity). For the mission, the Defense Department selected the Naval Research Laboratory's as yet undeveloped Project Vanguard, which won out over Wernher von Braun's team of German engineers at the Army Ballistic Missile Agency at Redstone Arsenal.[17] On December 6, 1957, before a host of reporters and a live television audience, an American Viking rocket rose only a few feet off its launching pad at Cape Canaveral, Florida, before disaster struck. Witnessing the launch from the relative safety of the blockhouse, located about three hundred feet from the pad, Kurt Stehling, head of the project's propulsion group, noticed flame shooting from the side of the rocket near the engine. "The vehicle agonizingly hesitated for a moment," said Stehling, "quivered again, and in front of our unbelieving, shocked eyes, began to topple." The rocket broke apart and struck the ground with a roar that could be felt by scientists safe behind the blockhouse's two-foot-thick concrete wall and six inches of bulletproof glass. "For a moment or two there was complete disbelief. I could see it in the faces. I could feel it myself. This just couldn't be," Stehling noted.[18]

Not everything went wrong with Project Vanguard. The grapefruit-size satellite survived the explosion, landed in some nearby scrub grass, and its transmitters began to faithfully broadcast its radio signals. The sight and sound of the forlorn American scientific apparatus prompted columnist Dorothy Kilgallen to ask, "Why doesn't someone go out there, find it, and kill it?"[19] Newspaper headlines across the country heaped scorn upon the effort, with the *Chicago Sun-Times's* cleverly reading, "Oh, What a Flopnik," and the *San Francisco News* calling the fiasco a "Cold War Pearl Harbor." *Time* magazine suggested that the satellite program be renamed "Project Rearguard." America's humiliation became complete at the United Nations when the Soviet delegation offered the United States financial aid as part of a Russian program to aid less-developed nations.[20]

Although the United States finally managed to place an object in space with *Explorer 1* onboard a Juno rocket on January 31, 1958, the American public still itched to overtake its Soviet foes in the space race. When the newly created National Aeronautics and Space Administration presented the country's original astronauts—Grissom, Slayton, and Cooper from the U.S. Air Force; Malcom Scott Carpenter, Walter M. Schirra Jr., and Alan B. Shepard from the U.S. Navy; and John H. Glenn Jr. from the U.S. Marines—at a 2:00 p.m. press conference on April 9, 1959, in Washington, D.C., the assembled members of the media actually applauded and cheered—an ovation that stunned the astronauts.

NASA

The three men responsible for the success of America's first Earth satellite, launched on January 31, 1958. At left is Dr. William H. Pickering, former director of the Jet Propulsion Laboratory, which built and operated the satellite. Dr. James A. Van Allen, center, designed and built the instrument that discovered the radiation belts circling the Earth. At right is Dr. Wernher von Braun, leader of the Army's Redstone Arsenal team that built the Redstone rocket.

"I've never seen anything like it, before or since," said Slayton, a veteran flyer from World War II. Loudon Wainwright, a reporter for *Life* magazine, which had signed the astronauts and their wives to an exclusive contract for their personal stories, described the seven men in a 1961 book as "perhaps the most adventurous, the most thoroughly courageous, the best-rounded group of explorers ever assembled anywhere at any time."[21]

The press's enthusiasm merely reflected the public's high regard for the brave pilots ready to risk their lives aboard America's finicky rockets, which showed an alarming tendency to immolate themselves on the launching pad. Becoming the country's newest heroes, noted Slayton, happened "without us doing a damned thing" except appear at a news conference, a situation the air force veteran termed as "crazy."[22] The esteem in which the astronauts were held was highlighted by the reaction of one audience to a speech given by Grissom, not known among the astronaut corps for his loquaciousness. Speaking before approximately eighteen thousand workers at General Dynamics in San Diego, where the Convair Division was building the Atlas rocket, Grissom uttered just three words: "Do good work." The Hoosier's remarks, perhaps the shortest pep talk in history, prompted the crowd to scream its approval so loudly that Grissom and other dignitaries were almost knocked off the stage.[23]

Grissom's taciturn nature was no secret to the other members of the astronaut corps. On weekends he and

Slayton would often climb aboard a jet and fly around the country. Glenn noted that when the two men flew on these coast-to-coast excursions they probably "made the least talkative flights ever made by two people anywhere." Even Grissom and Slayton joked about the silence, dubbing their flights as being "East Coast to West Coast in ten words or less."[24] Grissom always seemed uncomfortable with the public attention, particularly from the press, that came from being an astronaut. The negative publicity following his *Liberty Bell 7* flight only hardened his media shyness and led him to do whatever he could to blend into the woodwork. "As far as I know," said CBS television anchorman Walter Cronkite, "he was the only astronaut ever to don [a] disguise to duck the waiting press." Cronkite also remembered that Grissom faced the media responsibilities associated with a spaceflight with much more apprehension than the flight itself, and his answers to the press's questions were "cryptic and laconic." On one occasion when Grissom was set to board a commercial flight in Orlando, Florida, to visit an air force installation in Texas, he donned a disguise that included a floppy straw hat and sunglasses. When Grissom asked Slayton for his opinion about his outfit, the astronaut deadpanned: "You look just like Gus Grissom in dark glasses and a hat." In spite of his friend's skeptical assessment, Grissom managed to slip by the reporters and photographers who were lying in wait for him at the Orlando airport, a small victory that pleased the astronaut no end.[25]

For the most part, however, the astronauts faced a friendly response from the press. With the benefit of hindsight, Wainwright later reflected that he and the other staff members from *Life* came to their assignment with a different mindset than usual when reporting a story. "We had virtually abdicated skepticism," he said. "Possibly our attitudes had to do with the general innocence of the period or with a more ordinary need for heroes. Yet, from top to bottom, the *Life* group stood in some real awe of the Mercury pilots and were pretty wide-eyed about their mission." Also, because the magazine had bought the astronauts' stories, it and its staff were not looking to cause any problems with NASA. The *Life* team of reporters, editors, and photographers took upon themselves "the responsibility of telling the story in a positive way, one that would reflect credit on the men and the space program," said Wainwright. They believed it was their duty to protect what had become an extremely valuable national asset. He added that NASA was all too willing to aid in that effort as a way to win public acceptance, and increased government funding, for its program. All of these factors helped turn the reporters from observers to cheerleaders, Wainwright noted, and the interests of "patriotism and successful publishing seemed somehow to meld together . . . in a warm, red-white-and-blue glow."[26]

The public, too, was more than ready to embrace the astronauts, perhaps to counteract the swelling panic that gripped the nation following the Soviet Union's space triumphs. Faced with a public looking for heroes and a media unwilling to report on any negative personal qualities, there soon developed the "myth of the super-hero astronaut," noted *Apollo 7* veteran Walter Cunningham, who along with Donn Eisele and Schirra served as the backup crew to Grissom's *Apollo 1* flight. Most of the astronauts found the attention both flattering and easy to get along with, said Cunningham, but few could actually live up to the image projected by the media and NASA. "We weren't all simon-pure nor all hell-raisers," Cunningham noted in his book about the astronauts, aptly titled *The All-American Boys*. The great deeds accomplished by the American space program were "fulfilled by men who were all too human in their weaknesses as well as their strengths," he wrote.[27]

The myth of the super-hero astronaut endured for many years, egged on by continuing progress with the Mercury and Gemini programs and the promise of fulfilling President John F. Kennedy's goal of sending a man to the moon and returning him safely to Earth before the end of the decade with the mighty Apollo project. The deaths of Grissom, Chaffee, and White, however, came just before one of the most tumultuous times in the country's history. The year 1968 saw the launch of the Tet Offensive by the North Vietnamese against South Vietnam and its American allies, the assassinations of Martin Luther King Jr. and Robert Kennedy, large-scale riots by African Americans in a number of large cities, and police and protestors clashing at the Democratic National Convention in

Chicago. With the escalating involvement of American troops in Vietnam, NASA had to endure severe cuts in its budget, which fell from $5.17 billion in 1966 to $3.3 billion in 1972. Following *Apollo 11*'s achievement of a moon landing in 1969, the space agency found it harder and harder to find support in Congress for its programs, with the planned missions of *Apollo 18*, *Apollo 19*, and *Apollo 20* eliminated.[28]

As NASA suffered budget limitations—why spend more money on space when the United States had already beaten the Russians to the moon?—America's space heroes had their own problems. Fueled by the legacy of Vietnam and Watergate, the American media refused as it once did to turn a blind eye to the peccadilloes of those in the public eye, politicians and astronauts alike. Wolfe's critically acclaimed *The Right Stuff* not only penetrated the closed world of the test-pilot, fighter-jock fraternity, but it also laid bare the astronauts' extracurricular activities of "Drinking & Driving & the rest," complete with "juicy little girls" bragging about their sexual liaisons with the original seven astronauts by "going around saying, 'Well, four down, three to go!'"[29] But even before Wolfe's book, some astronauts had admitted their failings to the public. In his book Cunningham told about the "astronaut groupies" who worked hard to add as many space travelers to their scorecard as possible. Still, as a group the astronauts, Cunningham estimated, were no better or worse than the national average when it came to infidelity. "It is even possible, under the circumstances," he noted, "that our behavior was better than the gossip and suspicion implied." After all, astronauts had far more temptations facing them than the average businessman did.[30]

The deconstruction of the astronaut hero continued when Wolfe's book was made into a 1983 movie, which was written and directed by Kaufman. Originally, veteran Hollywood screenwriter William Goldman, who wrote screenplays for such films as *Butch Cassidy and the Sundance Kid* and *All the President's Men*, had been selected by United Artists producers Robert Chartoff and Irwin Winkler to pen the film's script. At the time Goldman became involved with the project (November 1979), radical Iranian students had seized as hostages diplomats and other employees of the American embassy in Iran. For the first time in his career, Goldman wrote in his book *Adventures in the Screen Trade*, he wanted to write a film that had a message. "I wanted to 'say' something positive about America," said Goldman. "Not patriotic in the John Wayne sense, but patriotic none the less." By telling the story of the astronauts, the screenwriter hoped to impart to viewers that "America was still a great place, and not just to visit."[31]

That effort came to naught when Kaufman, who had directed the critically acclaimed *Invasion of the Body Snatchers* (1978), was brought on board as director. The two men's ideas about the film clashed at once. When Goldman told Kaufman about his plans for producing a patriotic movie, the director blanched. Kaufman, according to Goldman, had been won over by Wolfe's depiction of Yeager as the country's greatest pilot, an iconic figure head and shoulders above all other flyers. "Phil's heart was with Yeager. And not only that," said Goldman, "he [Kaufman] felt the astronauts, rather than being heroic, were really minor leaguers, mechanical men of no particular quality, not great pilots at all, simply the product of hype." What Kaufman wanted to say, Goldman noted, was that America might have been a great country at one time, but those days were long gone. According to Kaufman, the story of Yeager was "the essence of what Tom Wolfe's book was about. It's about searching for the origin of that special quality. Whatever you may want to call it—grace under pressure—a kind of secret quality that was passed on from one generation of test pilots to the next." Goldman did not share the director's vision for the film and left the project.[32]

Kaufman's view of Yeager as being superior in ability to the men who eventually became astronauts permeates the film. One scene that typifies Kaufman's viewpoint comes when two hapless governmental representatives, played with comic aplomb by Jeff Goldblum and Harry Shearer, arrive at Edwards Air Force Base in the California desert to recruit test pilots for the new American space program. Walking into a local bar where the pilots congregate—Pancho's Happy Bottom Riding Club—the men and the program they represent are greeted with disdain by such top test pilots as Yeager and Scott Crossfield. "What you need," says Yeager, played by Sam Shepard, "is a little lab rabbit to curl up inside your

26

damn capsule with his heart going pitter-patter and a wire up the kazoo. I don't hold with it." Of course, the government does not want the "best" test pilots; Yeager is ineligible for the astronaut program because he did not attend college and Crossfield, as a civilian, failed to have the proper security clearance. Instead of the top pilots, the government had to, according to Kaufman, take such second-rate flyers as Grissom and Cooper. Cooper, played by Dennis Quaid, even acknowledges the disparity of talent between the two groups, noting to his friend Grissom, "Well, there sure is a long line of shit-hot rocket aces around here. A long line."[33] Why not attempt to jump ahead in line by volunteering for a project that had the potential for becoming a high priority with the nation's leaders?

Neglected in Kaufman's version of events are the many accomplishments of the pilots selected as astronauts, and the fact that while they were at Edwards both Grissom and Cooper were not in direct competition with Yeager, but *students* at the air force's test-pilot school there. After graduation, Grissom left Edwards for an assignment at Wright-Patterson Air Force Base near Dayton, Ohio. He was flying jets there when President Eisenhower decided in 1958 to draw upon the ranks of approximately five hundred military test pilots for the new astronaut corps. NASA's Space Task Group was pleased to have such qualified men to pick from, believing as it did that the eventual success of a mission could well depend on a pilot's actions in space. As Slayton notes in

NASA

The seven original Mercury astronauts join Wernher von Braun (far right) in inspecting the Mercury-Redstone hardware at the Fabrication Laboratory of the Army Ballistic Missile Agency in 1959.

his autobiography, some of the astronauts certainly did not have the same professional achievements to compare with test pilots such as Yeager and Crossfield. Others in the program, however, had solid test-flight credentials: both Schirra and himself had done frontline test flying, Shepard had been one of the first navy flyers to land on an angled-deck carrier, and Grissom had been involved with all-weather testing at the Wright Air Development Center at Wright-Patterson Air Force Base. "None of this was as spectacular as flying the X-

1, of course, but ninety percent of the test pilots in America never got close to stuff like that, anyway," Slayton said. "We were working test pilots who happened to get selected."[34]

Whatever the opinion on the piloting skills of the original astronauts, they achieved their mission in spite of a run of bad luck that would have daunted lesser men. Grounded during the Mercury program due to an irregular heartbeat, Slayton stayed the course, eventually becoming chief of flight-crew operations for NASA and finally making it into space as part of the crew for the Apollo-Soyuz Test Project mission in 1975. Shepard, the first American in space aboard *Freedom 7*, earned his nickname as the "Icy Commander" several times over after Ménière's syndrome, an inner-ear disorder, kept him from flying more missions and he took over for Slayton as head of the astronaut office. Given new life by a radical medical procedure that cured his inner-ear imbalance, Shepard, too, made it back into space, walking on the moon as commander of the *Apollo 14* mission.[35]

None of the original astronauts, however, endured Grissom's string of calamities and bad luck. In addition to the brouhaha and finger pointing over *Liberty Bell 7*'s blown hatch, he also suffered the embarrassment of being reprimanded by NASA officials and Congress for accepting and taking a few bites from a corned-beef sandwich smuggled aboard *Gemini 3* by crewmate John Young (thoughtfully provided by prankster Schirra from a Cocoa Beach delicatessen). Years later, with the hatch controversy still dogging his career,

Grissom became a forceful voice against using an explosive hatch on *Apollo 1*—a device that might have saved the crew from the toxic gases that killed them. Given Grissom's rotten luck as an astronaut, it seemed almost inevitable that someone would try to blame him for causing, at that time, NASA's worst disaster. One North American Aviation engineer hypothesized that Grissom had accidentally scuffed the insulation of a wire while moving about the spacecraft, which led to a spark and the subsequent fire. This hypothesis was immediately rejected by the NASA review board and a congressional committee investigating the Apollo tragedy.

Throughout his career, however, Grissom never let his misfortunes stand in the way of his stated purpose for accepting such dangerous assignments—patriotism. "If my country has decided that I'm one of the better qualified people for the mission, then I'm glad I can participate," he told a reporter from *Life* magazine.[36] For a short time, Grissom even considered leaving NASA to join other air force pilots in flying missions in the Vietnam War (a pilot friend warned him that Vietnam was nothing like Korea). Instead of returning to air combat, Grissom continued to strive to put America on the moon, giving his life in the process and earning a hero's burial at Arlington National Cemetery in Virginia, with the service broadcast nationwide on television. Neighbors from Mitchell joined President Johnson, members of Congress, and fellow astronauts at the funeral. It took NASA more than a year after the *Apollo 1* accident, during which time the spacecraft was extensively reworked, to launch another manned mission. *Apollo 7*, commanded by Grissom's friend Schirra, made 163 orbits during its eleven-day mission in the redesigned command module; America was back on its way to the moon. Years later, after six successful landings on the moon, Betty Grissom, reflecting on her husband, said: "I hate it that Gus is gone, but I guess the program was worth it. He wouldn't have had it any other way."[37]

2

Mitchell

LOCATED JUST A FEW MILES FROM DAYTON, OHIO, WRIGHT-Patterson Air Force Base served as one of the country's largest centers for aeronautical research and development during and after World War II. In the late 1950s, Capt. Virgil I. "Gus" Grissom, a veteran pilot who had flown a full tour complement of combat missions with the 334th Fighter-Interceptor Squadron in the Korean War, found himself stationed at the 8,400-acre base test flying a wide variety of the air force's jet fighters, a job that Grissom "thoroughly enjoyed."[1] One afternoon in January 1959 Grissom wandered into his squadron's operation office only to be greeted by the adjutant on duty with the question, "Gus, what kind of hell have you been raising lately?" A perplexed Grissom responded that as far as he knew, he had done nothing to merit such attention, although he wondered if perhaps he had failed to salute some self-important general. What had prompted the adjutant's question was a teletype message to Grissom's attention, marked top secret, ordering him to report to Washington, D.C. "What really intrigued me was the order that I should wear civilian clothing," noted Grissom. "By now I was as mystified as the adjutant, and the mystery wasn't much clarified by the instruction that I should discuss this assignment with no one. Just be there, and no questions asked."[2]

Returning to his home at 280 Green Valley Drive in Enon, Ohio, a Dayton suburb, to pack for his trip, Grissom did discuss his "weird orders" with his wife, Betty. Thinking of the most outlandish possibility she could, Betty asked her husband (prophetically as it turned out): "What are they going to do? Shoot you up in the nose cone of an Atlas [rocket]?"[3] Dressed in his best civilian suit, Grissom faithfully reported to the Washington address he had been given for interviews and briefings on this secret project. At the address he met a man who told him he worked with a government security agency and that he would soon be taken to a room with other people. Told not to discuss what his job was, Grissom became convinced that he "had wandered right into the middle of a James Bond novel." The mystery deepened as the Hoosier flyer was ushered into a large reception room packed with other men trying desperately to make small talk. It did not take long for Grissom and the others to figure out that they all shared the same occupation: test pilot. Finally, after undergoing private interviews filled with "all sorts of odd-ball questions," Grissom learned that he and the other test pilots were being considered for the fledgling American space program.[4]

Just a month before, on December 17, 1958, T. Keith Glennan, administrator of the new National Aeronautics and Space Administration, had announced that America's manned satellite program would be named Project Mercury. To find astronauts for the project, NASA had turned to the military services, with a committee screening the service records of 508 graduates of test-pilot school. Of that number, 110 met NASA's minimum requirements, including Grissom. Passing his initial screening in Washington, Grissom, and 31 other volunteers, accepted an invitation to undergo an extensive physical evaluation at both the Lovelace Foundation Clinic in New Mexico and the Wright Aerospace Medical Laboratory in Ohio.[5] Finally, on April 13, 1959, Grissom received the following orders: "Captain Virgil I. Grissom is relieved from assignment directorate of flight and all-weather testing, headquarters Wright Air Development Center [and is] assigned to Central Control Group, Headquarters USAF, Washington, D.C. with permanent duty station Langley Research Center, Langley Air Force Base, Virginia, for duty with the National Aeronautics and Space Administration Space Task Group." Not bad for a railroader's eldest son who may have built his share of model airplanes as a boy, but did not consider himself a "flying fanatic."[6]

✧ ✧ ✧

The rugged beauty and rolling hills of southern Indiana may be a scenic wonderland for visitors, but for residents the landscape has offered another attribute: a way to earn a living. The area is home to the famed Indiana building-stone district or "stone belt," a two-mile wide, thirty-mile-long strip running north to Putnam County and south to Owen, Monroe, Lawrence, Washington, Orange, and Crawford Counties. The first Lawrence County man to realize the potential offered by this natural building material—oolitic limestone—was Dr. Winthrop Foote, a Bedford physician, who operated the Blue Hole quarry on the eastern edge of that city in the early 1830s and brought the first stonecutter, a man named Toburn, to the area.[7]

The commercial market for limestone—described by one architect as "that astonishing material"—remained limited until the 1870s, due in large part to difficulties in transportation and competition from other building materials. Major fires in Chicago and Boston, combined with a revival of Gothic and Romanesque architecture styles, helped to increase limestone sales from 339,000 cubic feet in 1877 to approximately 5.5 million in 1896.[8] Eventually, limestone quarried in Indiana graced such notable examples of American architecture as the Empire State Building in New York, the Tribune Tower in Chicago, and the Pentagon and National Cathedral in Washington, D.C.

Other industries also contributed to the growth of communities in Lawrence County. For Mitchell, laid out in 1853 and incorporated as a town on December 23, 1864, the railroad—the Ohio and Mississippi Railway, to be exact—served as the impetus for its creation. The community was named for

Limestone quarry, Bedford, Indiana.

Main Street, Mitchell, Indiana.

Ormsby McKnight Mitchel, who served as chief engineer for the railroad's construction. Mitchel, an accomplished mathematician and astronomer who died while serving in the Union army during the Civil War, surveyed and platted the area that the town would occupy. The extra "l" in the town's name came later, compliments of a government clerk in Washington, D.C., who entered the town's name incorrectly. The town's early residents, as one local historian noted, became accustomed to the slow passage (it took all day to reach New Albany from Mitchell) of trains "with their balloon shaped smoke stacks and their canvas covered bow topped cabins which were about the size and shape of an ordinary wagon bed."[9]

Mitchell, which became a city on July 29, 1907, received

another economic boost in 1902 when the Leigh Portland Cement Company of Pennsylvania—attracted by the area's limestone and slate beds—opened a mill in the city. The firm added a second plant in 1905, and by 1916 it employed approximately 700 workers with a monthly payroll of more than $40,000. During its busy season, the cement operation shipped via the railroad 12,000 barrels of its product every day. A vibrant economy helped the community attract newcomers, and from 1900 to 1910 Mitchell's population doubled in size. Economic good news continued in later years as Ralph H. Carpenter, a Lawrence County blacksmith, came to Mitchell in 1918 and began producing school buses. The colorful product made by his business, later known as Carpenter Body Works, became a familiar sight for anyone driving into the community along State Road 37.[10]

In spite of the promise of good wages with the cement and bus companies, there were others who were drawn to Mitchell by the promise of steady work with the railroads. One of these men was Dennis D. Grissom, who had been born in nearby Martin County on October 14, 1903, the son of John and Melissa Stroud Grissom. In 1921 Grissom moved to Mitchell, where he began a forty-seven-year career with the Baltimore and Ohio Railroad, maintaining the line's signal system. His son, Norman Grissom, speculated that his father might have even lied about his age to obtain his job, "which people did routinely back then."[11] Three years after moving to the city, Dennis married Cecile King.

At about eight o'clock in the evening on April 3, 1926, at the couple's home on Sixth Street in Mitchell, Cecile gave birth by the light of a kerosene lamp to her first son (a previous child, a girl, had died in infancy), whom she and her husband named Virgil Ivan Grissom. Eventually, the Grissom family numbered four children, with Virgil joined by sister Wilma and brothers Norman and Lowell. A year after Virgil's birth, the Grissom family moved to an unpretentious wood-frame house on Baker Street (later renamed Grissom Street in the astronaut's honor). The house contained three bedrooms, a living room, kitchen, and bathroom. "It was very small for four kids to grow up in," noted Norman.[12] Reflecting on those years as the breadwinner for a growing family during the height of the Great Depression, Dennis said that he "worked six days a week at 50 cents an hour. Men got laid off all around me. I worried I'd be next, but at $24 a week, my family was well off."[13]

Mitchell proved to be a quiet place for Virgil Grissom to grow up in. The diminutive Grissom (the smallest astronaut at five feet, seven inches tall) later described his hometown as "small and unhurried," the kind of midwestern town where a person would not be surprised to run across Penrod and Sam, two of Hoosier author Booth Tarkington's famous characters. As the economic depression tightened its grip on the nation, the Grissom family, as did other families in the community, pinched pennies. The Grissom children became used to working in the family's garden, the produce from which their

Hamer's Mill, Spring Mill State Park, Mitchell, Ind.

Hamer's Mill at Spring Mill State Park.

mother canned for the winter months. Dennis Grissom and his brother raised a hog together, which they slaughtered in the fall for its meat. For entertainment, the Grissom children had the luxury of enjoying the woods and trails at nearby Spring Mill State Park. Although his family was "far from rich," Virgil remembered enjoying a "warm, comfortable family life," which was buttressed by his parents' strong religious beliefs.[14]

There existed in railroading families a long tradition of sons following in their parent's footsteps, but Virgil recalled no such pressures from his father. "In truth," said Virgil, "he encouraged us to think about some other careers in which he felt there were better chances of getting ahead."[15] Perhaps

Dennis had something like that in mind when the family took a ride one Sunday summer afternoon to Vincennes where Virgil enjoyed his first trip in an airplane. "He wasn't interested in becoming a pilot or anything back then," said the elder Grissom. "He just wanted to go ahead and fly in an airplane." The trip, however, must have made some impression on Virgil, as later he traded an air rifle for another ride, this time on a plane at the Bedford airport.[16]

To earn pocket money for attending movies and buying soft drinks at the Cargas Candy Kitchen on Main Street, Grissom delivered the *Indianapolis Star* in the morning and the *Bedford Times* in the evenings. For his *Star* deliveries, Grissom had to rise at four in the morning, riding his bicycle downtown to pick up his newspapers at Mitchell's bus station. The young newspaper deliveryman escaped some of the bitter cold of winter thanks to a kindly shoe cobbler, who gave Grissom a key to his shop, allowing him to fold his newspapers in comfort. Summer vacations from school for Grissom meant working at orchards in the area picking cherries and thinning apples and peaches at twenty-five cents per tree. His other jobs included working at a service station and clerking at the Mitchell Meat Market and Otha Fletcher's Clothing Store. "You can bet he didn't waste his money," noted his father. "Like several of the boys [in Mitchell] he worked at whatever he could get and saved all he could."[17]

In addition to his various jobs, Grissom, in those days known to his friends as "Greasy," also kept busy as a member

42

of Beaver Patrol of Boy Scout Troop 46, an association that almost cost him his life. One day while at a Boy Scout cabin near Mitchell, Grissom and his friends were busy practicing tying knots, an essential skill for any self-respecting scout. Jokingly rigging a hangman's noose, the youngsters slipped it over Grissom's head, threw the other end of the rope over a rafter, and pulled to see whether or not the knot would hold. It did; his face had already turned blue by the time his friends could release him. Years later at Purdue University, Grissom, during a much safer form of recreation—a card game—garnered a much more pleasant moniker than "Greasy." According to the story, a friend of Grissom's, looking at a scorecard upside down, mistakenly read "Gris" as "Gus." The nickname stuck.[18]

Reportedly equipped with an IQ of 145, Grissom was nevertheless, he later admitted, not much of a "whiz" in school. "I guess it was a case of drifting and not knowing what I wanted to make of myself."[19] His parents, however, remember that their son always brought home good report cards and stayed out of trouble. "We always knew where he was. There was a time to come in and he knew that was it," said Grissom's father. "We knew where he was going and what time he would be home."[20] Virgil's high school principal, George Bishop, agreed with the Grissoms' assessment, calling Virgil a "normal good pupil" who displayed an unusually good aptitude for mathematics. High school teacher Betty Beldon could remember numerous stories about the nonsense perpetrated by male students in her class, but these never seemed to involve Grissom, whom she described as "a good dependable boy."[21]

Standing only five feet, four inches tall and weighing just ninety-eight pounds when he entered high school at age fourteen in 1940, Grissom was too short to make the school's basketball team, the dream of many a Hoosier youth. "Maybe if I had even made the squad as a substitute," said Grissom, "I would have been encouraged to give athletics a try even though I was awfully small."[22] Instead of taking the court as a member of the team, he led his Boy Scout honor guard in carrying the American flag at the opening of games, impressing fellow student and future wife Betty Lavonne Moore, who played the drum in the school band and lived on Mitchell's outskirts with her mother, Pauline, father, Claude (a machinist at the Lehigh Portland Cement Company), and older sister, Mary Lou. Although Claude Moore managed to keep his job during the height of the Great Depression, the Moore family relied on its garden to supplement its diet. In addition to the garden, the Moores could obtain milk from a neighbor's cow and also kept some livestock of their own, including a few chickens and pigs, who always seemed able to escape from their pen on rainy days, remembered Betty. On such occasions, Pauline had to call her husband at work to come home and capture the escapees. "Of course, I always thought they [the pigs] were my buddies and she wouldn't let me help," said Betty. "She said, 'They'll run you over.' I said,

'Mother, they aren't going to run over me, I'm their buddy.' I don't think they would have done a thing to me, but she would always make me get back into the house."[23]

Grissom first met Moore when she entered Mitchell High School as a freshman, "and that was it, period, exclamation point!" said Grissom, a sophomore at the time, who described his courtship with Moore as a "quiet romance." From the moment he saw her, Grissom later told his wife, he decided that she was the girl he was going to marry.[24] Moore, who started out playing bells with the band but switched to percussion when one of the drummers graduated, regularly performed with her bandmates at the high school's basketball games. After finishing playing at halftime, the band would troop to an empty section of the arena to sit. "We really couldn't wander around," noted Moore, so Grissom would come up and sit with her for the rest of the game.[25]

In addition to courting the five-foot-tall Moore during his years at Mitchell High School, Grissom enjoyed a close friendship with Bill Head, who remembered that the two became friends as freshmen because of the school's policy of seating students alphabetically. The duo also often found themselves paired off in physical education class due to their small size, which also resulted in them facing each other in the school's intramural boxing championship in the flyweight division. "I managed to survive one round," said Head, "but in the second round, he [Grissom] knocked me cold." When he later related the story of the boxing match to an East Coast

IHS

*Visitors to Spring Mill State Park return from a boat trip
through Twin Caves.*

newspaper after Grissom had been selected as an astronaut,
Head noted that his friend suddenly had a number of
acquaintances eager to match their fighting skills against
Grissom. "I always told him he had more luck than most people have a right to have," said Head, who considered Grissom
more like a member of his family than friend. "He had a lot
of stick-to-itiveness to him. When he set out to do something,
he usually got it done."[26]

One incident that typified the "Grissom luck" came during a high school physical education class. The two friends
were clowning around before the class started when
Head smacked Grissom in the back and ran back into the

gymnasium, shutting the door behind him. In pursuit of Head, Grissom failed to stop his momentum in time to avoid the now closed door, throwing his hands in front of him to cushion the blow and smashing his hands through the door's glass window. Fortunately, Grissom escaped with no serious injuries.

Grissom matched his good fortune with an unflappable character. For fun, Head and Grissom would often jump on a motor scooter and head off to the airport in nearby Bedford where a local attorney would take them up in his plane for a dollar. On one flight with Grissom aboard, Head recounted, the plane came in for a landing but overshot the runway and had to swing around to try again. Unfortunately for the pilot, he had to quickly bank away in order to miss a large tree. As the pilot struggled to miss the object, Head observed his friend Grissom calmly waving to him from his seat in the cockpit. When the plane landed safely, Head asked his friend how he could manage to remain so composed in such a dicey situation. "What else am I going to do?" Grissom responded.[27]

Luck and pluck would be welcome attributes when Grissom and Moore started dating. Moore's mother maintained a healthy suspicion about "town kids" and kept a watchful eye on those families living in Mitchell who had earned bad reputations for themselves. With her mother's wariness in mind, Moore was leery of telling her mother about her new boyfriend (the only boy, in fact, she ever dated). "My thought was, my mother is going to throw a fit," she remembered. "Immediately it was: 'Well, he's not this one's son and not that one's, and I guess I don't know this family.' Since she didn't know that one, she gave in. I was sweatin' it out." Grissom soon earned the Moore family's trust, becoming a familiar figure by frequently bicycling out to their home to spend the day with Betty, then leaving his bicycle there and walking home. Claude Moore always suspected that Grissom left his bicycle behind so he would have an excuse to come back and see his daughter again. When he wasn't visiting Betty at her home, Grissom used his wages from his various odd jobs to take his girlfriend on dates, usually to the late show at the local movie theater, as well as theaters in nearby Bedford and Orleans. "We always had a new movie to go to," said Betty. "Probably in those days we saw every one of them."[28]

Although the war raging in Europe seemed light years away for a Mitchell high school student, Grissom did take time to read about the Germans' dreaded Stuka dive bomber and the brave "few" British pilots of the Royal Air Force. "Certainly flying sounded a lot more exciting than walking," said Grissom.[29] As did many Americans, Grissom learned about the Japanese attack on the American naval base at Pearl Harbor, Hawaii, on the radio as he and some of his school friends were gathered in the living room of his house. "They all wished they could go right away," noted Grissom's mother. Instead, Grissom had to wait until he was a senior in high school to enlist as an aviation cadet with the U.S. Army

Air Corps. In November 1943 Grissom and two of his friends, Bill Harrison and Harrison Conley, traveled to Freeman Field near Seymour to take their cadet examinations and physicals. It took another few months, however, until the trio finally received orders to report for induction on August 8, 1944, at Fort Benjamin Harrison in Indianapolis. Moore, who had been taught how to drive by Grissom, drove him to Indianapolis on the appointed day. Although Grissom never formally proposed marriage to Moore ("No, he didn't get down on any knee [to propose]," she said, "he wouldn't do that"), most people in Mitchell understood that the two would marry. His high school yearbook had even noted: "Virgil Ivan Grissom—Example of how a senior can become attached to a junior girl." Looking back on her engagement, Moore said, "I think he just decided we were always going to get married and that was it. We never really got mad at one another [enough] to leave, I guess."[30]

After their induction at Fort Harrison, Grissom, Harrison, and Conley were sent to Sheppard Army Airfield in Wichita Falls, Texas, for five weeks of basic training. After this initial course, Grissom received orders to report to Brooks Field in San Antonio. He had his first leave from the armed forces in December 1944, returning home for a visit before reporting for duty in January 1945 as a clerk typist at Boca Raton Army Air Field in Florida. As Grissom settled into his life in the military, Moore finished her senior year at Mitchell High School. Although she and Grissom had planned to marry after her graduation, Moore, not yet eighteen years old, needed her parents' permission. The couple granted their daughter's request, but her mother issued her the following warning: "I just want you to know that I'm not going to be a baby-sitter. I'm not going to raise your kids for you, and if you have any fights, don't come home." (Moore later told her husband that more marriages might be better off if all mothers gave their daughters the same advice.)[31] Grissom and Moore were married at 3:00 p.m. on July 6, 1945, in a double-ring ceremony in the parsonage at the First Baptist Church in Mitchell. Moore's sister, Mary Lou Fosbrink, served as maid of honor and Norman stood with his older brother as best man. A newspaper report on the ceremony noted that the bride was dressed in a "dress of powder blue, with white accessories and a corsage of pink roses." The couple had a short honeymoon in Indianapolis before Grissom had to return to Boca Raton. Moore returned to her job at the Reliance Shirt Factory in Mitchell.[32]

Although eager to become a pilot, Grissom found himself tied to a desk as a clerk instead of behind the stick of an aircraft. Two months after the war's end in September 1945, Grissom was discharged from the armed forces and returned to Mitchell where he and his new wife established a home in a small upstairs apartment on Main Street. Grissom soon was hired at Carpenter Body Works, one of the city's leading employers, putting doors on school buses. The early postwar years were a difficult time for Grissom. Frustrated with his

*Cecile Grissom waters her petunias on the front porch
of her home in Mitchell.*

dead-end job, he roamed the state looking for a new challenge. "He was going here, there and yonder," noted Betty. "He was probably gone three days a week off somewhere trying to find another job."[33] Although the air force had not taught him to fly, it did inspire Grissom to make aviation his career. To do that, he realized that he needed more than just a high-school education. "Betty and I talked it over and made up our minds," said Grissom, who set his sights on Purdue University in West Lafayette, Indiana, and a degree in mechanical engineering.[34]

As a veteran, Grissom could count on some financial support—approximately one hundred dollars per month—from the GI Bill of Rights. Given his short stay in the service, however, Grissom could not count on government aid for his entire stay at the university. He faced another hurdle in simply being accepted for enrollment. "The problem in high school was that he didn't have the money to go to college. He didn't get bad grades because he was stupid," said Betty, who noted that her husband never took books home with him and still made better grades than she did. "He just didn't figure he was going anywhere else." With at best an average record of achievement in academics during his high school days, Grissom and Head had to obtain letters of recommendation from Mitchell's school superintendent, C. W. Deckard. But when they sought the recommendation, the duo discovered that Deckard had left town for awhile and his secretary had turned the matter over to Bishop, the principal at the high school, who remembered at that time, before Grissom had become famous, that the two friends had been "troublemakers" in school. Appearing before a counselor at Purdue, Grissom and Head learned that Bishop believed the two had "sat too close together in school." The counselor informed them that, based on their letters of recommendation from the principal, the university would normally turn them down for admittance. Because they were both veterans under the GI Bill, however, Purdue had to admit them. The high jinks of high school were a thing of the past for the college-bound Grissom. "He knew what he wanted to do and what he had to do to get there. Nowadays I think people go to college with an attitude of 'Well, I'm not sure why I'm here, I have to go to college.' He went to college to get an education," said Betty.[35]

Acceptance at Purdue failed to end Grissom's difficulties. In the aftermath of World War II and the passage of the GI Bill, the university's enrollment skyrocketed. An admissions office accustomed to handling applications at no more than one hundred per day found itself swamped with twenty thousand applications during the 1946 summer session and the 1946–47 fall term. One history of the school noted that matters were further complicated by "having two generations of students on the campus simultaneously—the traditional eighteen-year-olds just out of high school and the veterans returning to resume interrupted education or enroll for the first time." The crush of students flocking to West Lafayette caused housing to be at a premium. To help stem the tide,

INDIANAPOLIS STAR

Gus Grissom (right) takes his father, Dennis, for a ride in a sports car during a visit to Mitchell in June 1962.

Purdue officials did everything possible, including placing bunk beds in dormitory attics, converting the second floor at the university's airport terminal into housing for fifty students, and turning a factory used during the war to fulfill defense contracts into a barracks for three hundred students.[36]

Even with Purdue's imaginative conversions, the region simply did not have enough housing—university owned or private—for everyone, as Grissom soon discovered as he prepared to begin classes in the fall of 1946. After looking everywhere for a suitable place for himself and his wife, Grissom finally found a room located in the basement of a house near campus. Unfortunately, he had to share the room with a male student, necessitating Betty's move from the couple's Mitchell apartment back home to live with her parents. After one semester apart, Betty joined her husband in West Lafayette and the couple eventually occupied a small one-bedroom apartment with kitchen. "It was hard on both of us, living in one room and trying to make ends meet," Betty later admitted. To supplement the meager allotment from the GI Bill, Betty worked as an operator with the Indiana Bell Telephone Company (her job included bus fare). She worked the 5:00 p.m. to 11:00 p.m. shift so her husband could study in the one room. "My greatest asset was that I had a working wife," said Grissom, who added to the couple's coffers by flipping hamburgers thirty hours a week as a short-order cook at a local restaurant, de-tasseling corn on a Tippecanoe County farm, and taking the night shift at a Monon Railroad roundhouse.

Grissom's doggedness impressed the restaurant's owner, who said that out of all the students who worked for him Grissom had been "the most dependable," as well as being "quiet and unassuming."[37]

Between work and school, there existed little time for a home life, noted Grissom. Betty remembered that she and her husband often ate breakfast at a small café near their apartment. While Grissom's other meals were taken care of at his job, Betty "ate an awful lot of hamburgers" at a local root beer stand. "If it was pouring rain or something," she added, "I didn't even go out to eat unless I had to go to work." Finances were tight for the young couple—on more than one occasion they had to decide whether to pay for books, rent, or food. For entertainment, the Grissoms took advantage of the sports programs at the university, attending Purdue football games and some wrestling matches.[38]

Reflecting on Grissom's career at the university for a 1967 issue of *Purdue Engineer* magazine, professors David S. Clark, Warren J. Luzadder, J. H. Porsch, and Paul S. Stanley said that like other postwar veterans at colleges and universities across the country following World War II, Grissom was more mature than younger students. Although Grissom was not "an exceptionally brilliant student," the professors admired his determination to succeed in his studies and gain the knowledge needed to further his career. "He knew exactly what he was going to school for and would let nothing get in his way," the professors said. "He hit the books instead of horsing around." The professors' further assessment of Grissom as "determined, hard-working, industrious, intent on doing everything to the best of his ability" would be echoed by others during his career as a test pilot and astronaut.[39]

By taking classes during summer sessions, Grissom graduated three months early, receiving his bachelor of science degree in mechanical engineering from Purdue in February 1950. "What I needed now was a job, and fast," said Grissom, "because I didn't want Betty spending any more of her life at a switchboard. She had made my degree possible." Even before graduating, Grissom discovered a tight job market, receiving only one offer, this from a brewery—a place of employment deemed unacceptable by his teetotaling mother. "I don't think his heart was in it," Cecile said of her son's job search. "He wasn't satisfied with civilian life and never would be. He loved flying and that was going to be his life." When a recruiting team from the U.S. Air Force visited Purdue, it found a willing recruit in Grissom, who after reenlisting traveled for basic training to Randolph Air Force Base near San Antonio, Texas, and then for advanced training at Williams Air Force Base near Phoenix, Arizona. "Only the color of the uniform was different," said Grissom, who donned air-force blue as an aviation cadet. As with his experience in being accepted at Purdue, Grissom made it into the air force by the skin of his teeth, joining the service early to avoid a deadline that would have denied entrance to married men.[40]

The service Grissom hoped to become a part of was a young one, having been created as a separate department of the U.S. armed forces in July 1947. Unlike the army or the navy, the air force had no service academy upon which to draw for its officer corps (the U.S. Air Force Academy did not come into being until 1955). Instead, the air force depended upon its aviation cadet program to train officers. Although the requirements for entrance into the program were not strict at first—a cadet had only to pass a physical and a two-year college equivalency test—it was a tough road for many recruits; approximately 50 percent washed out of the program. Once a cadet earned his silver wings, however, the road to success seemed limitless. "If an officer could fly well and was fortunate enough to see combat in Korea," noted John Darrell Sherwood in his history of air force fighter pilots in the Korean War, "there was no limit to how far he could rise."[41]

During the primary phase of his training, Grissom received instruction on the North American AT-6 Texan aircraft. The propeller-driven trainer gave him some trouble, particularly when it came to achieving the proper attitude for landing the airplane. In fact, Grissom's instructor even hinted that he might have to give up on his dreams of becoming a pilot and be happy with a position as navigator. "I don't want to be a navigator," Grissom told him. "I want to be a pilot." Sent aloft with a senior instructor to see if his problems could be corrected, Grissom continued to struggle with his landings. To help the cadet, the instructor pointed to an indicator—two small wheels—located to the left of the pilot's seat that could be used to help trim the plane. "No one had ever told me [about] this," said Grissom. "I had no idea what they were for." Armed with this new knowledge, Grissom experienced no further troubles in landing his plane and successfully soloed.[42]

While Grissom trained to be a pilot, a pregnant Betty went to live with her sister, Mary Lou, in Seymour, Indiana, where she earned her keep by doing housework. Although the Grissoms had been able to set aside some money from Betty's job as a telephone operator, money was tight on the $105 a month Grissom made as a cadet. Shaky finances played a role in the couple's decision to have Grissom stay in Texas instead of coming home for the birth of the couple's first child, Scott, who was born on May 16, 1950, at Schenck Memorial Hospital in Seymour. There existed another factor in the couple's decision: if Grissom left on leave and missed too many classes, he might be put back a class. "I think," Betty said during a telephone conversation with her husband, "maybe it would be best if you just stay there and get out as soon as you can. All new babies look alike anyway."[43] Six months after Scott's birth, Betty and her son flew to Phoenix to be with Grissom, living in a tiny apartment near the air base. "By that time I'm sure she must have felt that flying equaled poverty," said Grissom. In March 1951 he earned his wings, becoming a second lieutenant and receiving a salary increase to four hundred dollars a month. "We were practically millionaires!" joked Grissom.[44]

After receiving instruction in aerial gunnery at Luke Air Force Base in Arizona, Grissom, who had requested service somewhere in the Southwest, instead received an assignment to the Seventy-fifth Fighter-Interceptor Squadron at Presque Isle Air Force Base in Maine. The site had seen quite a lot of action during World War II because of a quirk in geography—it stood as the closest American air base to Europe. With the end of the war the base fell into inactivity. A new threat to the security of the country, the Soviet Union, resulted in the base being reactivated in November 1950 to defend the northeastern United States with the deadly new F-86 Sabre jets. The rush to whip the facility into shape for a new generation of jet fighter aircraft meant that amenities were few for the dependents of families assigned to Presque Isle, which included Betty and her son. While waiting for an apartment to become available at Presque Isle for his young family, Grissom shuttled back and forth on temporary duty to bases in Dover, Delaware, and McGuire Air Force Base in New Jersey. Finally obtaining an apartment at Presque Isle, the Grissoms were enjoying their new living arrangement and furniture when in December 1951 Gus received the call to another duty station thousands of miles from home: the Korean peninsula.[45]

On June 25, 1950, Communist North Korean forces, using small arms, artillery, fighters, bombers, and heavy T-34 tanks supplied by the Soviet Union, crossed the thirty-eighth parallel separating North and South Korea. The invasion had sparked an immediate response from the United Nations Security Council, which, at the strong urging of the United States, condemned the aggression. Acting without congressional approval, President Harry Truman ordered U.S. forces to aid the South Koreans. Fifteen other UN members joined American troops in the conflict. Americans were caught off guard by the conflict, with *Newsweek* magazine reporting that the news "hit the United States like lightning out of a clear sky." Roy Jolly, a member of an Evansville, Indiana, Marine Corps reserve company, spoke for many when he responded to reports about the fighting with a terse question: "Where's Korea?"[46]

As the meager American ground forces retreated from the South Korea capital of Seoul and struggled to maintain a foothold on the Pusan Perimeter, the U.S. Air Force scored its first aerial victory in the jet age. Early air battles in the war had pitted propeller-driven planes against one another: for the Americans, the F-51 Mustang and F-82 Twin Mustang (in the postwar years the air force had changed the designation for fighter planes from "P" to "F"), and for the North Koreans, Soviet-made Yak-3 and Yak-7 fighters. On the third morning of the war, North Korean IL-10 Stormoviks attempted to strafe and bomb the Kimpo airport just outside of Seoul. Lying in wait were four F-80C Shooting Star jets of the Thirty-fifth Fighter-Bomber Squadron. Capt. Raymond Schillereff gained credit for the first American air-to-air kill in a jet. Later, navy Panther jets, joined by U.S. Air Force and British planes, nearly wiped out the North Korean air force in a daring strike against an airfield near Pyongyang. As one historian noted, these early victories were "a good beginning for the Air Force in a bad war." As the first month of the war ground to an end, American aircraft enjoyed supremacy over the Korean peninsula.[47]

American air superiority was challenged when Soviet-built MIG-15 swept-wing jets, some flown by Russian pilots, entered the war in November 1950; they attacked several propeller-driven UN aircraft, which escaped the encounter without damage. Flying from Chinese bases north of the Yalu River (off limits to American aircraft), the MIGs had in one fell swoop, according to Robert Futrell, an air force historian, "rendered obsolete every American plane in the Far East," topping out at more than one hundred miles per hour faster than the F-80C. To meet this new threat, the U.S. Air Force hurriedly began to transfer its newest high-performance fighter to the theater: the North American F-86 Sabre. Although deficient in some respects to the Communist MIGs, which could out-accelerate and out-climb its foe, the U.S. aircraft enjoyed advantages in high-speed turns, had better visibility, a superior radar-ranging gun site, and highly trained pilots who had served in the previous war. By December 15, 1950, the F-86 had flown its first combat mission and, approximately a week later, pilots flying the new fighter shot down six MIGs. One Sabre pilot later claimed

Gun camera film from an F-86 shows a Communist MIG-15 pilot abandoning his aircraft after being hit by gunfire from the American plane.

that during the Korean War Americans had the luxury of "driving Cadillacs" while their opponents had to do with ordinary Fords. In the thirty months after the first F-86s had been deployed in Korea, American pilots had shot down 792 MIGs, while losing only 76 to enemy fighters.[48]

One of the F-86 units sent to Korea to match the MIG threat was Grissom's Seventy-fifth Fighter-Interceptor

NATIONAL ARCHIVES AND RECORDS ADMINISTRATION

Sleek U.S. Air Force F-86 Sabre jets patrol the skies over "MIG-Alley" in northwest Korea.

Squadron. The unit's squadron commander had broken the news by asking the pilots and other crew members if they would like to go to Korea. After a unanimous show of hands, the commander told the men, "Well, that's good, because that's where the whole squadron is going."[49] After enduring a stormy voyage aboard a transport ship, Grissom found himself not only in a strange country, but also in a strange world for a rookie aviator: the life of the combat pilot. Stationed at Kimpo Air Force Base, Grissom soon learned that although pilots were equals when it came to living arrangements, some pilots were more equal than others when it came to flying in combat.

High-ranking officers enjoyed some privileges in living

arrangements, but most air force pilots in Korea were quartered in metal Quonset huts that had been a staple for fighting men in World War II or prefabricated wooden huts made in Japan. These "hootches," as the living quarters were called, were inadequately heated and ventilated and lacked indoor plumbing and electricity. Privacy was at a minimum as well with typically six to twelve pilots sharing these primitive quarters. Morale among pilots remained high, however, as those stationed in the war zone were exempt from the more formal atmosphere that existed on air force bases back in the United States. Pilots could wear what they liked and drink what they liked. A pilot's only responsibility, noted Sherwood, was "to fly and fight: bases were merely a place to park one's aircraft, rest, recuperate, and prepare oneself for the next mission."[50]

The camaraderie of the barracks, however, turned into a highly structured caste system when it came to flying, the ethos of "The Right Stuff," captured so well by journalist and author Tom Wolfe in his book of the same name. Grissom, who flew an F-86 named for his son Scott, discovered this hard truth on his first combat mission in Korea. The unit he flew with, the 334th Fighter-Interceptor Squadron, had a rule that pilots who had not yet been shot at by a MIG had to stand up on the bus taking them back and forth between their quarters and the flight line for every mission. "I got to take a seat after my second mission," said Grissom, who wryly added that he still had ninety-eight more to go to fulfill his hundred-mission quota. He had learned, as Wolfe noted, that the "main thing was not to be *left behind*."[51] To his wife back home, Grissom wrote matter-of-factly about his combat experience. "I was flying along up there," he reported, "and it was kind of strange. For a moment I couldn't figure out what those little red things were going by. Then I realized I was being shot at."[52]

During his tour of duty, Grissom hoped for what every pilot longed for while flying in Korea—to down a MIG in combat and to become an "ace" after five kills. "When he first got to Korea he felt that he'd be an ace and he found out that isn't how things operate," said Betty, who had returned to Bedford to wait for her husband's return. "He said he wasn't about to be an ace."[53] What Grissom learned was that most of the air-to-air kills in Korea were accomplished by a small group of pilots, usually the most experienced ones in a unit. "We chased the MIGS around, and the MIGS chased us around," he said, "and I usually got shot at more than I got to shoot at them." Fighter tactics in Korea often dictated who would do the shooting. American F-86 fighters usually flew in a "finger four" formation with the lead plane responsible for shooting and the others in the formation acting as its eyes and ears. "I usually flew wing position in combat," Grissom noted, "to protect the flanks of other pilots and [to] keep an eye open for any MIGs that might be coming across." Although flying wing was not as glamorous as being the "shooter" in the group, it also had its share of danger, as Grissom later recalled: "Sometimes a bogey would sneak in and start firing at you before you could spot him. There was no time in a spot like that to *get* scared. You had just enough time to call your flight leader on the radio—right now—and tell him, in a calm voice that wouldn't rattle him, that it was time for him to break away fast and get out of there. You also had to remember to tell him which way to break. And you had to make sure to use the correct call sign so you wouldn't get all of the other planes in the flight breaking away at the same time and ruin the mission. This was a lot to do in a split second, and it was good experience." After the war, Grissom remained proud that he had never been hit by MIGs and neither had any of the leaders for which he had flown wing.[54]

Despite never shooting down a MIG in combat, Grissom earned promotion to second lieutenant on March 11, 1952. Later that month, he exhibited his piloting skills on one mission, which earned him a Distinguished Flying Cross. While escorting a photo reconnaissance flight, Grissom saw the aircraft being attacked by two MIG-15 aircraft as it left the target area. After dispatching two of his flight of F-86 jets to take care of the threat, Grissom saw two other MIGs joining the hunt for the American plane. Grissom again led his flight to intercept the threat, forcing the enemy to flee the engagement. "The superlative airmanship demonstrated by Lt. Grissom on this mission exemplifies his tour of duty," the citation for the award said, "reflecting great credit upon himself and his comrades-in-arms of the United Nations and U.S. Air Force."[55]

Approximately six months after his arrival in Korea, Grissom had completed his required one hundred missions, which meant a ticket back to the States. Still, the Hoosier pilot wanted more, requesting to fly twenty-five additional missions. "If you were a shoe salesman," he explained, "you'd want to be where you could sell shoes." With his request denied by the air force, he returned home and became an instructor at a base in Bryan, Texas. "When he got back from Korea," said Betty, "they [the air force] gave you your choice in the U.S. of where you wanted to go. The first time he got sent to Maine he said, 'I asked for the southwest, and I get the northeast. I guess I learned from this one.' I don't know what he put down, but we got sent to Bryan." It was there that the Grissoms' second son, Mark, was born on December 30, 1953.[56]

Teaching young aviation cadets how to fly proved to be even more dangerous than combat had been for instructor Grissom. "At least you know what a MIG is going to do," Grissom pointed out. "Some of these kids were pretty green and careless sometimes, and you had to think fast and act cool or they could kill both of you." One incident almost cost Grissom and one of his students their lives. Flying in a two-seat trainer, the cadet had been charged with the task of joining up on another pilot's wing while his teacher observed from the plane's rear seat. In the maneuver, the cadet was supposed to quickly approach the other plane and then throttle back and glide into position. "The cadet I was teaching came in *very* fast," said Grissom, "and then he throttled back. But he happened to be wearing an identification bracelet on his wrist, and the darned thing got caught in the handle that controls the flaps." One of the flaps broke off and the plane began to roll. Grissom grabbed the controls, reached for the flap handle, regained some control of the aircraft, and landed safely. "It was the kind of situation in which you don't have time to get scared until you're back on the ground," he said. "Then all you can do is have a beer and think it over."[57]

In addition to worrying about whether some young cadet might take her husband's life through carelessness or plain bad luck, Betty had to cope with a constantly changing schedule. She noted that the cadets were divided into a morning class and an afternoon class and Gus's schedule would switch every other week. "You were getting up with the chickens one time," said Betty. "Then the next week you were going to work at noon and getting home at 9:00 [p.m.]." Grissom also had to ensure his flight proficiency by putting in a number of hours in the air on weekends. "I had more wives look mad at me in those days because I didn't fuss about Gus being gone weekends flying," she said. "They always had a class that needed cross-country, so he could fly every weekend if he wanted to. He liked counting up all those hours of flying time. Gus enjoyed flying. So let him fly!" Betty remembered her husband one time sitting down to figure out his salary on an hourly basis—it came out to three dollars per hour. Instead of attending the normal rounds of parties and social

INDIANAPOLIS STAR

Grissom and his family visit his parents in Mitchell. On the steps of the home are (left to right, bottom row) Scott and Mark; (left to right, middle row) Gus and Betty Grissom; and (left to right, top row) Dennis and Cecile Grissom.

calls with other wives on the base, she preferred to stay at home with her two young sons.[58]

In August 1955 Grissom received orders to return to the Midwest, with the air force assigning him to the U.S. Air Force Institute of Technology at Wright-Patterson Air Force Base outside of Dayton, Ohio. Educating pilots had been a tradition at the airfield since 1919 (when it was known as McCook Field), with the establishment of the Air School of Application and its goal of giving "proper technical training to the permanent officers of the Air Service." Just a year before Grissom arrived at Wright-Patterson, Congress had passed and President Dwight Eisenhower had signed a bill giving the institute the right to grant degrees if it received accreditation from a nationally recognized association or authority, which it received from the Engineers Council for Professional Development. Grissom enrolled in a one-year program that saw him earn a bachelor of science degree in aero mechanics from the institute's School of Engineering.[59]

While studying at the institute, Grissom met and became friends with another student, a pilot named Gordon Cooper, who would join the Mitchell native as one of the original seven Mercury astronauts. Cooper described Grissom as "a heck of a nice guy, with whom I enjoyed working and playing. He was a little bear of a man and a country boy at heart, but when it came to flying he was steady and no-nonsense."[60] The two men were soon flying regularly together. When the telephone rang in the Grissom home Betty could usually tell when it was "Gordo" asking her husband to take another flight with him. "Gus was always too busy to get the plane reserved, but Gordo always came through," Betty remembered. It was when the two men were flying together that Grissom became involved in the only accident he suffered in an aircraft. Cooper was at the controls when the duo took off in a two-seat Lockheed T-33 "T-bird" jet trainer from the high altitude of Denver's Lowry Field in June 1956. The plane had just become airborne when it lost power. Grissom shouted out a warning to Cooper just before the plane hit back onto the pavement and skidded down the runway. Although the plane was destroyed in the crash, both men were uninjured. "What happened was that he didn't do his inspection," said Betty. "After that I think Gus started doing the inspection, no matter who he was flying with."[61]

After graduating from the institute, both Grissom and Cooper received assignments in October 1956 to the U.S. Air Force Flight Test Pilot School at the famed Edwards Air Force Base in California's Mojave Desert, an area seen as a wasteland to settlers but as "God's gift to the U.S. Air Force" by one of the school's commanders. The Rogers Dry Lake provided miles of natural flat surface for landing planes, especially those in need of emergency assistance. The base, however, received its true fame among the pilot fraternity back in 1947 when it was known as Muroc Army Air Field. On the morning of October 14, Capt. Charles "Chuck" Yeager became the first man to achieve supersonic flight—breaking the sound barrier—aboard the burnt-orange colored Bell XS-1 experimental aircraft, named *Glamorous Glennis* for Yeager's wife. After the XS-1 had been released from a B-29 bomber at twenty thousand feet, Yeager, nursing two broken ribs, fired the craft's four rocket engines in succession and observed the Mach needle reach .965 and then go off the scale. "We were flying supersonic!" Yeager noted in his auto-biography. "And it was as smooth as a baby's bottom. Grandma could be sitting up there sipping lemonade." Observers on the ground were surprised to hear a loud noise—the world's first sonic boom. A new age in flight had begun.[62]

In attending the test-pilot school at Edwards, Grissom and Cooper joined an elite group of flyers. According to a his-tory of the school, candidates for entrance "not only had to be outstanding pilots, but were expected to satisfy stringent aca-demic requirements as well—it was becoming increasingly obvious that only the very best and the brightest need apply."[63] For fledgling test pilot Grissom, the new assignment meant long hours of study, while for the rest of the family it meant another in a long series of moves. "We were a military family and we were pretty used to moving around," recalled Scott Grissom. "I think I had four separate first grade classes. It's always tough leaving, but we were military and that was pretty much how we approached things."[64] Chance played a role for the Grissom family when it came to housing at Edwards. Top-ranking officers at the base with children of two different sexes were eligible for a three-bedroom house, Betty noted. With two boys, it looked as if the Grissoms would be allotted a two-bedroom residence. The death of another test-pilot candidate, however, opened up one of the larger homes for the Grissoms.[65]

After successfully making his way through test-pilot school in May 1957, and reaching the rank of captain, Grissom and family returned to the familiar surroundings of Wright-Patterson, where he tested the air force's new generation of jet aircraft, including the sleek F-105 Starfighter, at the base's Wright Air Development Center. The Grissom family enjoyed being back at the base, but there were some anxious moments. Before leaving the house one morning, Grissom told his wife, "Well, I'm going to go out and fly the airplane today, I don't know if it's even going to get off the ground." If he had gone off to work as he normally had in the past, Betty said, she wouldn't have had a second thought. "That day I was a little nervous," she admitted.[66]

Life might have gone on as usual for the Grissom family if it had not been for a small, spherical object about the size of a beach ball with four whip antennae called *Sputnik*. On October 4, 1957, as Americans turned their attention to the World Series pitting the New York Yankees versus the Milwaukee Braves, the admittance of black students at Little Rock High School in Arkansas, and the premier of the television series *Leave It to Beaver* on CBS, the Soviet Union used an R-7 rocket to launch the world's first artificial satellite into an elliptical orbit around the Earth. When he learned the satellite had successfully achieved orbit, Sergey Korolyov, the leading designer behind the Soviet space effort, told those who had helped achieve the triumph: "Today the dreams of the best sons of mankind . . . have come true. The storming of space has begun." The person whose idea it was to launch a satellite for the International Geophysical Year of 1957–58, Lloyd Berkner, learned of the launch while at the Soviet Embassy in Washington, D.C. He told the crowd: "I have just been informed by the *New York Times* that a Russian satellite is in orbit at an elevation of 900 kilometers. I wish to congratulate our Soviet colleagues on their achievement." As the Russian success was being toasted in Washington, the news spread throughout the United States, and countless people looked to the skies to see if they could spy *Sputnik* as it made its way across the sky. One of the families who attempted to track the satellite was the Grissoms. "I think we found it once," said Betty. Soon, the Grissoms themselves would be front and center in the burgeoning space race between America and Russia.[67]

3

The Astronaut

IN JANUARY 1902, THE EDITOR OF THE JOURNAL *POPULAR Science News*, D. P. Doremus, received a manuscript titled "The Navigation of Space" from a Worcester, Massachusetts, high school student inspired by the writings of Jules Verne and H. G. Wells. The student proposed the idea of modifying Verne's concept of an immense cannon firing a craft to the moon by using successive smaller "cannons" to propel an object ever higher into space. "We may safely infer that space navigation is an impossibility at the present time," the student wrote. "Yet it is difficult to predict the achievements of science in this direction in the distant future." Although terming the piece "valuable," Doremus rejected the article. The setback, however, did not deter the author—Robert H. Goddard—from pursuing his dreams of sending rockets into space and becoming, through his work, the "Father of Modern Rocketry."[1]

By 1919, Goddard, a physics professor at Clark

Dr. Robert H. Goddard at a blackboard at Clark University in Worcester, Massachusetts, in 1924. Goddard began teaching physics in 1914 at Clark and in 1923 was named the Director of the Physical Laboratory.

University in Worcester, had published with the Smithsonian Institution a paper on using rockets to reach extreme altitudes, even postulating the possibility of reaching the moon with such craft. The claim was mocked in a *New York Times* editorial, which ridiculed Goddard's claims of a rocket functioning in the vacuum of space and accused him of "lacking the knowledge ladled out daily in high schools." Responding to this broadside, Goddard told an Associated Press reporter: "Every vision is a joke until the first man accomplishes it; once realized, it becomes commonplace." At the time of his death in 1945, Goddard held 214 patents in rocketry. Asked about the origins of their powerful and destructive V-1 and V-2 rockets that had hammered London at the end of World War II, a puzzled German scientist told his captors, "Why don't you ask your own Dr. Goddard? He knows better than any of us."[2]

Goddard was just one of many scientists around the world who dreamed of travel among the stars. As had Goddard, Hermann Oberth, a German-speaking Romanian, had devoured the works of Verne as a boy, particularly the novel *From Earth to the Moon*, reading it until he "knew it by heart." Trained in medicine, Oberth later switched to physics but had his dissertation involving flight by rockets rejected by the University of Heidelberg. Undeterred, the rocket enthusiast continued to work on the subject, eventually publishing in 1923 the book *Die Rakete zu den Planetenräumen (By Rocket to Space)*. The book inspired a number of rocket organizations to spring up throughout Germany; one young man who joined was Wernher von Braun. And years before in Russia, another space visionary, Konstantin Tsiolkovsky, had outlined details for the design of a spaceship using such fuels as liquid oxygen and liquid hydrogen. Tsiolkovsky, who published hundreds of works on spaceflight, predicted that in years to come men would "travel beyond the limits of our planetary system; they will reach other Suns, and use their fresh energy instead of the energy of their dying luminary."[3]

One of the many Russian scientists to be influenced by

Tsiolkovsky's work was Sergei Korolev, the guiding spirit behind the Soviet space program and the person responsible for *Sputnik*'s success. After *Sputnik* had successfully been launched from an R-7 intercontinental ballistic missile (ICBM) and signals from the satellite had been heard, the cautious Korolev had warned his comrades to hold off on celebrating until they could "judge the signals for ourselves when the satellite comes back after its first orbit around the Earth." When the familiar "beep-beep-beep" of *Sputnik* was finally heard the Soviet scientists knew they had triumphed over their western counterparts.[4]

In addition to stunning the American public and media (*Newsweek* termed the flight as the "greatest technological triumph since the atomic bomb"), the Soviet triumph caused great consternation for America's new rocket master: von Braun. Spirited into the country along with other German rocket scientists on September 29, 1945, von Braun had been working with the U.S. Army's ballistic missile program at Huntsville, Alabama, particularly the Redstone rocket. Hearing about *Sputnik* while entertaining Neil H. McElroy, the new Secretary of Defense, an aggrieved von Braun told him: "Vanguard will never make it. We have the hardware on the shelf. For God's sake, turn us loose and let us do something. We can put up a satellite in sixty days, Mr. McElroy! Just give us the green light and sixty days." Unbeknownst to those Americans lamenting the country's failure, the Soviet achievement had established quite by accident the principle of "freedom of space," paving the way for spy satellites to ply their trade when ready. Perhaps that is why President Dwight Eisenhower dismissed the cries of dismay from his countryman, telling reporters that the Soviets had "only put one small ball in the air." When asked if Communist triumph raised his concerns about national security, the president said it did "not raise my apprehensions, not one iota."[5]

The apprehensions of the American public, however, were increased when on November 3, 1957, the Soviet Union launched *Sputnik II* into space carrying a passenger: a dog named Laika (Barker). The Russian ability to place a heavy satellite (*Sputnik II* weighed more than a thousand pounds) into orbit heightened fears that the Communists would soon be dropping nuclear weapons on American cities and were close to achieving another first: sending a human into space. To a panicked country, Eisenhower's placid outlook on the situation seemed ill-advised and reinforced a view of the former World War II hero as a "'do-nothing,' golf-playing president mismanaging events." Democrats jumped at the chance to strike back at the Republican president, with Sen. Lyndon B. Johnson sponsoring hearings on the American defense and space program before the Senate Armed Services Committee. Each branch of the military service and any department associated with research inundated the federal government with plans for space travel. "It seemed to me that everybody in the country had come in with a proposal except Fanny Farmer Candy," an admiral said of those days, "and I expected them any minute."[6]

What the public did not know, however, was that America had moved ahead of the Soviet Union technologically. Russia had to use rockets with massive thrust in order to lift its bulky nuclear weapons. Thanks to advances in miniaturizing its nuclear arsenal, America needed smaller missiles to send the weapons to their targets. But with his approval ratings plummeting, Eisenhower moved to stem the rising tide of negative public opinion. The president turned to his new science adviser, Dr. James R. Killian, to devise a proposal for America's future space efforts. What emerged after much wrangling and speculation, especially among the various branches of the armed forces, all eager to be the one selected for the prestige of leading the country into space, was the use of an existing government research group, the National Advisory Committee for Aeronautics, which since 1915 had been devoted to advancing aviation technology. On July 29, 1958, Eisenhower signed into law the National Aeronautics and Space Act, which created a civilian space agency: the National Aeronautics and Space Administration. The president gave NASA the responsibility for the country's manned space effort and appointed T. Keith Glennan, former president of the Case Institute of Technology, as the agency's first administrator. NASA soon had at its disposal not only the test facilities and laboratories controlled by NACA and its eight thousand employees and $100 million annual budget, but also the air force's missile range at Cape

NASA

Hermann Oberth (forefront) with officials of the Army Ballistic Missile Agency at Huntsville, Alabama, in 1956. Left to right: Dr. Ernst Stuhlinger (seated); Major General H. N. Toftoy, commanding officer; Dr. Eberhard Rees, deputy director, development Operations Division; and Wernher von Braun, director, development Operations Division.

Canaveral in Florida and von Braun's team of German engineers at Huntsville (later renamed the George C. Marshall Space Flight Center). NASA's nonmilitary, public program stood in stark contrast to the Department of Defense's highly secret reconnaissance satellite effort. As NASA historian Roger D. Launius noted, the agency's program "dovetailed nicely into cold war rivalries and priorities in national defense."[7]

In addition to continuing a satellite program, which saw the successful launch of weather, communication, and scientific satellites, NASA developed plans to place a man into orbit. Even before NASA had been created, engineers of the Space Task Group, directed by Dr. Robert Gilruth, at NACA's Langley Aeronautical Laboratory in Virginia had begun work on such a project. Named Project Mercury for the Roman messenger god in December 1958 (the name Project Astronaut was rejected because it emphasized the man too much), the program set out to fulfill its gigantic task, including recruiting staff, designing what would go into space, and selecting a contractor to build the craft (St. Louis's McDonnell Aircraft Corporation signed a contract to build the Mercury capsule on February 13, 1959). "We had millions of things to do," noted Gilruth. "We had a tremendous job of recruiting, but it was made easy by the fact that there were a lot of people who wanted to do it. But it was still tough, and it was still hard to keep this organization efficient."[8]

Another key assignment for the STG involved selecting the people to operate whatever system was developed to take the leap into space. As engineers and scientists gathered at Langley to work on the hardware end of the operation, three men—Charles Donlan, Project Mercury assistant director, Warren North, a former NACA test pilot, and Allen O. Gamble, NASA manpower director and a psychologist—worked with military flight surgeons and psychologists to hammer out specifications for America's astronauts. At first, the group decided to open the position to individuals in the military and civilian life. "After all," said Gamble, "the President and Congress had bypassed the military in setting up the ill-starred Project Vanguard. More recently, they had done likewise in establishing NASA itself as a civilian agency, to operate publicly rather than in secret, 'for the benefit of all mankind.'"[9] On December 22, 1958, the group issued a draft announcement inviting people to apply for the position of "Research Astronaut-Candidate," a civil service job with a starting salary from $8,330 to $12,770, depending on qualifications. The announcement, actually published in the *Federal Register*, sought such professional qualifications as three years of work in physical, mathematical, biological, or psychological sciences; three years of technical or engineering work in a research organization; three years of experience operating aircraft, balloons, or submarines; completion of all work toward a doctorate in an appropriate science or engineering field plus six months of professional work; or physi-

Grissom stands ready to board an F-102 jet fighter. The Mercury astronauts lobbied successfully to be allowed to continue to fly while they completed their training.

cians with six months of clinical or research work.[10]

Although approved by Glennan, the plan also had to undergo the scrutiny of Eisenhower, who saw in it a recipe for disaster. According to Gamble, the president "scotched the idea of a public competition to select the first astronauts. As I heard it, his basic motivation was humiliation about Vanguard 1. Thus, he rejected anything premature or unproven. He wanted to announce a successful fait accompli. We had to limit our search to the *military*, and keep it *secret*."[11] Why not, Eisenhower insisted, use military test pilots? Gilruth called the decision "one of the best . . . he [Eisenhower] ever made. The test pilots were stable guys who had already been screened for security." In January 1959 the STG started reviewing the records of test pilots who met the following criteria: less than forty years old; less than five feet, eleven inches tall; excellent physical condition; holder of a bachelor's degree or equivalent; qualified to fly a jet; a graduate from a test-pilot school; and a minimum of 1,500 hours of flight time. From the beginning, noted George Low, NASA's chief of manned spaceflight, such standards "were established because of the strong feeling that the success of the mission may well depend upon the actions of the pilot; either in his performance of primary functions or backup functions. A qualified jet test pilot appeared to be best suited to this task." Or, as one air force general described the task, NASA was "merely looking for common, ordinary supermen."[12]

There were some on the search committee who were

hesitant to limit the search to just military test pilots, but Gamble outlined a number of "real advantages" to such a decision. All the records for the flyers were available for screening and evaluation in Washington, D.C. Military pilots, said Gamble, were "accustomed to secrecy and to following orders, so we could easily get them to Washington or elsewhere with no reasons given, and we could expect compliance without leaks to the press from them or from their probably reluctant survivors." Also, the test-pilot schools for the air force and navy had strong programs with high standards for entrance and for graduation. Finally, Gamble realized later, being in the military meant that the pilots were used to being moved about from location to location with little advanced warning, enduring long hours at work, unusual work schedules, and frequent absences from their families. "Thus," he said, "we would have a homogenous team, including their wives and families."[13]

A total of 508 military records were examined by Doctors Robert B. Voas, Stanley C. White, and William S. Augerson in Washington, D.C. Voas, a navy psychiatrist, had been in awe somewhat at his involvement in helping to select a future Christopher Columbus or Charles Lindbergh. Those chosen as astronauts would not only represent the program, he said, but "they'd possibly be American heroes." With that in mind, Voas received quite a scare when he reviewed material presented by his branch of the service. "One time when we went out to lunch and came back, and this big trolley with all the

Navy service records . . . disappeared," Voas remembered. "I thought my career had come to an end, but it turned out that someone, the cleaning woman or something, had moved the trolley out of the office while they cleaned up, so we got them all back."[14] After reviewing the records, 110 were found to meet the minimum standards (47 from the navy, 58 from the air force, and 5 from the marines). Missing from the list were pilots from the army, who failed to have the experience with high performance jet aircraft. A screening committee at NASA headquarters divided the potential candidates into three groups, with the first group of thirty-five "invited" to attend a briefing in Washington, D.C., on February 2, 1959, with a second group to follow a week later. "So when I say 'invited,'" noted Voas, "we didn't make any communication. They were ordered in by the Chief of Naval Operations or the Air Force commanding officer. They were just told to report to the Pentagon, and they were not supposed to be told why they were doing it and so on. This was being done in a top-secret form."[15]

The criteria established by NASA for its future astronauts had excluded some of the most famous names in test-pilot circles. Chuck Yeager did not meet the academic qualifications, and Scott Crossfield, another notable name among pilots, was a civilian. For Yeager, and some other test pilots, Project Mercury was treated as more of a joke than as a serious effort, given the fact that early indications pointed to a pilot having little role to play in the control of whatever was launched into

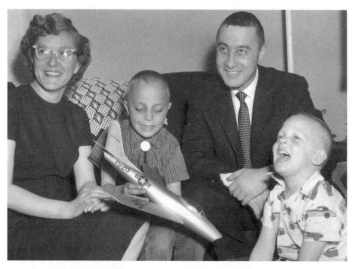

A happy Grissom family poses for a photographer shortly after Gus had been named as one of America's Mercury astronauts.

space. NASA's announcement that it intended to test whether it would be safe for a man to journey into space by first using chimpanzees as experimental subjects only sparked additional ridicule. Responding to other test pilots who rejected the chance to become astronauts, Yeager, in his autobiography, noted, "Hell, I don't blame you. I wouldn't want to have to sweep off monkey shit before I sat down in that capsule." The commanding officer at Edwards, Gen. Marcus F. Cooper, even warned two of his pilots—future astronauts Deke Slayton and Gordon Cooper (no relation)—to be careful not to volunteer for "some idiotic program" such as flying in space.[16]

The secret orders that had so perplexed Grissom's adjutant at Wright-Patterson Air Force Base became a little clearer for the pilot when another person at the base received a briefing on Project Mercury a week before Grissom was scheduled to attend. Initially, Grissom expressed similar skepticism as other test pilots had expressed about the program, believing it "sounded a little too much like a stunt instead of like a serious research program." He also worried that an astronaut would only be "a passenger," something he did not want to be. "I liked flying too much," said Grissom, adding that he had never been much of a science fiction fan. "I was more interested in what was going on right now than in the centuries to come," he said. After hearing his friend's enthusiastic report about the program, however, Grissom decided "there must be something to it. I got the same briefing myself the following week. And I liked the sound of it even more." Always interested in engineering, Grissom, now a captain in the air force, believed he possessed "enough flying experience to be able to handle myself on any kind of chute-the-chute they wanted to put me on. In fact, I knew darned well I could."[17]

At the briefings from NASA about Project Mercury, officials assured those assembled that they would play a significant role in piloting the spacecraft. Voas noted that in his presentation on the training program he attempted to "stress that it was built around the concept that they were important to the mission, you know, and not just passengers."[18] In addition to the briefings, those invited to Washington underwent a battery of interviews on technical matters, evaluations by psychiatrists, and a detailed interview with a flight surgeon. The personality tests included answering such true or false questions as "I often worry about my health" and "Strangers are trying to hurt me," and completing such sentences as "I am sorry that . . ." and "I can never . . . ." The candidates also underwent written tests designed to measure intelligence and engineering and mathematical ability. Of the sixty-nine men who had reported to Washington for the first two groups, thirty-two survived the initial evaluation (sixteen had declined to participate, six were too tall, and fifteen were eliminated by the testing), a number large enough for NASA to cancel a third call for volunteers. "We figured that with 32 men like this we could hardly go wrong," said Gamble. "All we had to do now was pick the very best from among these excellent candidates."[19]

Grissom was nearly removed from consideration early in the selection process when doctors discovered that he suffered from hay fever. "As far as I'm concerned," Betty Grissom quoted one doctor as saying, "you are out of the program right now." Thinking fast, Grissom had a ready answer to the doctor's concern: "There won't be any ragweed pollen in space." The logic proved unassailable; he remained as one of the men considered for selection as an astronaut. When he returned home to discuss the matter with his wife, Grissom noted NASA officials had stressed that any of the test pilots could always decline the invitation and return to their regular duty without any negative ramifications. When Betty asked her husband if being an astronaut was something he really wanted to do, and he responded that it was, she said: "Then do you even need to ask me?"[20]

For the next stage of evaluating the astronaut candidates, NASA divided the men into five groups of six each and one group of two and sent them for seven-and-a-half days of exhaustive testing at the private Lovelace Clinic in Albuquerque, New Mexico, which had been in operation there since 1922, for medical health and physiology testing, and then on for stress testing at the Wright Aerospace Medical Laboratory at Wright-Patterson Air Force Base. The Lovelace Clinic had conducted some early tests on space studies and on U-2 pilots. "Send them to Lovelace," said air force Brig. Gen. Don Flickinger, a flight surgeon. "They're used to keeping secrets." There existed another reason for sending the candidates to such a facility. Slayton noted that as a private clinic it did not have to turn over the data it collected on its subjects to the various military services, "so a guy could go through the tests somewhat secure in the knowledge that he wasn't going to screw up his flying career."[21]

Under the direction of Dr. A. H. Schwichtenberg, a retired air force general, the testing at Lovelace included such areas as the candidate's eyes, ears, nose, and throat; heart and circulation; nerves and muscles; and blood and tissues. Doctors ran seventeen separate tests on eyes alone and took thirty samplings of a candidate's blood, urine, and tissue. The men had to undergo a thorough series of X-rays and were poked and prodded in every available orifice, even offering sperm samples as "fertility base lines" for study after an astronaut orbited the earth. They had ice-cold water dripped in their ears to see if they were susceptible to motion sickness and had their body mass tested by being submerged in warm water. "If you didn't like doctors," noted Slayton, "it was your worst nightmare. Take the standard medical examination . . . and multiply it by ten. They had a captive group, and they exploited it." Another candidate, Wally Schirra, called the whole experience "an embarrassment" and "degrading." (Later, Dr. Randolph Lovelace joked that he hoped none of the candidates would ever give *him* a physical examination.) Only one of the thirty-two candidates, Jim Lovell, who eventually made it into space, failed the initial medical testing (Lovell had a minor liver ailment). Another future astronaut, Pete Conrad, did obtain some revenge on the doctors by convincing his fellow candidates to dine on spicy Mexican food the night before they were to undergo barium enemas so physicians could X-ray their intestines. Not surprisingly, Conrad failed to achieve his goal of becoming one of the first astronauts.[22]

The survivors of the Lovelace ordeal quickly developed a tradition of inviting for dinner at a local Mexican restaurant the new candidates who trundled into the clinic to undergo the brutal regime established by the scientists. At one of

The original seven Mercury astronauts with a U.S. Air Force F-106B jet aircraft. From left to right are: Scott Carpenter, Gordon Cooper, John Glenn, Grissom, Wally Schirra, Alan Shepard, and Deke Slayton.

these conclaves those who were finishing their time at the clinic, including Grissom, had at each of their feet a jug of urine they had been obliged to collect during their stay at the clinic in the interest of science. Unfortunately, sometime during dinner, Grissom accidentally knocked over his container. The quick-thinking crowd of test pilots had a ready answer for their friend's dilemma—order more beer. After a few rounds, and quick trips to the restroom, the jug had its requisite amount of urine for the physicians.[23]

If the medical tests at Lovelace were not bad enough, the candidates had to suffer another week's worth of stress and psychological trials at the Wright Aerospace Medical Laboratory. The candidates endured pressure suit, heat (baked in a room at approximately 180 degrees for two hours), isolation, and vibration tests, had their feet plunged into ice water, blew up balloons until they were out of breath, and walked on a treadmill until their heart rates raced to more than 180 beats a minute. Also waiting for the candidates were psychologists who interviewed them again and again. One of the psychologists, Dr. George Ruff, noted that at the beginning of the process he was certain NASA officials would never allow the thirty hours of psychiatric evaluation and psychological testing they had planned. "But we put it in," he said, "and lo and behold, they said OK, we'll do it." After a day of stress testing, the candidates would come back and be grilled by the psychologists. "To our amazement," said Ruff, "they did the whole program as we set it up. I felt it was a little bit like Parkinson's law. The amount of testing will expand to the amount of time psychologists are given to test. That is the reason so much was done."[24]

Grissom believed he had done well in almost all of the experiments at the Wright laboratory. The only one he did not do well in was the treadmill, where his heartbeat climbed to 200 beats per minute before the doctors stopped the test. "I was real disappointed in myself and thought I should have done better," said Grissom. He did do well on a trial called the "Idiot Box," an instrument panel jammed with lights, switches, and buttons the candidates had to push, pull, and click. "I guess they had taken everything they could think of that had ever gone wrong on an Air Force plane and put it onto one panel," he said. "Everything was out of phase, the lights were going on and the buzzers were sounding, and they watched you to see how you reacted in a clutch situation like this." The heat chamber proved to be the simplest test for Grissom to endure. He managed to keep cool despite the extreme temperatures by reading an old *Reader's Digest*, "just to keep from getting bored."[25]

As for the psychological tests, Grissom found them to be "a real bother." Although he had no idea what the doctors were trying to find out with their questions, Grissom attempted to "not give the headshrinkers anything more than they were actually asking for. At least, I played it cool and tried not to talk myself into a hole." In addition to honestly answering the questions posed to him, he tried not to get too carried away with his responses, being careful not to elaborate beyond what the doctors were asking for on such matters as the Rorschach inkblot tests. When all the evaluations were complete, Grissom remained optimistic about his chances of being selected. "I had compared notes here and there with some of the other fellows in my group, and I thought I had probably done as well as any of them had," he noted.[26]

Grissom's sense of his performance in the testing proved to be accurate. Late in March 1959, the selection committee at STG in Langley evaluated the thirty-one remaining candidates, which included eighteen recommended without medical reservations and thirteen recommended with medical reservations. According to Donlan, the committee hunted "for real men and valuable experience." He also noted that the testing done at Lovelace and Wright "had little to do with their actual selection; because the only question I ever asked finally was: 'Are there any physical or mental reasons any of these candidates should be dismissed?' If the answer to that was 'No,' they were on a list." Although STG had at first wanted to pick twelve men as astronauts, the figure had dropped to six when it became apparent that few, if any, of those selected would drop out of the program. The candidates were so outstanding, however, it proved difficult for the committee to pick just six, and so seven names were sent to Gilruth for his approval. On April 1, Donlan phoned the seven men chosen to train as astronauts for Project Mercury; all gladly accepted the offer. Along with Grissom, others picked for the program were Slayton and Cooper from the air force; Schirra, Alan Shepard, and Malcom Scott Carpenter from the navy; and John Glenn from the marines. After accepting his new assignment, Grissom sometimes lay awake at night wondering, "Now, why the hell do you want to get up on that thing [rocket] for?" The answer: "If my country decided that I was one of the better qualified people for this new mission, then I was proud and happy to help out."[27]

The seven men selected shared some similarities. All

GETTY IMAGES

Grissom, his wife Betty, and their two sons relax at their home in Virginia where he trained with the Space Task Group for a chance to become the first man in space. Ralph Morse, a photographer for Life, *captured the family on film as part of the magazine's exclusive contract for the astronauts' personal stories.*

were married with children and grew up in small-town America. The psychological testing conducted at the Wright laboratory also uncovered the fact that the seven all had a high degree of intelligence, with scores on the Wechsler Adult Intelligence Scale ranging from a low of 131 to a high of 141, and all had a slightly higher verbal IQ than those not selected for the program. Still, as Ruff noted in a later progress report, the astronauts were "oriented toward action rather than thought. They prefer action to inaction, and dislike assuming a passive role. At the same time, they are not overly impulsive, and can refrain from action when appropriate." In considering their physical attributes, all of the astronauts had brown hair, except for Glenn, whose red hair and easy grin gave him the appearance of the proverbial all-American boy. Grissom was the shortest astronaut at five feet, seven inches, and Shepard the tallest at five feet, eleven inches. They ranged in age from Cooper, the youngest at thirty-two, to Glenn, the oldest at thirty-seven.[28]

Seven days after receiving the call from Donlan, the new American astronauts, dressed in suits and ties instead of their usual military garb, reported for duty to Langley. At the first meeting, Gilruth met with the seven men and stressed that NASA had not selected them as merely "hired guns," but for their experience as test pilots and engineers. "This isn't the military, where direction comes from the top," Glenn quoted Gilruth as saying. "We want your direct input. Any problem you have with design, or anything we're doing, you let me know." The next day, April 9, the astronauts traveled to Washington, D.C., where they were to be introduced to the media at a press conference held on a stage in the ballroom at the Dolley Madison House, which housed NASA's headquarters at the time. Nothing could have prepared the men for the tumult that followed. At 2:00 p.m. the astronauts and NASA officials trooped onstage to meet the press. After press kits were distributed to the gathered horde of reporters, photographers, and cameramen, Glennan introduced the astronauts—an introduction greeted with applause by those assembled. As Tom Wolfe described the scene in *The Right Stuff*, not only did the reporters cheer "as if this were one of the most inspiring moments of their lives," but also some of the photographers, who moments before had crawled over one another in their haste to snap images of the astronauts, "let their cameras dangle from their straps, so that they could use their hands for clapping." Even Glenn, probably the most media savvy of the astronauts due to the attention he garnered for a record cross-country supersonic flight he made and a subsequent appearance on the popular television program *Name That Tune*, saw the instant favorable response as "unusual behavior" for the press. "Reporters didn't tend to give standing ovations to people they were covering," Glenn correctly noted.[29]

The questions posed to the astronauts strayed from the comfortable grounds of engineering and flying to more personal territory. The men were queried about their families' feelings on venturing into this new frontier, whether or not they smoked, their religious faith, and why they had volunteered for such a dangerous program in the first place. In his answers, Glenn hit all the right notes for the gathered reporters, comparing where the American space program stood at that time to the Wright Brothers standing at Kitty Hawk and tossing a coin to see who would be the first to take a powered flight. "I think we stand on the verge of something as big and as expansive as that was fifty years ago," said Glenn. He also received one of the biggest laughs of the afternoon when asked what had been the least-liked part of the testing. "It is rather difficult to pick one because if you figure out how many openings there are on a human body," Glenn observed, "and how far you can go into any one of them—you answer which one would be the toughest for you." Glenn's glibness with the press surprised his fellow astronauts. "He ate this stuff up," Slayton said of Glenn. Asked whether their wives had been behind their decisions to volunteer for the program, Slayton noted that the six of them had merely responded, "'Sure,' as if that had ever been a real consideration. Glenn piped up with a damn speech about God and family and destiny. We all looked at him, then at each other."[30]

Seated in alphabetical order, Grissom had the thankless task of following Glenn's loquaciousness. He and the others did their best in a setting none of them had ever handled before. Asked about the reaction of his wife and children to the program, Grissom noted: "My wife feels the same way, or of course I wouldn't be here. She is with me all the way. The boys are too little to realize what is going on yet, but I am sure they will feel the same way." As for his motivation for accepting his new assignment, Grissom noted that his air force career had been in service to his country and "here is another opportunity where they need my talents." The grilling from the assembled media horde took its toll on the usually taciturn Hoosier. Responding to the question about which of the tests had been the most difficult, Grissom agreed with Glenn about the dreaded probing of various orifices (one was nicknamed the "Steel Eel" by those who endured it), but also added, "To me I think this is the worst, here [the press conference]."[31]

The attention lavished on the astronauts by the media was soon unleashed on their families as well. Before that first uncomfortable press conference, Grissom had called his wife to warn her about the possibility of being "jumped on" by reporters. After a visit to her doctor's office to receive a shot of penicillin for a case of the flu, Betty had stopped at a grocery store for a few items when the first journalists—two from *Life* magazine—tracked her down, followed her back home, and helped her when more and more reporters arrived—a group she considered to be both rude and aggressive. "They [the media] took up residence on your property, in your driveway and that stuff," she remembered. "Shoot, you didn't invite them in, they just opened the door. *Life* didn't do that, they were nicer." One reporter even brought his typewriter with him and pounded out his story on top of the trunk of his car. Although the Grissoms had an unlisted number, the calls from the press grew so great that the phone company insisted the family have a new number. "The phone didn't ring for two or three days," Betty said. "I said, 'You know, they didn't call me back to tell me what my new number is.' I didn't even know it." She called the telephone company to ask about the new number, not knowing if they would believe her, but they gave her the information. "That was kind of funny," she said. "But at least the phone was quiet."[32]

Grissom's eldest son, Scott, found all the attention somewhat perplexing. To his way of thinking, his father's move from testing jet planes to going into space seemed like a natural evolution in his career. "I think probably the biggest shock to me was how the kids at school reacted to it," he said. "I didn't know quite what to do with that. As a family we were a very shy bunch and that was really unsettling." Of course, Scott Grissom had become accustomed to change over the years as a member of a military family, becoming very self reliant in the process. Once while living in Enon, Ohio, Betty became ill with the flu on her son's first day in second grade. When she asked her son if he could make it to school on his own, he answered with a confident, "Sure!" and made it to class with no problem. "Everything went smoothly," she recalled, "except for one thing: he was put into the first grade. But then at noon he decided he'd had enough of that and he got up and announced that they had it all wrong and that he belonged in the second grade."[33]

The incredible amount of press scrutiny even reached as far as Mitchell, Indiana. Grissom had called his parents and his in-laws the night before the press conference to tell them that he had been selected as an astronaut. The next day, the phone rang off the hook at the offices of the *Mitchell Tribune* with major newspapers and wire services all seeking background information on the small town's newest hero. "The day it was announced," said Norman Grissom, who worked at the newspaper, "I got calls from all over the country, even from a newspaper in London." Back at the Grissom residence, Dennis Grissom came home from work at his job at the Baltimore and Ohio Railroad to give an interview to a reporter from the *Bedford Daily Times-Mail*'s Mitchell bureau. While there, the reporter had to wait until Dennis (his wife had gone to a club meeting at a friend's home) finished three telephone interviews. Taking a break from the constantly ringing phone, Dennis said of his son: "Of course we're proud of him. This is what he wants. I know he'd have been disappointed if he hadn't been chosen." In a later interview with the *Indianapolis Times*, Cecile Grissom expressed some fears for her son's safety. When her son had called to tell his parents he had made the first cut of pilots to be considered for the space program, he had asked her why wouldn't she like to have one of her sons go into outer space. "I said I'd have to study that for awhile," she told the *Times* reporter, Nancy Lowe. "It would be an honor, but still. . . ."[34]

There was at least one man in Mitchell who had an inkling

GETTY IMAGES

Gus and Betty Grissom go for a bicycle ride. Gus borrowed his eldest son Scott's bike, while Betty rides her own.

of Gus's newfound fame before the rest of the town. Grissom's boyhood friend Bill Head had talked to him in Mitchell at his in-laws' farm shortly before the official announcement had been made. When Grissom told Head that he soon would be heading out west for some testing, Head, kidding, asked him if they were going to shoot him to the moon? Grissom grinned and replied: "No, but I'm going to get close." The confident assertion from his friend reminded Head of an incident from Thanksgiving Day 1949, when Grissom performed the duties of best man at Head's wedding. On that occasion, Grissom had been entrusted with holding onto the wedding ring for the ceremony. When the time came to hand over the beloved item, Grissom made a frantic search but "couldn't find the ring to save his soul," Head recalled. Grilled by Head on how he could find the moon when he couldn't find a ring in his pocket, Grissom pointed out that the moon was "a little bit bigger than a ring."[35]

There were some in the media who sought more than the normal access given by NASA to the astronauts and their families. Even before the names of the astronauts had been announced, *Life* magazine, under the direction of Ed Thompson, its managing editor, planned to see if their stories were available to the highest bidder. In hopes that such an arrangement could be made, editors at the weekly magazine—one of America's most popular periodicals—wrote drafts of potential contracts for the eventual space explorers. By the time the astronauts were named, however, according to Loudon Wainwright, one of *Life's* top writers and ghost-writer for many of the articles under the astronauts' bylines, those at the magazine realized "money offers would have to be made to the group as a whole and not to a single man." It would take years, perhaps, to pinpoint who would fly the first flights, said Wainwright. In addition, officials at NASA were concerned about what might happen if, for example, Shepard arranged a deal with the *New York Times* while Cooper sold his story to *Life*. A group contract with financial rewards for all, regardless of who flew first, might solve this difficulty and also "promote a sense of unity and teamwork among them." To start the ball rolling, *Life* editors drafted letters on the day of the public announcement of the astronauts' names outlining such an arrangement.[36]

On May 8, 1959, Walter T. Bonney, NASA's chief of information, sent to President Eisenhower's office a policy memorandum giving the astronauts the freedom, "singly and collectively, to make any agreement they see fit for the sale of their personal stories." The memo did note that all unclassified information about the astronauts in their official duties with the Mercury program "will be promptly made available to the public by NASA." The space agency wanted to have the astronauts accessible to the entire world as a stark contrast to the closed Russian program. Of course, as Wainwright pointed out, the contract with *Life* also proved to be a "superb vehicle" for NASA to be able to tell its story in the pages of one of the country's leading magazines to the

American people in a positive manner. The agency, he said, required "public awareness and acceptance to keep its programs going—and viewed favorably by Congress." What better way to reach the public than a magazine that reached six million to seven million readers a week?[37]

To ensure that NASA and the astronauts were well served in the journalistic rush for an exclusive, Bonney asked for assistance from Leo DeOrsey, a Washington, D.C., attorney whose clients included such celebrities as Arthur Godfrey and Edward R. Murrow. "I said to him in so many words, 'Leo, I want you to do a public service that you won't get a dime for,'" remembered Bonney. "I told him what the problem was, and he said he'd help. He was tremendously excited and enthused about what the boys were going to be doing." The astronauts and their wives met with DeOrsey to discuss their possible relationship at a dinner at a Washington country club. After dinner, DeOrsey announced to the group that there were two conditions he wished to state before he would agree to work with them. "Uh-oh, here it comes," Glenn remembered thinking. DeOrsey, however, surprised them all when his conditions were to accept no fee for his work nor any reimbursement for expenses. "Leo sat back with a deadpan expression," said Glenn, "and awaited our response. I thought I had missed something. Then we all looked at one another and, one by one, began to grin. Leo broke into a broad smile, and we all started laughing together." The astronauts were only too happy to accept DeOrsey's generous offer, signing an agreement with him on May 28 that gave all of them an equal share in whatever proceeds might come from "the literary work, motion pictures, radio or television productions, including personal appearances (other than those in line with their official duties)."[38]

DeOrsey set out to auction off the exclusive rights to the astronauts' personal stories to such interested parties as *Life*, *Saturday Evening Post*, *Look*, and *Newsweek*. Instead of a heated competition, however, only one of the periodicals— *Life*—seemed willing to meet DeOrsey's initial minimum asking price of $500,000, to be divided equally among the seven astronauts and their wives over the life of Project Mercury—quite a financial boon for a group of pilots making on the average of $10,000 per year. The magazine, part of Henry Luce's empire, trumpeted its triumph in its August 24, 1959, issue, noting, "*Life*, and *Life* alone," would have the inside details of the lives of these new American heroes. News of the arrangement brought outraged cries of protest from the rest of the media. "The story of what the Mercury astronauts do in Project Mercury belongs to the public," noted Alfred Friendly, *Washington Post* managing editor. "It cannot be sold by anyone to anyone." Friendly's opinion was later seconded by Turner Catledge, *New York Times* managing editor, who suggested that whatever property rights there may be in the astronauts' personal stories, those rights did not belong to the astronauts, but to the public footing the bill for the American space program.[39]

To celebrate its publishing coup, *Life* sent a contingent of writers, editors, and photographers to Langley for a get-acquainted party with the astronauts and their wives. In addition to discussing potential story ideas for the training period in which the astronauts would be involved before the first flights into space, the group from the magazine also attempted to answer questions about such a deal from some of the astronauts' wives, who "seemed to have more doubts about the ethical problems of the arrangements than their husbands—and certainly more than were admitted to by the people from *Life*—although no one, in his or her party glow, was suggesting that the contract that had brought them together should be canceled." Betty Grissom commiserated with those members of the press who were upset about the astronauts' deal with *Life*, but noted that if she gave an interview about her life to one reporter, hundreds of others would soon be clamoring for attention. In addition, the *Life* contract offered her family more opportunities to be together. "In fact," she said, "if we had not had the money, I don't know when we'd ever have seen Gus. Once we had the money, we could go to the Cape and spend a week or two and then come back."[40]

Whatever the nagging doubts expressed about the deal, *Life* quickly used its exclusive access to good advantage, featuring the astronauts on the cover of its September 14, 1959, issue, followed a week later by a cover story on the wives. These were the first in a long series of pieces on the space program and set the stage for the countless articles to follow that portrayed the astronauts as all-American boys possessing the steel-eyed courage and determination to battle the Soviet menace in the new frontier of space. Not surprisingly, the bland, Boy-Scout image developed in the pages of *Life* received its share of criticism from readers and other members of the press. Wainwright considered the criticism to be fair, explaining that one reason for it came from the approval power enjoyed by both NASA and the astronauts. Some of the astronauts, he said, were determined never to "seem anxious, fearful, naïve, immodest, irreverent, unkind, angry, jealous or in any way uncertain that the whole enterprise was going to come out just fine." Although the changes requested in copy by the astronauts were "rarely big" and in no way distorted the facts of the space program, they did tend to blur the distinctions among the seven men. "The pieces lost bite and humor, which were real qualities of a number of the pilots, because seeing their complaints or jokes in print often made them uncomfortable," said Wainwright.[41]

The article on Grissom, headlined "You Just Don't Have Time to Get Frightened," presented a family man with brown hair and brown eyes who just happened to be an experienced pilot with confidence in his ability to represent the United States in the space race and, possibly, risk his life in the effort. After detailing his days flying against MIGs in Korea, and subsequent much more dangerous duty of teaching rookie aviators piloting skills, Grissom turned to the dangers of entering the atmosphere aboard a spacecraft during reentry. Although

Grissom fixes a roof leak at his house after a heavy snow.

an autopilot had been designed to control the capsule during reentry, Grissom, not surprisingly for a pilot, stressed the need for manual control in case anything went wrong, a job "calling for absolute coolness and concentration." And even if he would be chosen to be the first into space, Grissom did not think he would be scared, pointing to a test flight he had made at Wright-Patterson that some had considered "downright suicidal." The night before the flight he had wondered if he would be scared on takeoff, but as it turned out he was far too busy doing his job to have time to be scared. "The best guess I could get was that the plane would fly," he told *Life* readers, "and it did. So will the capsule."[42]

Betty also expressed confidence in the space program for her article in *Life*, which appeared in the magazine a week after her husband's story. She dismissed the dangers involved in her husband's profession, noting that Grissom insisted flying was much safer statistically than driving a car and that he planned to make certain of coming back safely before he would let NASA shoot him into space. "I just accepted that and haven't worried any more about it," she said. Despite this attempt at putting on a brave face to a program fraught with potential dangers, Betty did convey some anxiety. In looking over the photograph of all seven astronauts on the cover of *Life*, Mark Grissom, then five years old, had pointed to Scott Carpenter and proclaimed he would go into space first and his father second. Grissom laughed and insisted he would be the first into space. "I guess I will worry if it is Gus," said Betty.

After this admission of fear, however, she added: "But I will be happy too, because I know this is what he wants to do."[43]

The cover shoot for the story on the astronauts' wives had caused some consternation among its intended subjects, who were to be photographed by famed *Life* lensman Ralph Morse. In addition to worrying about their hair and what clothes to wear, the wives had to ponder makeup ("I'm scrubbing my face, and that's it," Betty was heard to comment) and lipstick color. After enduring a five-hour session under Morse's relentless shutter, the women were aghast to see what the magazine had done to them. "And there we were," said Rene Carpenter, "seven broad, toothy smiles, sporting hideous lipstick in some never-before-glimpsed shade of red." When queried by the wives about what had happened, officials at *Life* explained that the lipstick color had been changed at the lab so all of them would be similar in appearance.[44]

Grissom's confident assertion of success for Project Mercury would soon be put to the test, as the astronauts underwent a grueling series of classroom work, training, and visits to the contractors responsible for producing America's space hardware. In addition to working with, and competing against, his fellow astronauts for the honor of being the first man into space, Grissom and NASA faced the continued threat of Communist Russia's dominance in the early days of space exploration. The Soviet Union, too, had its own set of astronauts, actually cosmonauts, training hard to win further glories for their country. As John F. Kennedy observed during his 1960 presidential campaign, "We are in a strategic race with the Russians and have been losing. If a man orbits the earth this year his name will be Ivan."[45]

4

Mercury

ON APRIL 27, 1959, THE SEVEN ASTRONAUTS, ON LEAVE FROM their respective military branches of service, reported to the Space Task Group at Langley Air Force Base to begin training for Project Mercury. They were housed in a two-story building dating from World War I in an office equipped with seven identical gray-metal desks, signs displaying their names and branches of service, and one secretary, seventeen-year-old Nancy Lowe. "She handled all our letters and reports," remembered Gordon Cooper, "and it was a real workload, with seven bosses, each of whom considered himself a leader—seven alpha males in the same pack."[1] Alan Shepard remembered that there existed some wariness among the seven, as they all were competing for the same job. "So on the one hand there was a sense of friendliness and maybe some support," he said, "but on the other hand, 'Hey, I hope the rest of you guys are happy because I'm going to make the first flight.'"[2]

Initially, the astronauts worked on becoming acquainted with NASA and their mission, and settled into their new homes. Gus Grissom and his wife and two sons joined the families of Wally Schirra and Deke Slayton in purchasing homes at a housing development called Stonybrook near Fort Eustis, not far from Langley in Newport News, Virginia, commuting to work together and becoming close friends. Cooper and Scott Carpenter made their homes at the Langley Air Force Base, and Shepard received an assignment to the naval air station at Oceana, Virginia. John Glenn chose to keep his family at their home in Arlington, Virginia, and he lived in bachelor officers' quarters at Langley.[3]

Joining the astronauts at the rapidly growing NASA were aeronautical engineers from all over the country, and even some from farther away. In February 1959 the Canadian government had decided to cancel a program to produce an advanced jet interceptor, the CF-105 Avro Arrow, putting numerous aerospace engineers, including some who had been hired for the project from Great Britain, out of work. Robert Gilruth, NASA administrator, heard about the available pool of talent from a Canadian acquaintance and moved quickly to snatch them up for America's new technological venture. "Here we were in the Space Task Group just absolutely strapped for top people, and so he suggested I might want to come up and talk with some of these people and recruit," Gilruth said. "It was a big break for us." Twenty-five Avro engineers initially accepted NASA's offer of employ-

The original seven astronauts in the familiar silver Mercury pressure suits, built by the B. F. Goodrich Company.

ment, and others would find jobs with the contractors connected with supplying the equipment for the space agency.[4]

Another addition to NASA's effort to conquer space proved to be a familiar sight to one of the astronauts. A North Carolina State graduate with a degree in mechanical engi-

NASA

Sam Beddingfield (left) helps John Glenn with a logo for his orbital Mercury mission.

neering in aeronautical options ("They didn't have an engineering department back then"), Sam Beddingfield after college joined the air force and received an assignment to test airplanes at Wright-Patterson Air Force Base. It was at the base where he met and became friends with Grissom. After his wife became pregnant, Beddingfield decided to leave the service and help operate a seven-hundred-acre farm his father-in-law had in North Carolina. "It took me about three days to realize I really didn't care about farming," he said. Hoping to find work at Langley Air Force Base as a flight research engineer, Beddingfield instead received the advice from the base commander to try his luck at NASA. According to Beddingfield, he responded to the advice with: "I don't know anything about rockets." The commander answered back: "They don't either."[5]

The first person Beddingfield saw when he arrived at NASA's small collection of buildings at Langley was Grissom. After he repeated to Grissom the remark he gave to the commander about not knowing anything about rockets, the astronaut assured him that would not be a problem. "He says, 'You're a civilian now?' I said, 'Yes, I got out of the military,'" Beddingfield recalled. "He says, 'That's perfect.' I said, 'What do you mean?' He says, 'You come into this job and if you don't like it, all you have to do is get up and walk out, and [there] ain't nothing they can do about it.'" Beddingfield ended up at Cape Canaveral in Florida in October 1959, where he oversaw the mechanical and pyrotechnic systems for the Mercury spacecraft, which included making sure the parachutes, explosive hatch, escape rockets, retro-rockets, and separation rockets functioned to perfection.[6]

The astronauts' early time working for NASA consisted of lectures and briefings on the systems involved with the blunt, cone-shaped Mercury spacecraft designed by Max Faget that would rocket into space, streak back to Earth protected by a heat shield, and finally plop into the ocean swinging under a parachute. The men received instruction on such subject areas as space physics, elementary mechanics and aerodynamics, basic physiology, navigating in space, principles of guidance and control, and elements of communication. They journeyed to Morehead Planetarium at the University of North Carolina for eight hours of instruction on star recognition and celestial navigation. The astronauts also read technical manuals from all of the contractors involved in producing hardware for the program; were fitted for their space suits at the Goodrich plant in Akron, Ohio; and visited the other facilities involved in producing the equipment, including McDonnell in St. Louis (spacecraft), Convair (Atlas rocket) in San Diego, Cape Canaveral (launch facilities) in Florida, and the Redstone Arsenal (Redstone rocket) in Huntsville, Alabama. On the visit to Convair, where Grissom made his famous "Do good work" speech, the astronauts learned just how popular they had become. When they arrived at the airport, they had signed autographs for two boys, the sons of a friend of Carpenter's. When the astronauts prepared to depart San Diego, the boys again showed up at the airport asking for more autographs. When Schirra asked them what they had done with the ones they had given them before, the boys noted: "We traded them. They're worth two toads apiece."[7]

There were some, however, who did not share the public's exalted view of the astronauts—other test pilots. Because they believed an astronaut would have little control over his machine, they derisively termed the craft and the person who manned it as "Spam in a can." In October 1959 Slayton and Chris Kraft, the person at NASA responsible for developing the worldwide tracking network and a flight control center for Project Mercury, traveled to Los Angeles to speak at the Society of Experimental Test Pilots annual meeting. "This was my chance to tell our side of the story and maybe change a few minds," said Kraft. "Deke was even more determined. He didn't like the Spam joke at all." Kraft's presentation went well, especially his statement that NASA planned to build a "procedures trainer" so astronauts and members of the flight control center could train together before a launch. Slayton, whose talk was titled "The Space Program: A Pilot's Point of View," lambasted those who believed anyone "'from a college-trained chimpanzee to a village idiot' could do as well in space as a trained test pilot." If the astronauts were eliminated from the equation, Slayton asserted, America would have to concede that man did not belong in space. "He didn't convert everybody," Kraft said of Slayton, "but he had most of them in his pocket when he was done talking."[8]

As Slayton tried to convince his test-flight brethren of the astronauts' role as pilot, the astronauts themselves were complaining about one element missing from their training program, created in part by Robert B. Voas, NASA's astronaut training officer. The issue would cause the first public relations crisis for the young space agency. As veteran pilots, the astronauts wanted flying high-performance aircraft to be part of their training, but they spent most of their time taking commercial flights to reach their various assignments. "We were fighter pilots and we longed to get back to flying," said Cooper. "We saw a dual purpose; we'd get where we needed to be quicker while keeping up our proficiency." The loss of flight time also meant a loss of flight pay, about $190 a month for an air force captain, for example, if he failed to fly at least four hours a month, Slayton noted. The matter came to a head when Cooper confided to New York congressman Jim Fulton during a lunch conversation about how flying was not part of the astronauts' training. The complaint reached Congress, which brought pressure to bear on NASA. "The higher-ups at NASA were none too happy," Cooper remembered, "but my fellow astronauts were delighted."[9]

Within a few weeks, the astronauts had access to some T-33 jet trainers and later to F-102 and F-106 fighters at Langley Air Force Base. Slayton and Grissom became big users of the aircraft, going to the base on a Saturday, taking off, "flying the plane cross-country until our fannies were tired," catching some sleep, and returning the next day, noted Slayton. "You might spend thirty hours flying in a short time, and by the time you got home you didn't want to look at an airplane for a while," said Slayton. "But that was the kind of thing we had to do." Through flying with him, Slayton said Grissom became his best friend among the seven astronauts, a friendship enhanced by also engaging in such activities together as hunting. On one occasion, the two were deer hunting in the Dismal Swamp in southern Virginia when Slayton heard Grissom fire his rifle and disappear from view for about an hour. Looking to find his friend, Slayton finally saw him labor out of the brush. Grissom told his friend he had shot a bear but couldn't find him. Finally locating the prize, the two men struggled to get the carcass from the swamp to the road and from there another seven miles back to their car. Upon reaching Grissom's garage, where they were preparing to skin their trophy, the men were stopped short in the pride at the size of their accomplishment by a comment from Scott Grissom, who exclaimed: "Hey, where'd you get that *cat*?"[10]

Voas and other members of the life sciences team at NASA were ambivalent about flying being part of the training regimen because they did not want to lose an astronaut in a crash. The astronauts were happy, however, and Voas even had the opportunity to fly with them. The uproar over the flying issue became the first indication of the power the astronauts enjoyed as America's newest heroes. "The public was going to focus on those astronauts and what they said and wanted and did," Voas said. "I think many . . . were not really recognizing how significant the power of the astronauts relative to public relations issues would be."[11]

Whether they were aware of the power they enjoyed or not, the astronauts took seriously NASA's original stated intention that it wanted to use their piloting and engineering skills. Because the Mercury project was too complex for any one person to understand, the astronauts allocated assignments based upon an individual's area of expertise and previous experience. "We tried to avoid going around like a patrol of Boy Scouts or 'Those Seven Little Dwarfs from Mercury,'"

NASA

A worker examines the retro-rocket and posigrade-rocket package used to de-orbit the Mercury spacecraft at the end of its mission.

said Schirra. "We tried to behave, instead, like seven vice presidents of a company. Each of us took charge of a different department." With their naval backgrounds, Carpenter handled communication and navigation; Shepard, tracking and recovery; and Schirra, the spacecraft's life support system and the astronaut's pressure suit. Glenn's prior involvement in aircraft design led to his role in the layout of the Mercury capsule's crew compartment, whose instrument panel alone had 165 different sets of switches, dials, buttons, and lights. Air force officers Slayton and Cooper were responsible for monitoring the Atlas and Redstone rockets respectively. With his background in mechanical engineering at college and Wright-Patterson Air Force Base, Grissom was tasked with monitoring the spacecraft's automatic and manual control systems. "Everything was parceled out fairly evenly," said Slayton. "We each went our own way, dug into our subject, and then made reports back to the others whenever we discovered something we thought they ought to know." One of his favorite memories of the Mercury program, Schirra noted, was how the seven astronauts, whom he described as "superachievers with super egos," put aside their differences to work together as a team and become as close as brothers. "But sibling rivalry is also part of brotherhood," he pointed out. "We had a lot of that."[12]

Whenever a problem occurred, the astronauts would gather together in their office at Langley and hold what came to be called a "séance," because, as Schirra noted, people believed they were "acting like swamis in there . . . and were pulling answers out from under the table." They tried to avoid nit-picking on minor matters, he said, but they "*never* avoided getting into technical arguments with each other when there was something big at stake." After hammering out any potential disagreements among them and coming up with a concrete proposal, the astronauts could then present a united front to NASA management. The astronauts had decided that since they were charged with the responsibility of flying and risking their lives in the capsule, "it ought to be something that *we* wanted, not just something that satisfied the slide-rule pilots," said Schirra.[13]

This strategy worked wonders after the astronauts' first look at some mock-ups of the Mercury capsule at the McDonnell plant. After reviewing the preliminary design, the astronauts used their backgrounds in engineering and testing jets to request several changes. In addition to revisions to the instrument panel and installing a manual control system in case the automatic system failed, the astronauts also sought to replace the two small portholes on the spacecraft with a large window they could use to orientate themselves and possibly correct the capsule's position. Glenn also pointed out that since one of them might be the first person in space, it was "unthinkable" not to have a window so whoever flew the mission could describe the sight for the waiting audience back on Earth. Another design change sought by the group involved replacing the side hatch, which had to be bolted on, with one incorporating shaped charges designed to blow the hatch off quickly in case of an emergency. Otherwise, an occupant of a Mercury spacecraft seeking a quick escape had to move a small pressure bulkhead in order to squeeze through a narrow opening through the antenna compartment at the top. Finally, they asked the engineers to stop calling Mercury a "capsule," preferring instead the more aeronautical term "spacecraft." (The astronauts were not the only ones who disliked using the word capsule. James McDonnell, the owner of the company making the craft, noted: "It sounds as if we were manufacturing a pill!")[14]

John F. Yardley, the lead engineer at McDonnell in the design of the Mercury spacecraft, said the astronauts were not yet the "Gods they became later, but their inputs were considered." Although it was too late to incorporate them into the Mercury craft designated for the first planned suborbital flight, the astronauts' suggestions for the window and hatch were implemented for subsequent flights. "We felt we would put man-in-the-loop," Schirra said. "We wanted to replace chimpanzees. We wanted to prove we could fly the vehicle, do something that man had never done before, of course. We wanted to be sure we could do it well. We knew the tools we needed."[15] After one trip to McDonnell, some of the astronauts sensed that the engineers working there were on pins and needles, just waiting for them to criticize another aspect of the spacecraft's design. Thinking fast, the astronauts decided to satirize their own seriousness by asking the engineers to consider how to handle a potential case of airsickness in the crew compartment. On the flight back to Langley, Glenn and Shepard grabbed a paper airsickness bag from the pocket of a seat and wrote on it: "Here is the answer to the airsickness problem. Please subject this specimen to environmental justification testing of salt spray, fungus, high and low temperatures, vibration, shock and capacity." Once they landed, the astronauts mailed the bag to a McDonnell vice president, whose reaction to the whole matter was not recorded for posterity.[16]

The spirit of cooperation shown among the astronauts in details on the spacecraft fractured when it came to extracurricular activities. In its coverage of the space program, *Life* magazine had presented the astronauts as pristine champions of the American way of life, fighting heroically against the Communist menace to capture the lofty frontiers of space. They were, as the magazine quoted a NASA official, "premium individuals picked for an unconventional task."[17] It proved to be an impossible image to live up to, especially with the temptations dangled before them on a daily, and nightly, basis. "Any one of us who was looking for companionship while he was on the road would not have to look very far," noted Glenn, who feared that just one unfavorable story in the media could tarnish the astronauts' image and place the entire project in serious jeopardy. The program already faced many critics, including those who favored using unmanned satellites instead of sending precious human cargo into space.

Delays with Mercury had also become part of the 1960 presidential campaign pitting Democratic challenger John F. Kennedy, who warned of a growing "missile gap" between the United States and the Soviet Union, against GOP candidate and incumbent vice president Richard Nixon. "If the program's most visible and highly regarded components—the astronauts—proved to have feet of clay," Glenn said, "I was afraid it would erode popular support and provide further grounds to attack the program."[18]

Matters came to a head during a visit by the astronauts to the Convair plant to meet with engineers working on the Atlas rocket. Previously, Glenn had voiced some concerns about the astronauts' behavior at one of the group's "séances" at Langley; he had also mentioned them to Lt. Col. John "Shorty" Powers, an air force public relations officer assigned as the astronauts' spokesman. During their visit to Convair, the group stayed in the Konakai, a hotel with a view overlooking the Pacific Ocean. Asleep in his room one night, Glenn remembered being awakened at 2:00 a.m. by a telephone call from Powers, who informed him that a West Coast newspaper had followed one of the astronauts and had taken incriminating photographs that it was prepared to publish on its front page the next morning. Glenn called the editor of the newspaper and pleaded with him not to run the story. "I talked about the godless Communists and how they were ahead of us," he said, "and how the press had to let us get back in the space race. I pulled out all the stops." It worked;

the article never appeared in print.[19]

The "séance" held at the Konakai the next morning became part of the astronauts' legend, becoming a key part of Tom Wolfe's book *The Right Stuff*. Instead of being prompted by a proposed newspaper article, however, Wolfe had the meeting inspired by Carpenter giving his room with a double bed at the hotel to another astronaut who needed it for his night's entertainment. Carpenter apparently related the story to Glenn "as an amusing local note." Whatever the reason for the gathering, both Wolfe and Glenn agree that at it the marine ripped into his mates for their supposed philandering, or, as he termed it, the failure by anyone to "keep his pants zipped." Although he said he did not intend to meddle in anyone else's life, Glenn did note that the astronauts were "public figures whether we liked it or not, and we had to act like it." According to Wolfe's account, Glenn's lecture was met by grudging support from Grissom and Slayton, and an angry rebuttal from Shepard, who told Glenn not to "foist his view of morality on anybody else in the group."[20]

Examining the methods used by NASA to prepare the astronauts for the rigor of spaceflight, it's a wonder the astronauts had any energy left for nocturnal adventures. At Edwards Air Force Base in California, the astronauts flew special parabolic flights in the rear cockpit of a two-seat F-100F jet trainer, which gave them about a minute's worth of weightlessness. Additional weightless flights were achieved in a padded rear compartment of a modified C-131 transport and a converted C-135 cargo plane. According to Carpenter, each of the astronauts had their own way of eating and drinking in this new environment. For example, Shepard enjoyed holding a bottle "a sporting distance" from his mouth and squirting it in, while Grissom "let some orange juice drift out of his bottle and enjoyed watching big bubbles of juice float around the cockpit with him."[21]

In addition to becoming familiar with the sensations of weightlessness, the astronauts visited the Aviation Medical Acceleration Laboratory at the Naval Air Development Centre in Johnsville, Pennsylvania, the site of the world's largest human centrifuge, called the "Wheel" by its test subjects. At the facility they endured the g-forces they would encounter with the liftoff and reentry during both Redstone and Atlas flights. In the forty-eight hours each of the men spent riding the centrifuge, they discovered that the force of 16 g was the limit to which they could function properly. As Glenn told a fellow pilot, even at 16 g it "took every bit of strength and technique you could muster to retain consciousness. I found there was quite a bit more technique involved in taking this kind of g than we had thought." To help them tolerate the crushing g forces, the astronauts learned a special breathing method to keep from blacking out during critical moments. They were assisted in this process by Dr. William K. Douglas, a NASA flight surgeon, who also participated in the centrifuge and other training undergone by the astronauts. As a flight surgeon, said Douglas, he

NASA

Mercury astronauts experience weightless flight on a C-131 aircraft flying a zero-g trajectory at the Wright Air Development Center. Weightless flights were a new form of training for the Mercury astronauts, and parabolic flights that briefly go beyond the Earth's tug of gravity continue to be used for spaceflight training purposes.

believed "you ought to do everything that your crews do, that you can, but you should never excel at it, at least not better than the crew does."[22]

Another fiendish training device concocted by NASA was an apparatus dubbed MASTIF, which stood for Multiple Axis Space Test Inertia Facility. As Grissom explained it, the trainer, located at an old wind tunnel at the Lewis Research Center in Cleveland, gave the astronauts their "wildest ride." Consisting of three frameworks of tubular aluminum, MASTIF had the ability to give its subjects a dizzying ride in three directions at once—yawing, pitching, and rolling. The astronauts used the device to train on the three-axis control stick used to control the Mercury spacecraft's attitude via hydrogen peroxide nozzles. "A mission on the MASTIF began like a carnival ride," said Grissom. "You tumbled slowly, twisted and rolled as your body lurched against the tight harness that strapped you to the couch. Then you rotated faster and faster until finally you were spinning violently in three different directions at once—head over heels, round and round as if you were on a merry-go-round, and sideways as if your arms and legs were tied to the spokes of a wheel." If an astronaut could not stop the insane gyrations by using the control stick, he was in immediate danger of becoming dizzy and vomiting. On especially rough rides, the astronauts wobbled off of the trainer and had to lay down on a cot provided by the technicians for at least a half hour "before everything stopped spinning," said Glenn. Despite the uncomfortable ride, Grissom said MASTIF provided the seven astronauts with more confidence in their ability "to pilot a spacecraft than any other test we took."[23]

For Schirra, the worst part of the training came during what he called "grueling" survival exercises in case an emergency reentry landed an astronaut in a desert. After a two-and-a-half day course of instruction at the air force's survival school at Stead Air Force Base in Nevada, the seven astronauts were left in the desert outside of Reno to fend for themselves with just a few rations, flares, and a parachute. To the surprise of the astronauts, an unexpected guest joined them on the expedition—Ralph Morse, *Life* magazine photographer. Although told by Powers that the survival exercise was to be off limits to the press, Morse, who had experience shooting combat in World War II, became determined to find the astronauts. Chartering a plane, Morse flew around the desert until he spotted a parachute, which the astronauts had spread out as a standard way of contacting search-and-rescue teams. To find his way back, Morse dropped from the plane one-pound bags of flour to mark each intersection, rented a jeep, and drove to the astronauts' base camp. In retaliation, Schirra and Shepard wired a smoke flare from the jeep's engine block to the fan belt and told Morse to move the jeep. "Ralph was still gloating and didn't suspect a thing," Schirra said. "He got in the jeep and hit the starter. Blam! He was engulfed in a blanket of green smoke. He started to back up in an effort to escape, but it was no use. He was covered with green dust, and the jeep had to be towed back to Reno and sold for scrap."[24]

Because they were so enmeshed in training, visiting contractors, and other public functions on behalf of NASA, the astronauts had little time left for a home life. Slayton estimated that during one four-month period the astronauts spent one day out of every three traveling on behalf of the program, and each of them had logged approximately twenty thousand miles.[25] As spouses of military pilots, the astronauts' wives were accustomed to frequent separations, with Betty noting

Wearing protective headgear fashioned from parachute material, the astronauts mug for the camera while participating in survival training in Nevada. Left to right: Cooper, Carpenter, Glenn, Shepard, Grissom, Schirra, and Slayton.

that her husband knew the time away from home "would not be a problem with me. I could take care of the situation at home." At first, she had waited for her husband to come home from his frequent trips before telling him of some of the mischief the two boys had concocted. "I thought this is not what he wants to hear when he comes home," she said. "I'm not going to do that anymore. I'm going to handle the situation." Gus tried to help as best he could, sternly reproaching his son Scott on one occasion, after he had talked back to his mother. "Scotty never did it again," observed Betty, "and I guess Mark learned from that. He never tried it." The astronaut used his engineering skills on one project with the boys, bringing home plans from *Popular Mechanics* for them to construct a small sailboat that Scott and Mark could pilot on a lake near their home. Painted yellow with parachute cloth for a sail, the boat underwent construction in the Grissoms' garage. "He spent a lot of time doing that," Scott said of his father. When Hurricane Donna hit the East Coast in 1961, the boat "actually blew out of our backyard and went to another part of the lake," he remembered. His mother and father piled into their car "in the middle of the eye of this hurricane to the other side of the lake to go get it! We loved that boat and that boat wasn't going to get away!"[26]

The astronauts' absences from home, and lionization by the rest of the public, led to rumors about their behavior, as Glenn had feared. Although none of the rumors ever made it into print during NASA's halcyon years, they did reach the wives back home. "It seems like the girls were all thrilled at meeting an astronaut," said Betty, "and of course the wives weren't thrilled because we had known them all our lives." She acknowledged that her husband might have found the attention "hard to resist," as the public treated him as a celebrity, while back home his family was waiting to greet him with its usual array of problems and complaints. After going through a "few hard months" of worrying about the situation, Betty decided there was little she "could do about it and I wasn't going to sit around and worry. Worry didn't help me a bit. I wasn't feeling sorry for myself. I just tried not to think about those possibilities."[27]

Grissom helps bring the boat he and his two sons built to a safe landing on a lake near the family's Virginia home.

As Project Mercury entered its second year, the astronauts found themselves spending more and more time at Cape Canaveral in Brevard County, Florida, an area known more for its citrus groves than its industry. Since a 1946 decision by a committee of the Joint Chiefs of Staff, the Cape had served as the location for the U.S. military to test its guided missiles. The launch complexes at the Cape were down the road from Cocoa Beach, which before the arrival of NASA had been a quiet tourist town on the Atlantic Ocean with few amenities. The area had begun to thrive, however, with the advent of the manned space program as NASA employees, contractors, politicians, military officers, and the media descended on the community. Guenter Wendt, a McDonnell Aircraft employee who worked at the Cape as pad leader for the contractor, said the area felt like a "boom town in the middle of a gold rush." From 1950 to 1960, Brevard County became the country's fastest growing county, with its population increasing from 23,653 to 111,435.[28]

A favorite spot for all concerned at Cocoa Beach was the Starlight Motel, managed by Henri Landwirth, a survivor of the Holocaust. After a long day of work at the launch facility (ten- to fourteen-hour workdays were the norm), workers met at the motel's bar, the Starlight Lounge, for drinks. At happy hour, from 5:00 p.m. to 7:00 p.m., anyone who bought a drink received a token for a free beverage. "Whenever contractor reps would come down from their home plants," said Wendt, "we would lube them up at the Starlight, then shake them down for their remaining tokens." To make his customers feel comfortable, Landwirth installed high-quality black lights in the lounge and employed some local artists to paint space scenes that would be highlighted by the special lights. "It was really unusual and helped create a unique atmosphere," noted Landwirth.[29]

The crew quarters for the astronauts were located at Hangar S, which was situated a few miles from the Redstone launch complex on the west side of the Cape near the Banana River. The former air-force hangar was a concrete-block building three stories tall equipped with large sliding doors; it had no air conditioning despite the brutal Florida heat and humidity. The area had been home to a large variety of snakes, and Wendt and others who worked there had a rule that if a worker "were pulling on a cable . . . and it pulled back, let go!" The quarters in the hanger for the astronauts were described by Shepard as "spartan, austere, nondescript and totally uncomfortable," with the room being reached by journeying down a dimly lit hallway, "an unpleasant walk during which we were assailed by hoots, screeches, screams, and howls" from the chimpanzees housed there. Soon, the astronauts abandoned the hangar for plusher accommodations at the Starlight and later at a Holiday Inn run by Landwirth. "Where the boys were," he said, "was where everybody else wanted to be." Although Landwirth proved to be the perfect host for the astronauts, even allowing Cooper to fill the motel's swimming pool with fish so he could cast his line while sitting poolside, the manager did put his foot down if his employees were given any trouble. "Customers I can always get! Good help is hard to find!" said Landwirth, who compared the shenanigans at the Cape to "a giant fraternity party."[30]

Landwirth enticed the astronauts from the Starlight to the Holiday Inn by promising them they would always be guaranteed of having a room. "No exceptions," Landwirth recalled. "When they were in town, they had a room." In one instance, however, the guarantee failed, giving flight surgeon Douglas his "greatest triumph"—beating Grissom to a hotel room. Showing up at the Holiday Inn one day without a reservation, Douglas discovered that he could have the room normally

Grissom studies diagrams of the Mercury spacecraft's systems in the office he shared with the other astronauts.

reserved for Grissom because the astronaut had called Landwirth to tell him he would not need the accommodation. "I got in it [the room] and about two o'clock in the morning in comes ol' Gus wondering, 'Who's in my bed?' Like the three little bears. And I said, 'Well, I guess I'll have to go out and sleep in the car.'" Realizing no rooms were to be had at that hour, Grissom told Douglas not to worry about it and one of the men took the couch while the other had the bed.[31]

Long days working at Cape Canaveral and enduring holds in countdowns and other delays were relieved a bit by practical jokes ("gotchas") the astronauts played on each other or any unwary NASA employee. "As I often said," Schirra noted, "levity is the lubricant of a crisis."[32] The tension was also eased for some via late-night drives in sleek and speedy Corvettes. The Corvettes came courtesy of a one-dollar-a-year lease from General Motors arranged by Jim Rathmann, winner of the 1960 Indianapolis 500 who owned a Chevrolet/Cadillac dealership in nearby Melbourne, Florida. "They were loaners, 'brass hat cars,' meaning we drove them for a year and either bought them or returned them to General Motors," explained Schirra. "It was a common automotive industry practice to loan cars and then sell them as 'executive driven.'" As someone used to being involved in a death-defying activity, the former racecar driver became close to Shepard, Cooper, Schirra (who preferred driving a Maserati), and Grissom. "Gus and I went all over together," Rathmann recalled, including trips by planes to racetracks around the country. "Gus was just a fun guy. He liked everything I did, and I liked things that he did." When at the NASA facility, Grissom would often visit the Rathmann home for dinner and conversation about the space program or auto racing, which Rathmann's wife, Kay, also enjoyed.[33]

The astronauts proved to be as fierce competitors with their cars as they were with who would fly the first Mercury flight, racing against each other on empty roads at Cape Canaveral. "They didn't speed," Wendt observed, "it was more like they just flew close to the ground. If an astronaut offered to give you a lift in his 'vette, you knew you were in for the ride of your life."[34] In one prank, Grissom, Cooper, and Rathmann conspired together to fool Shepard about the speed and performance of his Corvette. After being left in the dust in a couple of races against his fellow astronauts, a fuming Shepard took his car to Rathmann to see what was wrong. A supposedly concerned Rathmann told Shepard he would take care of the problem, but actually refrained from doing any work on the car. After picking up his car, and losing more races, Shepard again took it to Rathmann's dealership where it received a paint job reminiscent of the symbols marked on fighter planes during World War II to designate enemy planes shot down. In this case, however, instead of swastikas or Japanese flags painted on the side, Shepard had a few Volkswagens and bicycles emblazoned on the side of his car. An irate Shepard demanded a meeting with the three men in Rathmann's office, where he learned that they had changed the rear-end ratio of his car, giving it the ability to reach a top speed of 125 miles per hour, but also forcing the car to spend quite a bit of time to achieve that mark.[35]

On another occasion, Grissom again got the best of Shepard. According to Wendt, the two astronauts were at the Cape for testing of the Mercury-Redstone combination. While Shepard left early to get some sleep at his room at the Holiday Inn, Grissom remained behind in the capsule to finish the laborious procedure. Legend has it that it was well past midnight when Grissom sped from the Cape in his Corvette, gaining and losing a Cocoa Beach patrolman in the process. Upon arrival at the Holiday Inn, Grissom, thinking fast, parked his Corvette in front of Shepard's room, ran several doors down to his quarters and hid there with his lights out. When the patrolman arrived, he immediately identified which of the Corvettes had a hot engine and banged on the miscreant's door. A sleepy Shepard, unable to distinguish which Corvette was which in the dark, answered yes when the officer asked him if the car in front of the room was his, and was probably more than a little shocked to be placed under arrest. "I never did hear a credible account of how that episode was actually resolved," said Wendt, "but you can trust that Shepard was the king of revenge. He always got even."[36]

Rathmann and Grissom also sparred playfully with one another from time to time. Traveling to Cape Canaveral one rainy night in Grissom's Corvette after Rathmann had put new wide tires on the car, the astronaut, seated this time in the passenger seat, urged the former racecar driver to go faster. "Gus," Rathmann remembered saying, "these tires have no traction. So he said, 'Oh, you chicken, stand on it.' So I stood on it and sure enough we spun out, way off in the mud. It took two wreckers to get us out of there that night." A few weeks later, Grissom called Rathmann to let him know that he had arranged a trip for his friend aboard a T-38 Talon, a two-seat jet trainer used by the air force. After meeting Grissom at the hangar, Rathmann underwent a lecture by the astronaut about what not to touch in the aircraft and how to eject in case of an emergency. "I said, 'O.K., super.' I didn't even think about him doing any of the trick stuff," said Rathmann. Immediately upon takeoff, Grissom banked the plane until it seemed as if the wing was going to hit the runway. "Then he rolled it once and then went straight up. I thought I was going to slide backwards," Rathmann said. "When he went up and over, my belly almost left me, it was up in my throat. Anyway, I said, 'Put this mother back on the ground, take me back on the ground.' And then he started doing those spirals up there and that scared the living heck out of me. He got even with me and blamed me for that spin-out in the mud."[37]

The astronauts needed plenty of humor to cut the boredom and tension involved with testing the often cranky hardware on which they were gambling their lives. The lowest point for Project Mercury came during a test of the Redstone rocket and Mercury spacecraft (MR-1) on November 21,

GETTY IMAGES

Grissom participates in a launch simulation at the control center at Cape Canaveral in Florida.

1960, a few weeks after Kennedy had squeaked out a razor-thin victory over Nixon in the presidential contest. Schirra, who witnessed the test with the rest of the astronauts, called it "a memorable day, especially for someone who likes sick jokes." The launch, which was also the first trial of Kraft's Mercury Control Center, proceeded on schedule. At 9:00 a.m., with television cameras and reporters witnessing this milestone in America's space efforts, the Redstone's engines fired on schedule. Kraft, who had never witnessed a Redstone launch before, remembered having his eyes glued to the television screen on his console as the command to fire was issued. "Look at the acceleration on that son of a bitch!" Kraft remembered himself exclaiming as smoke obscured the launch site. Astounded engineers in the nearby block-house, however, saw MR-1 wobble a bit and settle back onto the pad after at most a four-to-five-inch liftoff. As the blast of the rocket engine ended, the escape tower atop the Mercury capsule blasted off on its four-thousand-foot flight—the acceleration that had so impressed Kraft. On schedule, the recovery procedures for the spacecraft kicked into gear, with the drogue parachute, main parachute, and reserve para-chute firing one after the other and drooping down onto the rocket "like Mrs. Murphy's laundry," Schirra noted. "The press had a field day," said Kraft. "It wasn't just a funny scene on the pad. It was tragic, and America's space program took another beating in the newspapers, on television, and in Congress."[38]

Perplexed engineers in the blockhouse debated the best way to relieve the pressurized propellant tanks on the Redstone, including having someone shoot holes in the rocket's liquid hydrogen tank with a rifle. That idea was quickly squashed as officials decided to let the heat of the sun eventually boil off the liquid hydrogen in the tanks through its relief valves. An investigation determined that a filed down plug at the end of a power umbilical cord had been the culprit, causing a millisecond delay that waylaid the launch sequence and caused the embarrassing scene of a Mercury capsule popping its top like an uncontrollable bottle of champagne. "Once we realized that the capsule had made the best of a confusing situation and had gone on to perform its duties just as it would have on a normal flight," Glenn noted, "we were rather proud of it." Learning from its mistake, NASA fixed the problem and successfully launched the Mercury spacecraft on a new Redstone on December 21, 1960.[39]

The problems with the MR-1 flight highlighted the precarious nature of the early days of spaceflight. Those who worked for NASA at the Cape often had to improvise to scrounge needed parts or fix damaged equipment. If a precise repair could not be made to meet a schedule, technicians could always turn to an old-fashioned remedy—liberal applications of green missile tape. "It got to the point that people said, 'If you don't have something taped up with green tape, it won't fly,'" Beddingfield recalled. Of course, for those such as Beddingfield, charged as they were with working on the delicate spacecraft, only the most stylish material—silver tape—would do. Joe W. Schmitt, a NASA equipment specialist responsible for overseeing the astronauts' space suits, proudly remembered an instrument panel he used to check out the suits. "I made that out of a three-quarter inch plywood board and I mounted various flow meters and pressure gauges on there and valves of various kinds," said Schmitt. Although crude in design, he said the panel "got the job done." Because NASA in those days had yet to develop a large bureaucracy, workers had a direct voice in the operation. When a problem did occur, said Beddingfield, everyone would "pile into a big conference room and have heated arguments on how to fix it. . . . We really debated. I mean pretty vigorous arguments, and a lot of it in not the classical English language even. But once we decided, everybody would go that way."[40]

The glitches endured by Project Mercury failed to halt the march to manned flight. At the end of 1960, Gilruth called the astronauts together and asked them for their opinions on which of them should be first into space (they couldn't pick themselves). Such a peer vote proved to be upsetting to one astronaut: Glenn. "Months of training," said Glenn, who picked Carpenter in his evaluation, "were being reduced to a popularity contest. After my comments at the séance about everybody's needing to keep their pants zipped, I could imagine where I'd stand in a peer rating." A bemused Slayton later observed that Glenn had figured "he had made all the right moves to win the first Redstone, provided the decision was made from the top. He just figured wrong. Well, it wasn't the last time John ran for something without having the votes he needed." A curious Kraft asked Gilruth what the astronauts had said about each other, but could only get the cryptic reply: "It was interesting."[41]

Finally, late in the afternoon on January 20, 1961, the day before Kennedy was inaugurated as the country's thirty-fifth president, Gilruth gathered the astronauts together in their Langley office to inform them of his decision. Although NASA had initially wanted to keep secret which astronaut would be the first to fly until the morning of the actual liftoff, Gilruth said the first man into space and his backups should have priority time on the Mercury trainers and so, based on the peer ratings, on evaluations from the astronauts' training officers, and his personal judgment, he had decided the names of those who would make the first three flights. After asking them to keep the flight order confidential, Gilruth indicated Shepard would make the first suborbital flight, Grissom the second suborbital mission, and Glenn would serve as backup for both. Silence greeted Gilruth's call for questions; he thanked the assembled men and left the room. "Well, there I am looking at six faces looking at me and feeling, of course, totally elated that I had won the competition," said Shepard. "But yet almost immediately feeling sorry for my buddies because there they were. I mean, they were trying just as hard as I was and it was a very poignant moment because they all came over, shook my hand, and pretty soon I was the only guy left in the room." Shepard went home after the meeting and his face told the story of his selection; his wife, Louise, knew he had been selected as the first into space even before he could open his mouth to tell her.[42]

For those close to the program, including the astronauts' wives, the flight order seemed to be preordained, with all three military services represented—Shepard, navy; Grissom, air force; and Glenn, marines. "When you think about the president being navy," Betty noted, "you kind of knew who was going to be first. It was politics."[43] The process also came under question by someone who lost out on the potentially historic inaugural ride into space: Glenn. The day after Gilruth's announcement, Glenn drove *Life* writer Loudon Wainwright from Langley to National Airport in Washington, D.C. "He seemed very tense and preoccupied," Wainwright said of Glenn, "and as he drove . . . his face was taut and unsmiling. I remember that he slammed the steering wheel hard with his bare hands a number of times." At first, Wainwright thought Glenn was angry over not being able to clearly hear Kennedy's inaugural address on the car's radio because of static, or perhaps responding to the new president's eloquence. Later, he learned that the astronaut was "simply furious because Shepard, and not John Glenn, had been chosen as the first American to go into space."[44]

Remembering the drive with Wainwright, Glenn said his mind was on the fact that Gilruth would not have asked for a

From left to right, astronauts Glenn, Grissom, and Shepard stand in front of a Redstone rocket ready for launch.

peer vote unless he meant to use it in making his decision. The next day, Glenn wrote Gilruth a letter expressing how unfair he thought the peer vote was and the reasons why he might have been ranked low in such a ranking. "I said I thought I might have been penalized for speaking out for what I thought was the good of the program," he said. "It was a strong letter, because I felt strongly." Glenn gave the letter to Gilruth but heard nothing more about it as time passed. "We were all following Al now," Glenn said. "The decision was made, and we were a team, so we went back to work."[45]

Although insiders at NASA knew the order of the flights, the general public was informed on February 20, 1961, that three astronauts—Glenn, Grissom, and Shepard—had been selected as the prime candidates for the first ride on the Redstone. *Life* magazine had a field day with the new hero order, splashing the three astronauts on the cover of its March 3, 1961, issue with the headline "Astronaut First Team." Inside the magazine, each of the prime candidates for the fifteen-minute ballistic flight were profiled by Wainwright and photographed by Morse at work and at home with their families. Glenn was described by the magazine as "a stern and single-purposed individual about as relaxed in his particular search for destiny as a launched rocket," while Shepard possessed "an easy charm and speaks out with poise, authority, and often humor," but still seemed to be "wary, a cool studier of the situation."[46]

The story on Grissom, titled "A Quiet Little Fellow Who

Scoffs at the Chance of Becoming a Hero," described the astronaut as "a little bear of a man" who seemed lost in the shadow of his more outspoken space comrades. *Life* labeled Grissom as someone who refused to take himself too seriously. In a comment that would be repeated by many who came to know Grissom in the years to come, the magazine noted: "He doesn't talk unless he has something to say and his comments are always exactly to the point." Grissom downplayed his role as a hero and mocked those who compared the astronauts to such figures as Christopher Columbus, the Wright brothers, and Charles Lindbergh. "They did it themselves," he observed. "We didn't think up this thing. We're just going to ride the capsule." The astronaut was candid about the potential dangers involved in spaceflight, indicating he expected to "be scared when I get in there, but I don't worry about being scared. I won't be scared very long. I know it's going to work." Although Grissom called his involvement in the space program "the best thing that's ever happened to me," he did lament the amount of traveling he did and the time it took him away from his two sons. The magazine also depicted the Grissom family as "country folks" uninterested, as the astronaut said, in "fads or frills or the P.T.A. We don't give a damn about the Joneses."[47]

The distinction that developed in the public's eye, fueled by *Life* and other members of the media, between Glenn, Grissom, and Shepard, and the four remaining astronauts, sparked some discontent. Although Slayton knew that a problem with an irregular heartbeat meant he would probably not be selected for the first flight, he still called NASA's decision to name only the candidates for the first flight one of the agency's "classic Mickey Mouse routines." For his part, Schirra said after *Life* issued its cover with the three primary astronauts the other four "were devastated."[48] The astronaut corps, however, had other pressing problems to worry about. The new Kennedy administration seemed poised to scuttle the program. The president's scientific adviser, Jerome Wiesner, who favored using unmanned satellites to explore space, urged Kennedy in a report on the program to not "effectively endorse this program and take the blame for its failures," instead pinning any difficulties on President Dwight D. Eisenhower's reign. The administration also seemed to shortchange the space effort when it named James E. Webb, a former budget director in President Harry Truman's administration and State Department official with no scientific training, as NASA's new director. (The appointment, however, turned out to be a godsend for the space agency. As Slayton noted, "Webb wasn't technically trained, but he knew how to get things done.")[49]

In addition to pressure from its own government, NASA had the added anxiety of not knowing for certain what the Soviet Union had planned for its next space spectacular. The Soviet Union had also selected military pilots for its manned space vehicle, called Vostok, in which the pilot would eject after reentry and land via a parachute. Evaluated from

The original 1960 group of cosmonauts is shown in a photo from May 1961 at the seaside port of Sochi. Sitting in front from left to right: Pavel Popovich, Viktor Gorbatko, Yevgeniy Khrunov, Yuri Gagarin, Chief Designer Sergei Korolev, his wife Nina Korolev with Popovich's daughter Natasha, Cosmonaut Training Center Director Yevgeniy Karpov, parachute trainer Nikolay Nikitin, and physician Yevgeniy Fedorov. Standing the second row from left to right: Aleksey Leonov, Andrian Nikolayev, Mars Rafikov, Dmitriy Zaykin, Boris Volynov, German Titov, Grigoriy Nelyubov, Valeriy Bykovskiy, and Georgiy Shonin. In the back from left to right: Valentin Filatyev, Ivan Anikeyev, and Pavel Belyayeu.

October 1959 to January 1960, the twenty men eventually selected as Soviet cosmonauts were trained in a Moscow suburb. The cosmonauts, fondly called "my little swallows" by Sergei Korolev, the Russian space program's chief designer, were under strict orders to keep their mission a secret, even from their families. By May 1960, Korolev had targeted six of the cosmonauts for extensive training for the first

Ham, the first chimpanzee ever to ride into space, is shown off by his trainer at Cape Canaveral, Florida.

Vostok flight from the Baikonur Cosmodrome in Kazakhstan. By mid-January 1961, the group of six had been trimmed to three, and in early April a state commission, which included Korolev, had selected Yuri Gagarin as its choice to beat the Americans into space.[50]

Before sending humans into space, however, NASA had decided to test its systems using chimpanzees—the primates housed near Hangar S that had discomforted Shepard and had delighted those test pilots not chosen for the space program. On January 31, 1961, a chimpanzee named Ham rode the Redstone rocket into space, equipped with a small card proclaiming "Have Missile, Will Travel." Problems developed early into the flight, as the rocket consumed its fuel faster than anticipated and the escape tower blasted the capsule higher than anticipated, to 157 miles instead of 115 miles, placing a greater g-load on Ham. In addition, the onboard automatic equipment malfunctioned, rewarding Ham's flawless performance not with banana pellets but with electric shocks to the soles of his feet. Despite the breakdowns, the only injury Ham had to contend with was a bruised nose. Concerned about the Redstone's performance, however, Wernher von Braun and other engineers at the Marshall Space Flight Center called for another unmanned flight, and Wiesner and other officials sought more tests involving monkeys. "We were furious," remembered Kraft. "We had timid doctors harping at us from the outside world, and now we had a timid German fouling our plans from the inside." A perturbed Shepard later recalled: "We had 'em [the Russians]. We had 'em by the short hairs, and we gave it away." Instead of having Shepard blast off from the Cape, NASA, on March 24, launched another rocket, labeled a Mercury Redstone Booster Development flight, which qualified the vehicle for manned missions.[51]

On the morning of April 12, the American space program's worst fears were realized when the twenty-seven-year-old Gagarin, after urinating on the tires of a bus taking him to the launchpad (instituting a cosmonaut tradition), lifted off on his successful one-orbit flight. As Gagarin passed over the Pacific Ocean, Radio Moscow announced to the world: "Today, 12 April 1961, the first cosmic ship named Vostok, with a man on board, was orbited around the Earth from the Soviet Union." Seeking a comment on the Soviet success from NASA, an enterprising reporter phoned Powers at 4:00 a.m. A sleepy Powers, in a widely disseminated quote, said: "We're asleep down here." Grissom had more time to think about his response to Gagarin's flight than did Powers, telling the media, in a statement issued by NASA's public information office, that he was disappointed about the country's runner-up position in space compared to the Russians. "Now I intend to keep on doing just what I have been doing to get on with the job—working just as hard as I can," said Grissom. "I think the public has to make up its own mind about this Soviet achievement. I think I am doing all I can do to help."[52]

At a press conference following Gagarin's mission, Kennedy expressed the same frustration felt by many

Americans about the country's continued second-rate status in space compared to the Russians. "However tired anybody may be, and no one is more tired than I am, it is a fact that it is going to take some time [to catch up]," Kennedy told reporters. "As I said in my State of the Union message, the news will be worse before it is better." The president did attempt to reassure the American public, noting he did not "regard the first man in space as a sign of the weakening of the free world." Kennedy warned, however, that the Communists' "total mobilization of man and things" over the last several years posed a "source of great danger to us."[53]

Two days after the Soviet success, Kennedy met in the evening in the Cabinet Room at the White House with aide Theodore Sorenson, budget director David Bell, science adviser Wiesner, Webb, and NASA deputy administrator Hugh Dryden to discuss "the next steps in the space race." Also joining the meeting was Hugh Sidey, a *Time-Life* correspondent, who reported details of the conversation in his book on the Kennedy administration. According to Sidey, the president asked those assembled if there was any part of the space race where the country could catch the Soviets. "What can we do? Can we go around the moon before them? Can we put a man on the moon before them?" pondered Kennedy. Dryden noted that the one hope in achieving success might lie in a crash program similar to the Manhattan Project during World War II, which developed the atomic bomb. Such an effort, however, he said, could cost as much as $40 billion and had no guarantee of beating the Russians. "The cost," Kennedy said. "That's what gets me." At meeting's end, the president appeared anxious to do anything it might take to pass the Russians in space. "If somebody can just tell me how to catch up," said Kennedy. "Let's find somebody— anybody. I don't care if it's the janitor over there, if he knows how." Glancing at each of the assembled men, the president added: "There's nothing more important." According to Sorenson, the meeting set the stage "for the full-scale inquiry which would be necessary before a final and precise decision could be made" on what to do with the American space effort.[54]

Setbacks continued to plague the Kennedy administration. On April 16, a group of Cuban exiles landed at the Bay of Pigs in an aborted attempt to inspire a popular uprising against that country's Communist leader, Fidel Castro. The Central Intelligence Agency–inspired invasion was a debacle, with more than a thousand exiles ending up as prisoners of Castro. After the Bay of Pigs disaster, Kennedy sent Vice President Lyndon B. Johnson a memo asking if there were any space programs in which the United States could achieve "dramatic results in which we could win," including placing a laboratory in space, a trip around the moon, landing a rocket on the moon, or even landing a man on the moon. Kennedy proclaimed at a press conference that if America "could get to the moon before the Russians, then we should." According to Wiesner, the Bay of Pigs fiasco did play a role in advancing the American space program. "I think the President felt some pressure to get something else in the foreground," said Wiesner. At an April 24 meeting with space experts and others, Johnson forcefully led the discussion around to a determination to pursue landing a man on the moon. A cautious Webb questioned Johnson's enthusiasm, noting, "I think when you decide you're going to do something and put the prestige of the United States government behind it, you'd better doggone well be able to do it."[55]

NASA, too, experienced dramatic failures, with one leading some to believe that one of the original seven astronauts had been incinerated. On April 25, NASA launched a Mercury capsule (equipped with a "crewman simulator") aboard a new thick-skinned Atlas rocket to test the spacecraft's environmental control system. Just forty seconds into its flight, the Atlas rocket failed to roll and pitch to achieve its proper flight position and a range safety officer sent a self-destruct command to the missile. Observing the launch from unique vantage points were Cooper and Grissom, who were each flying F-106 jets in an effort to monitor the launch. "Gus was to approach at five thousand feet, ignite his afterburner, and climb up in a spiral alongside to observe this early phase of flight," explained Cooper. "I would take over from the fifteen-thousand-foot level and continue observing the big bird." As the Atlas exploded without warning, the escape rocket on the capsule fired, pulling it within fifteen feet of Cooper's aircraft. Grissom had been congratulating himself on his fine view of the launch when the rocket exploded. "Reacting automatically, without really thinking," said Grissom, "I pulled up and over and went away from that place fast. From the ground, they told me later, it looked as if I'd simply flown straight into the fireball." A physician friend of the astronaut, watching the launch from Cocoa Beach, turned to his wife and told her there were now only six astronauts. Miraculously, said Grissom, neither he nor Cooper suffered any damage to their planes. "Just how big a miracle I realized when I flew down to see how the spacecraft was doing as it floated on its chute toward the water," he said. As he followed the capsule's descent, Grissom remembered thinking that there were very large seagulls in the area flying around his jet. "And *then* it hit me—these were no seagulls," Grissom recalled. "They were chunks of the exploded Atlas, falling."[56]

With the debate still raging about the country's failures, Shepard, Grissom, and Glenn continued to prepare for a journey into space by using simulators at Langley and at Cape Canaveral, with Shepard, as the prime pilot, flying 120 simulated flights. To keep the mood light as he prepared for a planned launch on May 2, Shepard repeated his favorite routines from comedian Bill Dana, who had entertained the astronauts, and the entire country, with his character José Jimenez, a very reluctant Mexican spaceman. As the astronauts joked about potential disasters on the launchpad, however, some in the Kennedy administration advised delaying the flight or, if it was permitted to continue, closing it to the press. The president made the decision to proceed with the launch ("Why postpone a success?" asked one space official) and kept it open to the media. The choice to have an open program seemed unusual to those such as Slayton who were used to military flight tests. "It was a great idea—unless something went wrong," said Slatyon. A low cloud cover over the launch site, however, caused the mission to be canceled. By that time, Howard Benedict, an Associated Press reporter, had uncovered the name of the first American into space and put Shepard's name out on the AP wire.[57]

Three days later, on May 5, Shepard awoke at 1:10 a.m., showered, shaved, and along with Glenn, Douglas, and others, had a breakfast consisting of orange juice, filet mignon wrapped in bacon, and scrambled eggs. At 3:55 a.m. Shepard left for the launchpad aboard a transfer van (likened to a "cramped cattle car" by Shepard), which also included fellow astronaut Grissom. To relieve the tension, Shepard and Grissom performed one of Dana's José Jimenez routines. Shepard, playing the part of Jimenez, asked Grissom, playing the straight man, what it took to be an astronaut—courage, perfect vision, low blood pressure, and four legs. "Why four legs?" Grissom asked. "They really wanted to send a dog," Shepard responded, "but they thought that would be too cruel." After admiring the rocket, Shepard and the others rode the elevator to the white room surrounding the spacecraft, which Shepard had named *Freedom 7* (seven because it was Mercury spacecraft number seven). Grissom had

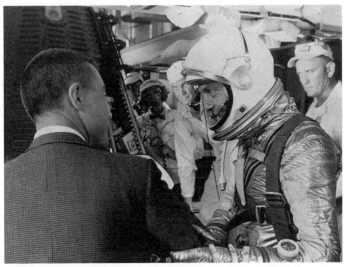

NASA

Grissom wishes Shepard a safe flight just before insertion into the
Freedom 7 *spacecraft. John Glenn and Guenter Wendt wait in the*
background to help Shepard into the capsule's small cockpit.

planned on relating to Shepard an old test-pilot slogan as he
went up in the elevator on the way to the capsule. "Test pilots
have a gruff saying which they like to use sometimes when
they see a buddy going out to wring out a new airplane. 'Go
blow up,' you tell him," said Grissom. "It sounds cruel, but
not to the other test pilot. He knows he may blow up anyway,
and you're just using it as a little joke to help him relax."
When the time came, however, Grissom discovered he had a
few butterflies in his stomach and could not joke with
Shepard as planned.[58]

After climbing into the tight confines of the spacecraft, Shepard received handshakes and wishes of good luck from Grissom, Glenn, and others. Technicians gathered for the launch shouted "Happy landings, Commander!" Shepard also discovered a taped message on the instrument panel compliments of Glenn: "No handball playing in this area," which lampooned one of Shepard's favorite forms of recreation and the capsule's cramped conditions. As delays mounted in the countdown, Shepard, wearing a parachute in case of an emergency, discovered he had to urinate—a problem in a space suit without adequate plumbing to handle such a situation. As NASA officials wondered whether they should scrub the launch, Shepard put an end to the discussion by relieving himself in his suit. When high pressure readings on the Redstone's fuel tank caused a stop in the countdown, an impatient Shepard bellowed: "Shit! I've been in here more than three hours. I'm a hell of a lot cooler than you guys. Why don't you fix your little problem and light this candle?" NASA quickly got back on schedule and, at 9:34 a.m., Shepard, watched by millions of people on television, lifted off on his flight into history. From the Mission Control Center, an excited Slayton proclaimed: "You're on your way, José!" Just fifteen minutes and twenty-two seconds later, and after reaching an altitude of 116.5 statute miles, *Freedom 7* made a successful splash landing in the Atlantic Ocean. Shepard may not have known it at the time, but America was on its way to the moon.[59]

5

Liberty Bell 7

THE "UNQUALIFIED SUCCESS" OF ALAN SHEPARD'S *FREEDOM 7*
flight prompted President John F. Kennedy to set America's
course for the moon. After receiving the National
Aeronautics and Space Administration's Distinguished
Service Medal from Kennedy in ceremonies at the White
House, Shepard and the other six astronauts met with the
president, his staff, and space-agency officials in the Oval
Office. As First Lady Jackie Kennedy escorted the astronauts'
wives on a tour of the White House, the president discussed
Shepard's flight and asked for a briefing about future plans.
"Now, you don't think he was excited? You don't think he was
a space cadet?" exhorted Shepard. "Absolutely, absolutely!"
In fact, shortly after Shepard's May 5, 1961, mission, James
Webb, NASA administrator, and Robert McNamara, secretary of defense, had sent a memo to the president outlining
recommendations for America's space program. The memo
stressed that manned spaceflights would have a positive

NASA

President John F. Kennedy in his historic message to a joint session of the Congress, on May 25, 1961, declared, "I believe this nation should commit itself to achieving the goal, before this decade is out, of landing a man on the moon and returning him safely to the earth."

effect on the nation's standing in world opinion. "It is man," the memo argued, "not merely machines, in space that captures the imagination of the world. Dramatic achievements in space . . . symbolize the technological power and organizing capacity of a nation. It is for reasons such as these that major achievements in space contribute to national prestige."[1]

On May 25, Kennedy, recently back in Washington, D.C., after a two-week trip abroad, spoke to a joint session of

Congress on "Urgent National Needs." In his speech, the president promoted to legislators what he called "the freedom doctrine," delineating ways in which the country could use economic and social progress here and elsewhere to combat the perceived threat of the Soviet Union, and calling for increased funding for civil defense to protect people in case of a nuclear strike. Late in his talk, Kennedy turned to space matters, pointing to the recent dramatic developments in that area by both countries. He then established as a national goal of "before this decade is out, of landing a man on the moon and returning him safely to the earth. No single space project in this period will be more impressive to mankind, or more important for the long-range exploration of space; and none will be so difficult or expensive to accomplish."[2]

Although Kennedy at first believed his speech had failed, telling aide Theodore Sorenson that the reaction to plans for reaching the moon had been met with a "something less than enthusiastic" reception by lawmakers, Congress did move quickly to give NASA the increased funding that it needed for the complicated and exhaustive program, known as Project Apollo. With just fifteen minutes worth of time in space, America had set course for one of the major undertakings of the twentieth century. The decision proved to be a wise one in terms of catching up with the Russians. As NASA historian Roger D. Launius noted, a lunar landing presented to the United States "a reasonable chance of overtaking the Soviet Union in space activities and recovering a measure of lost status."[3]

The difficulties posed in a journey to the moon were gigantic, so gigantic, in fact, that NASA had urged the president to change an original deadline of arrival on the moon by 1967 to by the end of the decade, which gave the agency, according to Webb, an "administrative discount." The NASA administrator also increased the estimated costs for the lunar voyage from between $8 billion to $12 billion to a total of $20 billion. Webb's conservative approach to the bold adventure outlined by Kennedy seemed to be the right course to take, especially with NASA's limited experience in spaceflight. And, as the next mission would prove, there was still much to be learned and improved upon about this new technology if the deadline was to be met successfully.[4]

NASA's next venture into the heavens involved another suborbital flight similar to Shepard's mission. Designated as Mercury-Redstone 4 (MR-4), the flight was originally scheduled to liftoff from Cape Canaveral on July 18, 1961. This time, however, there would be a new astronaut aboard— Grissom—and several changes with the capsule, designated as Spacecraft Number 11, which had been finished by McDonnell Aircraft Corporation in May 1960. Instead of the two ten-inch side ports Shepard peered through on his flight, Grissom's spacecraft had a large viewing window designed by the Corning Glass Works of Corning, New York, which gave the astronaut a field of view of thirty degrees horizontally and thirty-three degrees vertically. The window's Vycor glass outer panel could withstand a temperature between 1,500 and 1,800 degrees Fahrenheit. Also available to the astronaut was a new rate stabilization control system, giving the astronaut finer control of the pitch, yaw, and roll thrusters through his hand controller.[5]

The biggest change, and the one that gave Grissom his greatest difficulty on the flight, came with the addition of a new hatch, built by Honeywell's ordnance division in Hopkins, Minnesota. Both Ham's and Shepard's flights had used a mechanically operated latch mechanism that weighed sixty-nine pounds (too heavy for the planned orbital flights to come), as compared to the explosive hatch cover used on Grissom's spacecraft, which weighed just twenty-three pounds. Seventy quarter-inch titanium bolts secured the hatch to the Mercury craft. Each of the bolts had a tiny hole drilled into it to provide a weak point so that when a mild detonating fuse, installed in a channel around the hatch, was activated the bolts would fail and the hatch would be blasted away from the spacecraft at a distance of approximately twenty-five feet. There were two ways to activate the hatch. Inside the capsule, an astronaut had within six to eight inches of his right arm access to an igniter that needed only five pounds of force to activate after removing a safety pin (forty pounds of force would be needed with the pin in place). If the astronaut happened to be incapacitated, rescue crews could get the hatch open by removing a panel from the side of the capsule and pulling a lanyard, which required forty pounds of force.

Inside the capsule, the astronaut had available to him a new life raft, developed by the Langley Research Center and the Space Task Group and weighing just three pounds and four ounces, and the instrument panel included a new Earth-path indicator showing the spacecraft's position (a required piece of equipment for future orbital flights). Grissom's space suit also had some new features, including an enhanced wrist fitting for improved movement and a convex mirror, which came to be known as a "hero's medal," worn on the chest to allow an onboard camera to record both the astronaut *and* instrument readings.[6]

Before immersing himself in training for his mission, which included a hundred simulated flights on the procedures trainer, Grissom spent most of his time worrying about his spacecraft. "I made a point of attending production meetings at the McDonnell plant in St. Louis," he noted, "supervising some of the engineering work periods and fretting a little over whether all of the critical parts would arrive from the subcontractors on time and get put together." His presence at the plant, he believed, just might make the McDonnell workers "a little more careful than they already were and a little more eager to get the work done on time if they saw how much I cared." Grissom's hands-on approach was a character trait familiar to his fellow astronauts. As Scott Carpenter observed, Grissom may not have talked much, "but when he did talk it was worth listening to" as he had "strengths unequaled by the other guys." Despite Grissom's constant oversight of the capsule, however, there were some problems. Somehow the controls were switched in assembly, with the craft yawing to the left when it should have yawed to the right. "This sort of thing should not happen even on automobiles," said Grissom, who ensured that the mistake was corrected. In addition, Grissom noticed that the attitude controls failed to immediately center themselves after he yawed the spacecraft, a quirk he noted for the flight ahead.[7]

McDonnell delivered Grissom's spacecraft to Hangar S at Cape Canaveral on March 7, 1961, after which NASA engineers removed some of its components, tested them, and put them all back together again. Some of the engineers were perfectionists who wanted to "stop the show and redesign the whole system from scratch," Grissom observed. He worked to reassure the engineers that if a system satisfied the person charged with flying the spacecraft, "it ought to satisfy them." Grissom also spent his time at the Cape working with Chris Kraft and his mission control staff on a preliminary flight plan. "Grissom was good," said Kraft. "We'd heard that he was a pilot's pilot, a talented engineer and easy to like." Kraft attempted to give Grissom the same advice he had given Shepard but was interrupted by the astronaut. "Al told me all about it," said Grissom. "He said that if anybody was a f—kup, I should just say it." Kraft laughed and told Grissom they should get along just fine. Luckily for those involved in running simulations for the mission, Grissom did not have any complaints, and Kraft

Deke Slayton (left) discusses a point with Chris Kraft at the Mercury Control Center.

reported that "we were increasingly happy with him."[8]

During the month of June, Grissom endured a series of nagging problems that threatened to delay his mission. First, the Marshall Space Flight Center in Huntsville, Alabama, anticipated some problems with the Redstone rocket, indicating it might not make it to the Cape by the promised date of June 22. Technicians were also unsure about how to test some minor new items for Grissom's space suit. Finally, the astronaut discovered the clock in the spacecraft, a standard eight-day aircraft timepiece responsible for keeping track of his mission's elapsed time, had rusted and a replacement could not be found before July 4. Luckily, an old friend came through for Grissom. Sam Beddingfield promised to secure the necessary part even if he had to steal one. "I do not think Sam was a thief," Grissom recalled, "but we got our clock." The other problems were solved as well and the staff at Marshall delivered the Redstone on time. As Grissom observed the rocket's arrival, Paul Donnelly, the spacecraft test conductor, jokingly told him they would not launch the missile without him. "Hell," Grissom responded, "I've already ridden it bareback all the way from Huntsville." His concern about the rocket also translated into other areas, as Grissom's biggest worry was something might happen that would keep him from making the flight. The cautious astronaut gave up water skiing, one of his favorite pastimes, and even began to carefully observe speed limits in his Corvette.[9]

On July 1 technicians moved the spacecraft out of its hangar and mated it with the Redstone rocket on Pad 5. "It was the happiest moment to date for me," observed Grissom, adding that his mission was proceeding on schedule. The astronaut almost missed the big event, as he had locked his hard hat—a required piece of equipment for anyone on the pad—in his office and forgotten the key. Fortunately, someone loaned him the necessary equipment and he managed to view the operation. At a meeting that day Grissom convinced NASA technicians to forgo changing the position of a fixed camera in the capsule. "I insisted it was too late in the game to start changing relay panels around and cutting wires and adding things," he said, "especially since we knew everything was now in good shape." Grissom clinched his argument by pointing out changing the camera would make it harder for him to get in or out of the already cramped spacecraft.[10]

For the next three weeks, the Redstone and capsule underwent numerous tests to ensure their compatibility and to familiarize the astronaut with the launch crew. On July 7, Grissom participated in a test of the radio frequencies to be used for the launch, which closely patterned the procedures to be used for the actual flight. "It was quite a sensation," he remembered. "There I was, perched up on top of that slender 70-foot booster with nothing to hold it upright and steady but a half-load of fuel in the tanks. I think a fairly strong wind could have pushed it over, otherwise." The removal of the gantry gave Grissom quite a start as it seemed that he was moving and the gantry was standing still. With the gantry gone, the astronaut noticed only a slight sway to the rocket in the summer breeze and "some clouds floating peacefully by."[11]

The flight plan for Grissom's mission differed somewhat from what Shepard had flown. NASA officials realized they had expected too much of Shepard during his short time in space, particularly during the five minutes of weightlessness he experienced. For Grissom, his flight plan "weeded out" a number of communication checks, giving him additional time for observing the ground below through his new window. Also, when Shepard switched from automatic to manual handling, he had control of only one axis at a time, while Grissom would attempt to take over all three axes (roll, pitch,

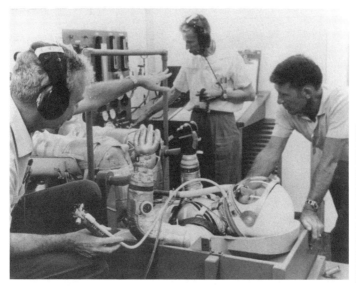

PHOTOGRAPH BY NASA, INDIANA HISTORICAL SOCIETY, C9154

Grissom undergoes an inflation test of his Mercury pressure suit. Assisting with the test are (left) Dr. William K. Douglas, (center, back) Joe W. Schmitt, and (right) Wally Schirra.

and yaw) at once. "I also planned to fire the retro-rockets manually instead of automatically as they had been fired on Freedom 7," said Grissom. At the meeting some of the engineers expressed concern about a minor problem with the capsule's oxygen system, but an impatient Grissom argued against any changes. Hoping to fly home so he could spend time with his family over the weekend, the astronaut told the group he was satisfied with the spacecraft and asked them not to "fiddle" with it while he was gone.[12]

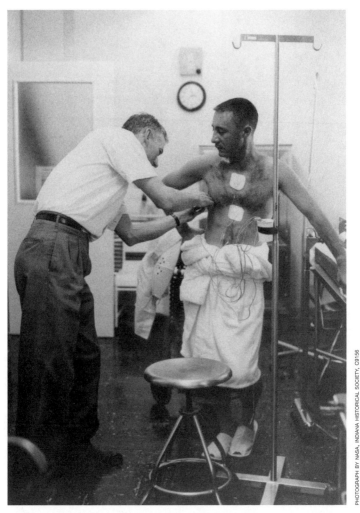

PHOTOGRAPH BY NASA, INDIANA HISTORICAL SOCIETY, C9156

Space suit technician Joe W. Schmitt attaches sensors to Grissom's body during a dress rehearsal for the astronaut's Mercury mission.

Grissom spent a quick weekend at home, using some of the time to continue practicing on the air-lubricated free-attitude (ALFA) trainer at NASA's Langley facility, picking up his oldest son, Scott, from a Boy Scout camp, and taking Betty out to dinner. During his visit home, Grissom also discussed with Betty what to take on his flight as souvenirs for Scott and Mark. Grissom wanted to take a hundred dollar bills for his sons and their friends, but the family could not afford such an expense. Instead, the astronaut decided to take two rolls of Mercury dimes (one hundred in all), which he would stuff in a pocket in the leg of his space suit. Before leaving to return to the Cape, Grissom drove his two sons to Sunday school and informed them that he would soon be making a flight into space similar to the one recently made by Shepard. "Scott, who was eleven, said 'Gee, that's great, Dad,'" Grissom recalled. "But that was about it. I guess they have about as much emotional display as their father does." Talking to his wife later, however, Grissom learned that the boys were quite excited when she picked them up, with seven-year-old Mark, sworn to secrecy about the mission by his father, whispering in her ear, "Daddy's going!"[13]

On July 15 Robert Gilruth, Space Task Group director, made the official announcement of Grissom as the prime candidate for the MR-4 mission, with Glenn once again serving as backup. "I assumed after serving as Al's backup that I would be named to make the second flight," Glenn noted in his memoirs. "Again, I was surprised and disappointed when it went to Gus and I was named backup for the second time." As last-minute testing continued at the Cape, both Grissom and Glenn went on low-residue diets "so that no matter which of us went on the flight we would not find ourselves embarrassed by too many natural functions," said Grissom. The astronaut also made a decision on a name for his space-craft—*Liberty Bell 7*. Grissom said he selected the name "Liberty Bell" because of the spacecraft's actual resemblance to a bell. The number seven came from a suggestion by Glenn that all Mercury missions should use the figure to honor the seven original astronauts. With a name selected, one of the NASA engineers suggested painting a crack on the capsule, just like the real Liberty Bell. "No one seemed quite sure what the crack looked like," Grissom observed, "so we copied it from the 'tails' side of a fifty-cent piece." After the mission ended with *Liberty Bell 7* sinking beneath the waves of the Atlantic Ocean, Grissom said a joke went around the Cape "that that was the last capsule we would ever launch with a crack in it."[14]

On July 17, the day before the scheduled launch, Grissom relaxed in the crew quarters at Hangar S, which were equipped with a bed, television, radio, and reading matter. Before retiring early for the next morning's liftoff, Grissom and Glenn pondered a solution to a problem that had beset Shepard on the pad—what to do if nature called while sealed in the capsule? According to Glenn, the two men went to a medical laboratory next door to the crew quarters and worked to design their own "urine collection device." The astronauts took some condoms, cut the receptacle ends off of them, and "cemented some rubber tubing that ran to a plastic bag to be taped to his [Grissom's] leg," said Glenn. William Douglas, flight surgeon for the astronauts, sent nurse Dee O'Hara into Cocoa Beach to buy a panty girdle for Grissom to wear to hold the jury-rigged contraption in place during the mission.[15]

Unfortunately for Grissom, bad weather caused NASA to scrub the launch, a decision relayed to the astronaut by Douglas at 10:30 p.m. There was some good news, however, as the decision to delay the launch came before the Redstone had been loaded with its corrosive fuel mixture of liquid oxygen and alcohol/water, which meant only a twenty-four-hour postponement instead of forty-eight hours. Grissom tried to relax the next day by doing some fishing. "I caught one bass, but the fish did not seem to enjoy the weather any more than I did, so I threw my one fish back and went to another meeting," he noted. On the evening of July 18, Grissom watched *The Life and Legend of Wyatt Earp*, starring Hugh O'Brian, on television before retiring at 9:00 p.m. (to save time for the next morning's launch, he showered and shaved before going to bed). Even before Douglas came in the room to wake him at 1:10 a.m., Grissom said he had awakened, wondering about the weather. Douglas reported that both Shepard and Grissom "appeared to have been sleeping soundly. There was no startle reaction on awakening, and the immediate post-waking state was characterized by eager anticipation and curiosity as to the progress of the countdown."[16]

Douglas informed Grissom that NASA officials had moved the scheduled liftoff time up one hour in hopes of getting the mission under way before bad weather settled over the Cape. The schedule called for Grissom to eat breakfast and then undergo a physical examination. "Apparently someone forgot to pass the word about the earlier launch time, because breakfast was not ready at 1:45 [a.m.] as it was supposed to be," said Grissom. Instead of eating, Grissom donned a bathrobe and Douglas started the physical, which was designed to determine any ailment that might necessitate calling on Glenn to take over the mission. The only hitch in the examination came when Douglas expressed surprise at Grissom's low blood pressure. "Well," said Grissom, "I can try to boost it up a little for you." Also before breakfast, the astronaut spoke to "consultant headshrinker" George Ruff about the upcoming trip into space. "He made me recite my feelings, and then we played some little games with words and numbers—to make sure I was completely sane, I guess," Grissom said. The brief psychiatric examination noted "no evidence of overt anxiety" by the astronaut, who was aware of the dangers posed by the flight "but saw no gain in worrying about them."[17]

For his high-protein breakfast of fruit, steak, eggs, juice, and milk, Grissom was joined by Glenn, Carpenter, and Walt Williams, Mercury operations director. After Grissom finished his meal, doctors began gluing sensors onto his body. The sensors monitored the astronaut's vital signs during the mission. "The only thing I remember about this period was that everybody seemed to be winking or grinning at me," said Grissom. "They seemed to feel they had to cheer me up. I thought to myself that they were the ones who looked a little shaky, and it tickled me to realize that almost everybody in the place was nervous but me." By 4:15 a.m., Grissom, now in his space suit, climbed into the same transfer van he had ridden to the pad in with Shepard. Just inside the van's door, one of the NASA technicians had thoughtfully stenciled a sign reading "Shepard and Grissom Express," which pleased the astronaut.

There was a brief delay after the van arrived at Pad 5 as Grissom awaited the final word to take the elevator up the gantry and climb into his spacecraft. During the wait, astronaut Deke Slayton, stationed in the nearby blockhouse for the launch, came into the air-conditioned van to update Grissom on the weather forecast. "It didn't look too good for making visual observations through the capsule window," Grissom remembered. "The entire Atlantic coast from Canaveral on north would be obscured by clouds." Still, local weather conditions were reported to be good and, at 5:00 a.m., word finally came from NASA officials that Grissom could proceed on his mission. After a quick look at the Redstone, the astronaut was headed for the elevator when he heard a round of applause from the workers gathered around the launchpad. "I must admit this choked me up a little," admitted Grissom. "It was a darn fine feeling, as I looked down and saw them staring up at me, that I had all those people pulling for me." Douglas handed the astronaut a crossword puzzle book thoughtfully provided by Beddingfield, who included the following note: "Since the flight load has been reduced, we did not want you to get bored."[18]

Upon reaching the third level of the gantry, Grissom stepped from the elevator, walked across a platform, and wiggled into the *Liberty Bell 7*, a compact craft that, as Guenter Wendt, McDonnell Aircraft pad leader noted, "you get in with a shoehorn and get out with a can opener." Before technicians bolted on the capsule's hatch, Glenn slipped his fellow astronaut a note that highlighted Grissom's speech-making success at the Convair plant. The note read: "Have a smooth apogee, Gus, and do good work. See you at GBI [Grand Bahama Island]." The only problem occurred when Grissom noticed "the troops" leaving behind fingerprints and noseprints on the capsule's new window after peering in at him. Wendt promised the astronaut that the window would be cleaned before he blasted off. Overhearing his complaint over the radio circuit, another technician joked to Grissom that NASA would install window wipers on the spacecraft in time for the next launch.[19]

Back at her home in Newport News, Virginia, Betty had been up since 6:00 a.m. to prepare for the big day. As she switched on the television to watch her husband ride the

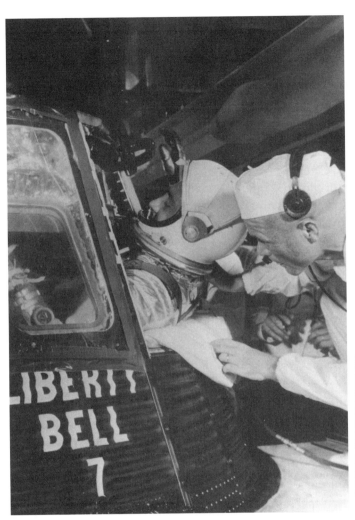

Backup astronaut Glenn helps Grissom into the Liberty Bell 7 *capsule on the morning of July 21, 1961.*

PHOTOGRAPH BY NASA, INDIANA HISTORICAL SOCIETY, C6419

Redstone into space, she was joined by Jo Schirra, Marge Slayton, and Rene Carpenter. "The girls and I went into the den and sat around the television set drinking coffee," Betty recalled. NASA concerns about the weather caused the countdown to be placed on hold for five minutes just ten minutes and thirty seconds before launch. After NASA called for a thirty-minute hold, Grissom hit his "lowest point," as he realized the weather probably would not improve. As the delay stretched on, Carpenter, from his position in the Mercury Control Center, arranged for Betty to talk with her husband. "I was very nervous," she said. "I wanted so much to think of just the right thing to say—something funny. But we really couldn't hear each other very well and I never did think of anything very good to say to him."[20]

After NASA officially canceled the mission, Grissom returned to the astronaut crew quarters at Hangar S where he was visited by Williams, who explained why he had made the decision to call off the launch. "Of course I was disappointed that the flight did not go," a space agency spokesman quoted Grissom as saying. "But I know the operations director [Williams] had good reason for canceling. I have confidence in his judgment and I support him fully." Grissom did not look forward to spending another forty-eight hours at the Cape, the time it would take for workers to purge the Redstone of its volatile fuel, clean out its tanks, and start all over again. "But I felt sure we would get it off the next time around," the astronaut said of his MR-4 flight. "And we did."[21]

Early in the morning on Friday, July 21, Grissom underwent the regular launch routine, finally climbing into the spacecraft at 3:58 a.m. Before embarking on his dangerous mission, Grissom seemed to keep his sense of humor. Beddingfield remembered talking to his friend about the necessity of having a personal parachute with him in the cabin. "OK, we'll get it put in, but I don't think it'll do you any good," Beddingfield recalled telling Grissom, as he did not believe the astronaut would have time to strap on the parachute in case of an emergency. "And his retort was, 'Well, it'll give me something to do until I hit,'" said Beddingfield. Once again, holds delayed liftoff. While technicians were installing the seventy bolts to attach the hatch to the capsule, one of the bolts became cross threaded and NASA called a hold to assess the situation. Engineers decided one missing bolt would not jeopardize the mission, and the countdown proceeded. Other delays were called to turn off the pad searchlights so telemetry from the flight would not be affected and to let some clouds pass by. As Grissom waited, he did deep-breathing exercises and flexed his arms and legs to keep from getting stiff. Carpenter also managed to arrange another telephone call with Betty. "I asked him if he was all right," she said, "and he said he thought if everyone stopped talking to him, he just might fall asleep. This was his way of saying that he was relaxed. Then he talked to the boys for awhile." When NASA announced another delay, Betty stopped watching television and went to her kitchen to soft boil some eggs. Called

PHOTOGRAPH BY NASA, INDIANA HISTORICAL SOCIETY, C6409

*A Redstone rocket launches Grissom on his fifteen-minute
suborbital flight.*

back to the television by Marge Slayton, Betty forgot about the eggs on the stove until five minutes before the launch. She ran to the kitchen and discovered her soft-boiled eggs were now hard boiled.[22]

At 7:20 a.m. Eastern Standard Time, MR-4 lifted off Pad 5 under the 78,000-pound thrust of the Redstone's single rocket, built by the Rocketdyne Division of North American Aviation. Grissom, who later said he felt "a bit scared," reported to mission control: "This is Liberty Bell 7. The clock is operating." Alan Shepard, serving as capsule communicator (CapCom) for the mission, responded by referring to comic Bill Dana's reluctant astronaut, saying: "Loud and clear, Jose, don't cry too much." As the Redstone climbed to 36,000 feet and reached the speed of sound, Grissom experienced none of the vibration problems Shepard had endured on his flight, thanks to the improved aerodynamic fairings between the capsule and rocket and extra padding around the astronaut's head. The Redstone's engine, which boosted Grissom (the third human to reach space) thirty-miles-per-hour faster and one-and-a-half-miles higher than Shepard's flight, shut off 142 seconds into the MR-4 mission. Grissom, who experienced a "brief tumbling sensation," could hear the escape tower fire and the bolts holding it onto the spacecraft blow. "The firing of the escape-tower clamp ring and escape rocket is quite audible and I could see the escape rocket motor and tower throughout its tail-off burning phase and for what seemed like quite some time after that climbing off to my right," Grissom noted in his post-flight report. "Actually, I think I was still watching the tower at the time the posigrade rockets [which separated the capsule from the Redstone] fired, which occurred 10 seconds after cutoff. The tower was still definable as a long, slender object against the black sky at this time."[23]

The spacecraft's new window gave Grissom an excellent view during the mission. The blue sky at launch gave way to a darker and darker blue as the rocket climbed into space. At approximately two minutes after liftoff, when the spacecraft had climbed to an altitude of 100,000 feet, Grissom reported that the sky "rapidly changed to an absolute black." As he looked out his window, the astronaut spied what appeared to be a faint star, equal in brightness to Polaris, a fact he reported to mission control. Glenn had bet Grissom a steak dinner that during the flight he would be able to see a star during daytime. Grissom knew he should theoretically be able to see stars, but believed his eyes would not adjust to the darkness enough to view them. Later, Grissom learned that he had actually won the bet, as the "star" he observed was actually the planet Venus. As for his observations of the Earth, Grissom had some trouble at first in identifying any land masses because of an extensive cloud cover over the Gulf of Mexico coastline between Apalachicola, Florida, and Mobile, Alabama. "Even so, the view back down through the window was fascinating," he said. "I could make out brilliant grada-tions of color—the blue of the water, the white of the beaches and the brown of the land."[24]

The astronaut's earth observation tasks were made a bit difficult by the spacecraft's control system, which seemed "sticky and sluggish" to Grissom. Unlike Shepard, who maneuvered the capsule only one axis at a time, Grissom attempted to take control in all three axes. Both the yaw and pitch control, however, overshot their marks. These problems, combined with continuing to observe the earth through the window, put the astronaut slightly behind schedule and he had to abandon the planned roll maneuver. "It was just sheer amazement [at the scenery]; that's all it was," he said. Grissom did manage to fire the retro-rockets manually and as the first one fired he saw the spacecraft yaw to the right. "I had planned to control the spacecraft attitude during retrofire by using the horizon as a reference; but as soon as the right yaw started, I switched my reference to flight instruments," he noted. As the retro-rockets burned out and dropped away from the capsule, Grissom could clearly see Cape Canaveral come into view. "The Banana and Indian Rivers were easy to distinguish and the white beach all along the coast was quite prominent," he observed. "I could see the building area on Cape Canaveral. I do not recall being able to distinguish individual buildings, but it was obvious that it was an area where buildings and structures had been erected."[25]

As the g forces built up during reentry, Grissom noted that the instruments reported some oscillations but he could not feel any difference inside the spacecraft. Nine minutes and forty-one seconds into the flight, the capsule's drogue parachute deployed, slowing the capsule before it released. The main parachute followed and Grissom felt a slight jolt and bumping as the parachute "dug into the air, but this was no problem. The capsule started to rotate and swing slowly under the chute as it descended. I could feel a slight jar as the landing bag dropped down to take up some of the landing shock." After opening his helmet's faceplate and preparing for splashdown, Grissom reported to mission control that he observed a triangular rip in the parachute measuring about six inches by six inches. Despite the tear, the main parachute did its job and, at fifteen minutes and thirty-seven seconds into the flight, the spacecraft hit the Atlantic Ocean with what Grissom called "a good bump." Everything seemed to be going as planned. As Kraft at the control center later observed, Grissom, the Redstone, and the capsule had all performed "perfectly" up to that point.[26]

Liberty Bell 7 nosed over under the water with Grissom laying on his left side and head down. Although the astronaut heard "a disconcerting gurgling noise," no water made its way into the spacecraft. The capsule slowly righted itself as the impact skirt, which had helped cushion the landing, filled with water and began to act as a sea anchor. When he was sure the recovery section had cleared the water, Grissom deployed the recovery aids and ejected the reserve main parachute. "I felt I was in good condition at this point and started to prepare myself for egress," he reported. The astro-

194

naut disconnected the oxygen inlet hose into his helmet; unfastened the helmet from his space suit; released the chest strap, lap belt, shoulder harness, and knee straps; and disconnected the biomedical sensors. Grissom considered not bothering with unrolling a rubber neck dam fastened to the exterior of his suit to keep air in and water out in case he went into the water during the recovery, a device Wally Schirra had helped to develop. "It's a chore to secure the dam, and I didn't think I would need it," he noted. "Fortunately I reconsidered." With those tasks done, Grissom remained connected to the spacecraft at only two points, an oxygen inlet hose used to cool his space suit and a helmet communications lead for talking to the recovery forces. He then turned his attention to the hatch, releasing the restraining wires at both ends and tossing them at his feet. Next, he took the Randall knife from the door and placed it in his survival pack. Finally, Grissom removed the cover and safety pin from the hatch detonator.[27]

As the astronaut made his final preparations to complete his mission, Sikorsky UH-34D helicopters from the aircraft carrier USS *Randolph* circled the scene, including one piloted by Marine Lt. Jim Lewis, who was responsible for recovering the capsule and its occupant. Lewis had rehearsed recovery procedures with the astronauts in the waters off of Langley Air Force Base and expressed confidence about his mission. According to the recovery plan, Lewis would move near the spacecraft, have his copilot John Rinehard cut off its high-frequency antennae, hook onto a Dacron loop at the top of the recovery section, and hoist the capsule out of the water. Once the helicopter had snagged its quarry and lifted it out of the water, the astronaut would be given the signal to blow the hatch, after which he would exit the spacecraft, grab a horse collar, and be winched aboard the helicopter.

As Lewis, whose call sign for the mission was *Hunt Club 1*, neared the spacecraft he communicated directly with Grissom, who asked the pilot to give him five minutes to mark various switch positions before he hooked onto *Liberty Bell 7*. NASA had requested that Grissom accomplish this task because on Shepard's flight some of the readings had been "jiggled loose" on the trip back to the recovery aircraft carrier. About twelve seconds later, Grissom again radioed Lewis: "OK, give me about another 3 or 4 minutes to take these switch positions, then I'll be ready for you." Struggling to mark the settings on the switch chart with a grease pencil while wearing his bulky gloves, Grissom, from time to time, also had to deal with his neck dam, which ballooned due to the space suit's ventilation. Approximately ten minutes after splashdown, Grissom had the following conversation with the recovery helicopter:

"OK, Hunt Club. This is Liberty Bell 7. Are you ready for the pickup?"

"This is Hunt Club 1; this is affirmative."

"OK, latch on, then give me a call and I'll power down and blow the hatch, OK?"

"This is Hunt Club 1, roger, will give you a call when we're ready for you to blow."

"Roger, I've unplugged my suit so I'm kinda warm now."

"1, roger."

"Now if you tell me to, ah, you're ready for me to blow, I'll have to take my helmet off, power down, and then blow the hatch."

"1, roger, and when you blow the hatch, the collar will already be down there waiting for you, and we're turning base at this time."

"Ah, roger."[28]

Lying flat on his back waiting for the helicopter's call that it had hooked onto the spacecraft, Grissom turned his attention for a second to the knife he had placed in his survival pack, wondering if he could carry it out with him as a souvenir instead of leaving it in the spacecraft. "I heard the hatch blow—the noise was a dull thud—and looked up to see blue sky out the hatch and water start to spill over the doorsill," he told NASA officials. Acting on instinct, Grissom quickly tossed his helmet to the floor, grabbed the right side of the instrument panel, and exited the spacecraft. "I have never moved faster in my life," he noted. "The next thing I knew I was floating high in my suit with the water up to my armpits." Grissom reported that although the cap and safety pin were off the detonator, he did not believe he hit the button to blow

A marine helicopter from the USS Randolph *attempts to lift the* Liberty Bell 7 *capsule from the Atlantic Ocean after the hatch mysteriously blew off the spacecraft at the end of its mission.*

the hatch. "The capsule was rocking around a little, but there weren't any loose items in the capsule, so I don't see how I could have hit it, but possibly I did," he later said in a debriefing aboard the carrier.[29]

From the pilot's seat aboard *Hunt Club 1*, Lewis saw the capsule sinking beneath the waves. "I had to dip the chopper's [three] wheels into the water in order to get my co-pilot to hook the cable on to it. Fortunately, the first time John tried, he managed to hook-up while the capsule was totally submerged," Lewis remembered. Although at first entangled in a line attaching a dye marker to the capsule and afraid he might go down with his ship, Grissom managed to easily free himself and swim away from danger. When he saw Lewis's helicopter struggling to save *Liberty Bell 7*, the astronaut swam back to try and help in the recovery operation, but before he reached his destination Rinehard had sliced off the capsule's antennae with a special squib-activated cutter and snagged the capsule. "Now I thought, 'Those boys have really saved us after all,'" Grissom recalled. The astronaut became puzzled, however, when the helicopter did not seem to be lowering a collar to hoist him aboard.[30]

What Grissom did not know was that Lewis had quite a struggle on his hands with *Liberty Bell 7*. In addition to the water inside the sinking spacecraft, the helicopter had to contend with a landing bag filled with approximately four tons of seawater. Lewis believed he could generate enough lift to raise the spacecraft from the water and return with it to the

Randolph. The pilot managed to lift the capsule from the water a few times, but just as the water began to drain from the spacecraft and landing bag, a swell would rise up and fill them back up again. "It was a battle we were beginning to lose," he observed, "and the readings from my cockpit instruments were not encouraging." Even before he pulled the capsule from the water, Lewis had noticed a chip detector warning light on his instrument panel, which indicated excessive wear on the helicopter's engine and gave him only five minutes of flight time before the engine quit and he crashed. "I told John to stop lowering the sling for Gus," said Lewis. "I said we've got a sick bird and better not bring him onboard because we probably won't get back to the carrier without swimming." After calling on another helicopter to come in and rescue the astronaut, Lewis also noticed the helicopter's cylinder head temperature rising and its oil pressure falling. He ordered Rinehard to cut the capsule loose, declared an emergency, and safely made it back to the carrier as the $2-million *Liberty Bell 7* sank in 2,800 fathoms of water. Later, mechanics discovered that *Hunt Club 1*'s engine was fine; the chip indicator light had been triggered by mistake.[31]

Grissom did not know of Lewis's difficulties, and Lewis was unaware of the astronaut's predicament. In previous recovery training missions, Lewis had observed that the astronauts "floated very well in their suits." In this case, however, Grissom discovered he had inadvertently left open an oxygen inlet connection, which allowed both water to seep into his space suit and air to seep out, retarding his buoyancy. He successfully closed the inlet, but some air also seeped out of the neck dam, causing Grissom to sink lower and lower in the water. He regretted the weight of souvenirs he had stored in the left leg of his suit, including rolls of dimes, small models of the capsules, and two sets of pilot's wings. The rotor wash from the helicopters, described by one NASA official as "like being in a little bit of a hurricane," kicked up so much spray that it made it hard for the astronaut to move in the water. Waves broke over his head, causing Grissom to swallow seawater and cough. The American space program was about to suffer its first casualty. "I thought to myself, 'Well, you've gone through the whole flight, and now you're going to sink right here in front of all these people,'" recalled Grissom, who expressed doubt that anyone in the recovery team would have time enough to save him. He also worried if there might be any sharks in the water and recalled a time when he and Schirra, both of whom were wearing flippers at the time, helped save Deke Slayton, who could not swim, from drowning during a recovery training exercise. "I wanted someone to do this for me," Grissom said.[32]

Struggling to stay afloat (he later said his time in the water "seemed like an eternity"), Grissom noticed a second helicopter hovering nearby and tried to get the crew's attention by waving his arms. Instead of coming to the astronaut's aid, the crew merely waved back and snapped photographs of the action. "I wasn't scared now. I was angry," said Grissom. "Then I looked to my right and saw a third helicopter coming my way and dragging a horse collar behind it across the water." In the doorway of the helicopter Grissom spied George Cox, the marine pilot who had handled the recovery hook for both chimpanzee Ham and astronaut Shepard. "As soon as I saw Cox, I thought, 'I've got it made,'" said Grissom. But there were still some tense moments ahead for the floundering astronaut. The rotor wash from the other helicopters made it impossible for Cox to get the horse collar closer than approximately twenty feet to Grissom, who swam hard to make the connection. When he arrived at his salvation, the exhausted astronaut realized he had put the collar on backwards. "But I couldn't have cared less," he said. "I knew it would hold me." Cox later told Grissom he had been dragged in the water for about fifteen feet before finally being lifted free, something the astronaut was too fatigued to remember. Safely aboard the helicopter, Grissom shook Cox's hand and said, "Boy, am I glad to see you." The astronaut then grabbed a Mae West life jacket and put it on. "I wanted to make certain that if anything happened to this helicopter I would not have to go through another dunking," he said. "I spent the entire trip back to the carrier buckling that life jacket." Once safely on the *Randolph*, the first words out of Grissom's mouth, as reported by the Associated Press, were: "Give me something to blow my nose. My head is full of water."[33]

Back at Cape Canaveral, mission control technicians and other NASA officials involved in the MR-4 mission were struggling to understand what had gone wrong in the

PHOTOGRAPH BY NASA, INDIANA HISTORICAL SOCIETY, C6418

Close to drowning following his escape from his sinking spacecraft, Grissom is finally pulled from the water by a recovery helicopter.

Atlantic. Gene Kranz, an assistant flight director during the Mercury program, remembered that he and his fellow controllers "sat helpless" as Grissom fought to survive. "I kept murmuring aloud at the console, 'Dammit, get Gus, forget the damn spacecraft,'" Kranz recalled. Excited voices over flight director Kraft's communication lines were buzzing that the capsule had sunk and recovery forces were trying to retrieve the astronaut. "I remember thinking, *I hope it's not a body they're recovering*. The next minute dragged on forever," said Kraft. "Then we heard it. Gus was aboard the chopper. They were returning to the ship."[34]

Betty and her two sons were anxiously watching the flight from liftoff to splashdown. A tense silence filled the house

Betty Grissom waits at her Virginia home to hear the results of her husband's Mercury mission.

until they heard that the capsule's parachute had opened and everything seemed to be going well, at which point Scott and Mark began to clap (Scott later told newsmen that he also whistled). "When we heard that Gus was staying in the capsule for a while," Betty recalled, "I really didn't think that anything might be wrong. I just assumed he was taking some last-minute readings." When she finally did learn that *Liberty Bell 7* had been lost at sea, Betty said she was "heartsick" because she knew her husband would feel the same way. "I wondered if, accidentally, Gus might have done something wrong," she said. "I knew if he had he would never forgive himself." Before a crowd of newsmen in front of her home, she added that she "almost cried" when she heard her husband's spacecraft had been lost, but the tensest moment for her came during "the last few seconds before liftoff." The news conference ended on a humorous note, as one reporter told her about Grissom tidying up the capsule the day before his flight and asking her if he was that way at home. Betty smiled and admitted: "He does not pick up things around the house very well."[35]

Grissom's parents began their vigil at their Mitchell home at 5:00 a.m., joined by their son Norman and his wife and daughter; their daughter, Wilma Beavers, and her three daughters visiting from Baltimore; their in-laws, Claude and Pauline Moore; and Ruth Sorrells, Gus Grissom's aunt. "There was very little conversation," recalled Norman. "We were all pretty nervous." Gus's father Dennis echoed those remarks, noting he would not want to go through such an experience too many times again. "It was the longest 15 minutes I ever lived through," he said. "You wouldn't realize this unless you had a son up there." Claude pointed out that those gathered at the Grissom residence for the launch certainly went through a lot of coffee and cigarettes during the mission. Asked about their reactions to a possible moon flight by their son, the Grissoms had radically different reactions, with Dennis supporting one if the astronaut could be returned safely, and Cecile franking stating: "No. Never." Other residents of the southern Indiana community were so relieved to hear that their hometown hero had made it back to Earth in one piece that they organized an impromptu parade, which featured Grissom's parents, a fire truck, brass band, antique cars, and scouts of both sexes. Factory sirens and whistles and the siren at city hall blared as the parade made its way through the community. As the *Indianapolis Star's* Bob Collins reported the details, the parade was supposed to go up and down Main Street twice. After passing the cheering crowd, estimated at five thousand in number, the first time, however, the parade took its time returning, prompting policeman George Stillman to observe: "I don't understand it. They said they were coming back." Some people had even left for home when the parade finally showed up again.[36]

On the *Randolph*, Grissom, still in his soggy space suit, received a congratulatory telephone call from Kennedy, who had watched the mission from the Oval Office. The president expressed to the astronaut his "great pleasure and satisfac-

Grissom starts to get out of his pressure suit as two medics aboard the aircraft carrier wait to start his physical checkup.

tion" with the MR-4 mission. Later that day, Kennedy signed into law an approximately $1.7 billion appropriation act for the Apollo lunar program. Just fifteen minutes after his harrowing experience on the ocean, Grissom underwent a physical examination conducted by the same doctors—Jerome Strong of the army and Robert Laning of the navy—who had examined Shepard on the USS *Lake Champlain* after the first Mercury flight. The physicians found Grissom had a temperature of 100.4 degrees Fahrenheit and a pulse rate that ranged from 160 initially to 104. "On general inspection," the doctors reported, "the astronaut appeared tired and was breathing rapidly; his skin was warm and moist." His condition proved to be consistent, according to the medical staff, with his ordeal and exposure to seawater. Grissom's pulse rate may have raced a bit more when one of the carrier's officers returned the astronaut's helmet to him and reported that a crew of the destroyer USS *Cony* had found it floating alongside a ten-foot-long shark. The return of his helmet proved to be small consolation to Grissom, who noted that in all his years of flying, including combat missions in Korea, *Liberty Bell 7* had been the first craft he had ever lost.[37]

After eating his second breakfast of the day and taking a quick nap, Grissom, joined by Lewis, departed the carrier on a Gruman S2F Tracker aircraft for a debriefing on his mission at Grand Bahama Island. Preparing to leave the *Randolph*, Grissom smiled and gestured to Admiral John Clark on the ship's bridge. As he climbed onto the plane, the ship's bells rang out twice and an announcement over its loudspeaker noted, "Captain United States Air Force departing," an honor usually given only to navy admirals. On the flight to Grand Bahama Island, Lewis said that the astronaut expressed appreciation for the efforts made to save the capsule. "While we all would have preferred to have the spacecraft," said Lewis, "what resulted, given the circumstances, represented excellent results. The mission could certainly be considered a success, because given the fact that problems developed, all of our contingency procedures worked and we brought Gus back." Upon arrival at the island, Grissom underwent a medical examination by Douglas and checks by an ophthalmologist, a neurologist, and a psychiatrist. Douglas noted that the astronaut "seemed to be recovering rapidly from the fatiguing effects of his flight and the postflight water-survival experience." Grissom and others involved in the MR-4 recovery operation were also questioned about the experience by Robert F. Thompson, head of the Space Task Group's recovery operations branch.[38]

With all of this activity swirling around him, Grissom found time to telephone his wife, who had been inundated since her husband's return from his mission with laudatory messages and a frequent stream of visitors. "I heard you got wet. Are you all right?" Betty asked her husband via the staticky ship-to-shore connection. Grissom responded he was fine, jokingly adding that the water had been warm and he always enjoyed swimming. Although she dreaded to do so, Betty finally asked the question most people had on their minds—was the hatch mishap his fault? "He told me there had been some malfunction in the capsule, and I was glad for his sake that he was not to blame," she said. Continuing the conversation, Betty informed her husband of the parade held in his honor in Mitchell and the receipt of congratulations from Indiana's governor, Matthew Welsh, and the state's two U.S. senators, Vance Hartke and Homer Capehart. Grissom responded by asking her to keep track of the calls, and then turned to more mundane matters. Noting that a hotel laundry had lost two pairs of his slacks and that he needed some shirts, he asked his wife to bring some clothes down to him when she visited him at the Cape. "When I said goodbye, I added 'I love you.' There was nothing more important to say than that. I'm not used to yelling it, but I did," Betty said.[39]

NASA plans called for Grissom to remain at Grand Bahama Island for forty-eight hours after his arrival. The following day, however, doctors decided to let the astronaut return to the Cape for a press conference and other ceremonies, as he seemed to be recovering as well as Shepard had after his mission. After arriving at Patrick Air Force Base near the Cape, Grissom received a quick hug from his wife before journeying to Cocoa Beach's Starlight Motel. At the start of the press conference there, Grissom received NASA's Distinguished Service Medal for his "outstanding contribution to space technology" from administrator Webb and a handshake from Robert Gilruth, Space Task Group director. Grissom then underwent a trial he had dreaded since first becoming an astronaut—questions from the assembled media horde. In spite of his disregard for the spotlight, the astronaut, noted a reporter from the *New York Times*, "gave a calm, methodical and often humorous report" on his MR-4 flight. With his short frame and crew-cut haircut, the reporter continued, Grissom resembled "a fighter pilot giving a matter-of-fact briefing to intelligence officers on a just-completed mission."[40]

Through garbled transcriptions of the astronaut's conversation with the recovery forces, there were some in the press who believed Grissom had purposely blown the hatch early. The astronaut immediately set them straight, noting: "I was just lying there minding my own business when—pow!—the hatch went. I looked up and saw nothing but blue sky and water coming in over the sill," said Grissom. "My one thought was to get out of the capsule." Although space agency officials had initially assured those concerned about the astronaut's stay in the water that he had been in no danger, reporters learned Grissom had come close to sinking for good beneath the waves. Grissom told them that the "best thing" he did all day was to roll up the neck dam on his space suit. Asked by one reporter if he felt in danger anytime in the water or during the flight, Grissom, with a smile, truthfully responded: "Well, I was scared a good part of the time. I guess this is a good indication." The reporter, perhaps taken back a bit by the astronaut's response, said, "You were what?" Grissom again said, "Scared, OK." The room, which also included his fellow astronauts and NASA officials, erupted in laughter over his honest answers. After all, the veteran of combat flights in Korea added, "I have been scared a few times before." Later, in an article about his experience in space for *Life* magazine, he noted: "I said I was scared and I meant it. If a guy isn't a little frightened by a trip into space, he's abnormal." Kraft agreed with Grissom's view, noting that you could not place a man on a rocket in 1961 and not be nervous. "Because if you weren't nervous," said Kraft, "you didn't know what the hell the story was all about. I wouldn't say he [Grissom] was afraid,

Joined onstage by NASA officials, Grissom answers questions from the media about his ill-fated Liberty Bell 7 *flight.*

but if he wasn't somewhat afraid, again, he didn't understand the problem, and Gus understood the problem."[41]

Further questions about the astronaut's behavior once he splashed down in the Atlantic were fueled in part in subsequent years by an incident after the press conference involving Grissom and his wife Betty—an incident featured prominently in both Tom Wolfe's book *The Right Stuff* and the movie of the same name directed by Philip Kaufman. NASA had wanted to give the Grissom family some privacy following the intense media scrutiny after the *Liberty Bell 7* mission so it arranged quarters for them at a VIP guesthouse at

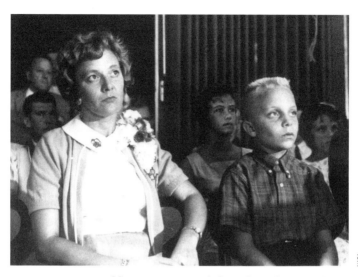

Betty Grissom and her son Scott watch from the audience at the press conference following Gus Grissom's Mercury mission. Writing about the experience later, Betty recalled being struck by "a manipulated sourness in the demonstration."

Patrick Air Force Base, which included a fully stocked refrigerator. Both the book and the movie have the couple arguing, with Betty, allegedly upset at not receiving an invitation to the White House for a visit with the president and first lady, railing against NASA and the military for having somehow violated the "military wife's compact," treating her not as the spouse of a hero but as "Honorable Mrs. Squirming Hatch Blower." Betty, however, remembers looking at the food in the refrigerator and laughing about it with her husband, asking, "They think I'm going to cook? They were trying to be nice, but that's not what's going through your mind, you don't want to start cooking." With no easy access to a beach for her children and with her husband returning immediately to work the next day, Betty asked to return to Cocoa Beach with the other astronauts' wives and families at the Holiday Inn, which she did. "It was just a conversation," Betty noted, disparaging Wolfe's depiction of her as being difficult.[42]

The hatch incident did have an effect on others in the Grissom family as well. Scott recalled that he and his brother Mark were immediately picked on at school by kids who blamed the astronaut for losing the capsule. He even asked his father about whether he was to blame for the loss of the spacecraft, and received a strong rejection of any such responsibility for the glitch. "There wasn't any way he had anything to do with the blowing of that hatch," Scott told an interviewer. "I believed him and I still do!"[43]

Back home in Indiana, and elsewhere, the questions about the hatch incident failed to deter those who wished to honor Grissom for his space achievement. The city of Mitchell intended to invite its hometown hero as the guest of honor of its fifteenth annual Persimmon Festival. Gov. Matthew Welsh wanted Grissom to first visit Indianapolis for a public welcome on Monument Circle attended by governors of neighboring states before assuming his duties in his home community. When Jack New, Welsh's executive secretary, called NASA to seek permission for the visit the space agency responded with a flat no. New quoted a NASA spokesman as saying that Grissom and the other astronauts were "priceless" and far too busy with their duties preparing for the first orbital flight for any public appearances. Other such requests following Shepard's flight had also been squelched by NASA. Not to be outdone by the Hoosier State, Newport News, Virginia, where Grissom made his home, designated the astronaut as its honorary mayor and named a new branch library in his honor. "I cannot think of any better way for our city to show its appreciation to Capt. Grissom and his fellow astronauts and all of the personnel of NASA than to name the new Debigh branch library the Virgil I. Grissom Library," said J. Fred Christie, Newport News city councilman.[44]

Some may have wanted to honor Grissom, but there were others ready to denigrate his performance. Grissom's comments about feeling scared during his spaceflight and splashdown proved to be much too honest an assessment for those in the test-pilot fraternity, who believed any such confession by a flyer was a sign of weakness. In his book *The Right Stuff*, Wolfe reported that the "True Brothers" at Edwards Air Force Base were laughing at the astronaut's explanations. It was obvious—to them at least—that Grissom had "screwed the pooch." Even if they doubted he had blown the hatch deliberately, there existed among the Edwards test pilots the belief that Grissom just might have panicked enough ("you have to be *afraid* to panic, old buddy") to have logic escape him and cause him to blow the hatch in his rush to leave the capsule. "Maybe the poor bastard just wanted out, and—bango!—he punched the button," Wolfe wrote. The author also questioned whether Grissom might have hit the hatch activator by accident as he tried to remove the Randall knife from the survival kit as a souvenir. (The astronaut had said in his report to NASA that he thought about removing the knife, but never indicated he had started to do so.) Wolfe also pointed to Grissom's high heart rate before and during the flight as confirmation of the astronaut's panicked state. Left unsaid, however, was Grissom's history of having an abnormally high heart rate, including during a treadmill run as part of the testing he underwent to become an astronaut.[45]

NASA officials downplayed the loss of the capsule, with Williams pointing out that the agency obtained "a great deal of data telemetered from the ship in flight." Still, the Space Task Group sought to obtain an answer to the hatch mystery by appointing a review committee, which included Schirra and Beddingfield. The committee subjected the hatch to extreme conditions but could not get it to malfunction. Grissom, dressed in his full space suit, climbed into a production spacecraft similar to the one he flew and repeated the actions he had made during his flight. At no time did he come anywhere near the hatch activator. Schirra also tried his luck, but no matter how hard he wriggled around in the spacecraft he could not inadvertently trigger the hatch's detonation. Possible reasons for the hatch's premature release included the exterior lanyard becoming snared in the straps holding the landing bag to the capsule; the ring seal being omitted from the activator, causing it to be triggered with very little pressure; static electricity generated by the helicopter; and chemical action of the seawater on the capsule's explosives. Although Beddingfield noted that the committee could not prove which hypothesis was correct, he and others believed Grissom's story. "Gus and I had flown together a lot," said Beddingfield, "so I knew whatever happened he would tell me. He said, 'I didn't fire that hatch.' So, I believed him."[46]

A NASA official closely involved in the recovery, Thompson, who debriefed Grissom and others involved in the incident at Grand Bahama Island, simply believed that the astronaut had been trying to do too good of a job and had gotten "out of sequence" during the operation. He likened the situation to a gun equipped with two safeties. Once those safeties were disengaged, it could fire even if a person did not pull the trigger. "Did Gus push the plunger?" Thompson asked. "No, he didn't push the plunger. Did he get out of sequence? Yes." Discounting any notion of "panic" on the astronaut's part, Thompson noted that once the cover and safety pin were removed, no spring, just two O-rings, held the plunger in place. The bobbing of the capsule in the water was so forceful that the plunger "just slid in," Thompson noted. "So, you know, there's no doubt in his mind but what he did not activate the door, and that's correct. He did not push the plunger and activate the door."[47]

According to Kraft, inside NASA there existed "two vehement camps" with opinions on what happened. One side believed Grissom had either panicked or hit the switch by accident, causing the hatch to blow. Another faction pointed to some unknown problem with the machine and held the astronaut blameless for the accident. Wendt, known as the "Pad Fuehrer" for the meticulous way he ran his operation, belonged in this camp, pointing to the external lanyard becoming tangled in the straps of the landing bag as the most likely culprit. "We will never know for sure," said Wendt, "but I suspect it was nothing more than a freak accident." Kraft talked to Grissom, read all the reports on the incident, and chose to believe the astronaut's account. "I trusted Gus's professionalism," he said, "and it was best for the program, considering all the circumstances, for Flight to take his word and tell everybody to put it behind us." Thompson agreed, noting they decided not to let the incident bog down NASA's efforts. "We didn't have a federal investigation case over the thing," he remembered. "Just made a judgment call and went on with the program." Thompson noted that Grissom "was one of the better people we had, and I think that that whole incident allowed the program to move on and not damage that individual, which was the right thing to do." Recovery procedures, however, were changed so that astronauts would refrain from removing the cover to the igniter until the time came to blow the hatch, and navy crews would be tasked with getting the occupant first and the capsule second. And, because other than the hatch incident Grissom's flight had gone well, Kraft recommended to Williams that NASA proceed on to orbital flights using the Atlas rocket.[48]

Grissom returned to his duties, assisting the other astronauts in preparing for orbital flights. His near-death experience, however, would not be the last time astronauts experienced difficulties in the Mercury program. As Glenn prepared for reentry on his three-orbit flight, technicians in mission control received indications from their instruments that the heat shield on his spacecraft, *Friendship 7*, had come loose. Leaving his retropackage on in hopes that it would hold the shield in place, Glenn survived reentry and became America's newest hero; the telemetered data had been incorrect—the heat shield performed its job perfectly. With Slayton grounded due to a heart ailment (idiopathic atrial fibrillation) and given a new job as head of the astronaut office, Carpenter took his place on *Aurora 7* for another three-orbit mission. On his flight, Carpenter experienced problems with his equipment and had problems aligning his spacecraft for reentry, resulting in his being approximately 250 miles off course. An anxious television audience held its breath, unsure of whether Carpenter had survived, but NASA tracked the wayward capsule and had a recovery team in the area within an hour. Equipment malfunctions also plagued Gordon Cooper's flight on *Faith 7*, in which he made twenty-two orbits of the earth. At one point during the mission's end, Cooper radioed to mission control: "Well, things are beginning to stack up a little. ASCS inverter is acting up and my CO_2 is building up in the suit. Partial pressure is decreasing in the cabin. Standby inverter won't come on line. Other than that things are fine." Cooper handled all the glitches thrown at him with aplomb and made a successful splashdown.[49]

One of the Mercury missions added another chapter to the mystery of *Liberty Bell 7*'s hatch mishap. Upon the completion of his six-orbit textbook flight on *Sigma 7*, Schirra, who joked with controllers on the ground about flying in "chimpanzee configuration" when he switched to auto mode during his flight, landed in the Pacific Ocean just northwest of Hawaii, and awaited pickup by the aircraft carrier USS *Kearsarge*. The ship hoisted the capsule, with Schirra still inside, and deposited it on one of its aircraft elevators. The astronaut had a nasty surprise when he pressed the igniter to blow the hatch. The recoil proved to be so forceful that it cut through the reinforced-metal glove of his space suit. "When Gus came aboard the carrier after my recovery (he'd been in Hawaii, I think), he had the biggest smile on his face when I showed him this cut hand because there was not a mark on his body after his problem with his hatch," Schirra pointed out. "I said, 'Gus, look at my hand, it really kind of hurt.' He knew exactly what I was telling him." In fact, all of the astronauts—Glenn, Schirra, and Cooper—who activated the explosive hatch on their spacecraft suffered cuts or bruises on their hand from the recoil of the igniter.[50]

The intense pressure and tension surrounding each of

PHOTOGRAPH BY NASA, INDIANA HISTORICAL SOCIETY, C9152

Gordon Cooper examines the gloves he would use on his Mercury orbital mission. Cooper named his spacecraft Faith 7.

the Mercury launches and recoveries called for something or someone to lighten the load with humor. On both Shepard's and Grissom's missions, the names for their spacecrafts had been sprayed on via a stencil cut. On Glenn's flight, the marine became determined to have his capsule's name hand painted. The decision prompted a "good bit of 'joshing,'" with both Shepard and Grissom making "comments that a stencil wasn't good enough for John, that he had to have his name hand painted by an artist," noted Cece Bibby, the artist who did the work. An employee of Chrysler's missile division, which had won a contract with NASA to provide workers for its publication group, Bibby met Grissom one day on the staircase after leaving the astronaut office. The astronaut asked her about how her work was going on the "'Boy Scout's' capsule. Then he said he thought what I really should do was paint 'naked ladies' on the capsule because it would really shake John up, since he was so 'straight arrow,'" she noted. Bibby told Grissom his idea was not a good one, to which he answered by calling her "chicken." She reminded him, however, that her job would be in jeopardy, not his, as NASA would not fire an astronaut. "An artist was another matter," said Bibby, nicknamed Baby by most of the male employees at the Cape. "He just chuckled."

Grissom's chance remarks did prompt an idea for Bibby to play a joke on Glenn by using the capsule's periscope. The artist drew a small painting of a naked lady, with pillows placed in strategic locations, and the caption: "It's just you and me, John Baby, against the world." Bibby gave a print of the drawing to one of the white room engineers on the launchpad so he could put it on the periscope and remove it before the countdown. Although NASA scrubbed Glenn's flight, the astronaut caught a good view of Bibby's work. "When I went to work the next morning there was a note taped to the lamp on my drawing board," said Bibby. "The note was from John telling me he had gotten a big kick out of the drawing and that he was going to have it framed for his den at home." For Glenn's liftoff on February 20, 1962, Bibby provided another drawing, this one of an older woman holding a bucket and mop with the caption, "You were expecting someone else, John Baby?" She also provided a naked woman to grace the periscope for Carpenter's mission.

The rash of unclad women reached its fever pitch when NASA printed a safety manual for its launchpad personnel. Some enterprising employee added a smiling, buxom blonde woman (wearing no top) to a photograph of space agency technicians in hard hats. "Well, you can imagine in which direction the finger of blame was pointing," said Bibby. Fortunately, NASA had farmed out the production of the manual to another contractor, and Bibby's art department had not been involved in any work for the publication. The furor over the manual "cured" Bibby of painting nude women. Later, Grissom apologized to Bibby about his dare, indicating he never realized such a storm would result from his suggestion. He told her he had admitted to NASA officials

Garbed as vaudevillians, Grissom and Shepard engage in a bit of horse-play during the early days of the Mercury program. When Grissom gave the photos to Cece Bibby, she asked him what they were up to. He just said, "Fun and games, baby [her nickname], fun and games."

that he had been "the one who instigated the whole thing. He even told them he had called me a 'chicken.'"[51]

The Mercury program ended as a triumph of American ingenuity and technology. The time had come for the next step toward the moon: Project Gemini. Two men would be going into space together to test procedures to be used for the proposed trip to the moon. Still smarting from the roasting he had received following his Mercury mission, Grissom became determined to make his mark on this new space effort. While the other astronauts were still concentrating on the Mercury missions, Grissom had turned his attention to Gemini, working quite closely with McDonnell Aircraft in the design of the new two-man spacecraft. "He was angry about being blamed for his spacecraft having sunk," Schirra said of his friend, "and he was fighting to come back out of the pack. Gus was a tiger. He wanted the first Gemini flight, and by God he got it." Grissom achieved the honor of flying the first Gemini mission, but only after another of the original seven had his astronaut career derailed by illness.[52]

6

Gemini

THE AMBITIOUS GOAL OF LANDING A MAN ON THE MOON AND returning him safely to Earth by the end of the decade created a myriad of problems for the National Aeronautics and Space Administration to ponder as Project Mercury ended its brief forays into the unknown of space travel. If the agency's Project Apollo was to be successful, there were a number of unexplored areas to be examined, including the main basic question: how does one get to the moon? Three methods were under consideration, including the use of a giant booster, the Nova, with forty million pounds of thrust, to send a spacecraft directly to the moon, land, and return to Earth (the direct-ascent approach). Another proposal (Earth-orbit rendezvous) involved using the Saturn 5 rocket already being developed by NASA to send the necessary craft for the trip to the moon into orbit, have them rendezvous, assemble into one unit, refuel at a space station, and then blast its way to the lunar surface. Finally, the team at the space agency's rendezvous panel at the Langley Research Center, under the direction of John Houbolt, championed a lunar-orbit rendezvous plan whereby the lunar spacecraft would be sent to the moon, where a small lander or "bug" would detach and land on the lunar surface. After exploring the surface, the astronauts would leave in a small section of the lander and link up with the main spacecraft for the return voyage home.[1]

After initial objections by Wernher von Braun and other rocket scientists at the Marshall Space Flight Center, the lunar-orbit rendezvous plan won acceptance (even from von Braun) at a June 7, 1962, meeting at the Marshall center. The NASA decision, however, received criticism from an old foe—Jerome Wiesner, President John F. Kennedy's science adviser, who believed the plan posed grave dangers to the astronauts responsible for fulfilling the lunar mission. The matter came to a head in September 1962 when Kennedy, Wiesner, other dignitaries, and NASA officials visited von Braun at the Marshall center for a view of the mock-up of the Saturn 5 rocket's first stage. The president casually asked von Braun about the disagreement over the lunar-orbit scheme. "I was starting to tell Kennedy why I thought they were wrong when Jim Webb [NASA administrator] came up, saw us talking, thought we were arguing, and began hammering away at me for being on the wrong side of the issue," Wiesner recalled. "And then I began to argue with Webb." The contentious debate, overheard by the assembled media, became public, but the president knew how it would end. "Jerry's going to lose, it's obvious," Kennedy told a foreign dignitary on Air Force One. "Webb's got all the money and Jerry's only got me." The president proved prophetic; in November Webb announced NASA's decision to use the lunar-orbit rendezvous plan.[2]

Robert Gilruth, Space Task Group director, noted that he became convinced the choice for the lunar-orbit rendezvous "was the way to go" because it required less weight to be fired toward the moon. More important, in his view, the plan called for one machine designed specifically for landing and taking off from the moon, and another for flying there and reentry to a water landing back home. "An additional bonus was that it allowed the tremendous industrial job to be divided between two major contractors since there would be two spacecraft," Gilruth said, "thereby giving each one a more manageable task." Still, the plan prompted its own set of issues to be examined, as there existed a huge gap between NASA's short experience with Mercury and the long voyages to the moon to come.[3]

As early as 1959, NASA had studied the possibility of an advanced Mercury spacecraft equipped to carry two astronauts—Mercury Mark 2, an intermediate program to build upon the equipment and lessons learned from America's previous spaceflights. For this new effort, NASA needed to determine if astronauts could work in space for the approximately fourteen days it would take for a journey to the moon and back, if an astronaut could leave the capsule and perform

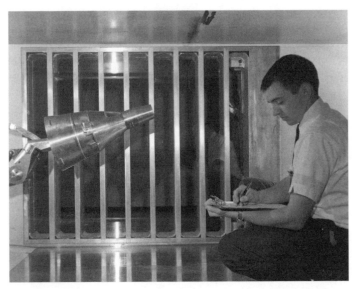

NASA

A model of a Gemini capsule is tested in a wind tunnel at NASA's Langley Research Center.

extravehicular activities, if rendezvous and docking could be accomplished, if two spacecraft could be controlled in flight while docked, if ground crews could track and communicate with two spacecraft, and if a controlled reentry could be made following a high-speed lunar flight. On December 7, 1961, NASA announced its plans to develop a two-man spacecraft launched by a modified U.S. Air Force two-stage intercontinental ballistic missile, the Titan 2, manufactured by the Martin Company. Just eight days later, McDonnell Aircraft Corporation (where Grissom's brother, Lowell, worked as a senior systems analyst), which had proved it could build dependable space vessels in the Mercury program, won the contract to develop the two-man vehicle, which would rendezvous in orbit and dock with an Agena target vehicle launched by an Atlas rocket. In addition, a program-naming committee discarded the old Mercury Mark 2 designation for a new title: Gemini, for the third constellation of the Zodiac, featuring the twin stars Castor and Pollux (Alex P. Nagy at NASA headquarters won a bottle of Scotch for coming up with the name). For NASA administrator Webb, Gemini served not only as a training program for Apollo, but also as "insurance" in case the moon effort failed. "Mercury would not have led us very far," said Webb. "With Gemini, we would have learned a great deal about spaceflight and its capability. If we had an insuperable obstacle and had to stop Apollo, if our equipment wouldn't work or it is too difficult a job . . . we would have still done the next most important thing."[4]

In addition to juggling the finish of Mercury, the start of Gemini, and the future moon missions of Apollo, the approximately 750 NASA employees also had to contend with a move from facilities at Langley, Virginia, to a new Manned Spacecraft Center located near Houston, Texas. A site selection committee had been working at NASA for some time seeking a site to house the agency's burgeoning space program. In August 1961 the committee evaluated approximately twenty cities as possibilities for the new center. A month later, Webb sent a memorandum to President Kennedy indicating that the command center for NASA would be located about twenty miles southeast of Houston on one thousand acres of land near Clear Lake donated by Rice University (the federal government purchased an additional six hundred acres of highway frontage). Although there were technical factors in Houston's favor, politics played a major role in its selection, as the area's congressman, Albert Thomas, held a key post on the House appropriations subcommittee, and Vice President Lyndon B. Johnson also called the state home. "We've got to get the power," Webb explained to Gilruth, who would serve as MSC director. "We've got to get the money, or we can't do this program."[5]

The astronauts were used to receiving perks with their newfound status as American heroes in the battle with the Soviet Union, and the pattern continued with the move to Houston. A real estate developer named Frank Sharp offered the original seven spacefarers free, fully furnished homes in a housing development to be called Sharpstown. According to Lt. Col. "Shorty" Powers, NASA's public relations representative, he had received approval from the space agency's counsel, but negative media reaction to the deal caused the astronauts to decline the offer. As Powers later admitted, he may have acted rashly in going through with the offer because "nobody gives you anything for nothing, and it was obvious Mr. Sharp certainly had plans for exploiting the fact that the seven astronauts lived in his development."[6]

Instead of Sharpstown, the Grissom family and their dog,

a basset hound named Sam Bass, moved to a three-bedroom home in a development called Timber Cove near Seabrook, Texas, just down the road from the new NASA facility. Other astronauts in the development included John Glenn, Scott Carpenter, and Wally Schirra. The Schirras and the Grissoms bought three lots side by side then divided the lots in half for their homes. "I liked contemporary design," noted Betty Grissom, "so Gus and I built a one-story, flat-roof, white brick home that has wisteria vines creeping up on the outside and ceramic in the entry way." The ceramic floor indicated her practical nature, as she did not want to spend her time waxing the floor, while the home's orange door reflected her whimsical nature. "Maybe it looks like a 'farout' house you wouldn't expect two small-town products to live in—but it has the hominess of oaks and pines around it," Betty said, "and sometimes you can hear the squirrels playing on the roof." The nearby Clear Lake soon drew the Grissom family to its waters, where they enjoyed water skiing, except for Betty. "I tried it, but I drank too much of the lake and quit," she noted.[7]

Joining the original seven astronauts in the exodus to Houston was a new crop of star voyagers selected by NASA to help crew the ten manned Gemini missions. For this next group of astronauts, the space agency opened applications to military and civilian test pilots, raised the height limit to six feet, lowered the age limit from forty to thirty-five, and allowed college degrees in physical and biological sciences as well as engineering. After reviewing 253 applications, NASA selected thirty-two men to undergo medical evaluation at the Aerospace Medical Science Division at Brooks Air Force Base in Texas, as well as written tests and personal interviews. In September 1962, NASA picked nine men for the program, including such familiar names in space history as Neil Armstrong, Frank Borman, James Lovell, Tom Stafford, and John Young. Deke Slayton, NASA director of flight crew operations, assigned Grissom to supervise the new group—known to the general public as the Gemini astronauts—as he had become very involved with the Gemini program. In spending time with the Mercury veterans, Stafford noted that they were "very friendly" to the new recruits, "even Gus Grissom, who had the reputation of being tough to take. He didn't offer much in the way of conversation, but he was pleasant." Grissom's sometimes wicked sense of humor, however, came to the fore during the selection of another group of astronauts: the fourteen selected by NASA in October 1963 for the Apollo program. Schirra and Grissom served as part of an interview team for the selection process and questioned candidate Edwin "Buzz" Aldrin (the second man to walk on the moon), who came to the interview dressed in a sport coat and tie with his flight wings and Phi Beta Kappa key. "Aldrin," Schirra quoted Grissom as asking, "we've already read your résumé. Why are you wearing it?"[8]

Following his flight on *Liberty Bell 7*, Grissom realized that he probably would not be assigned another Mercury mission, and if he wanted to fly again he would have to look elsewhere. "I didn't have a job, and if there's one thing I can't stand is sitting around and doing nothing," said Grissom, who received a promotion to major from the air force in July 1962. Because he knew James Chamberlin, program manager for Gemini, "quite well," Grissom began to spend more and more time working with NASA technicians and McDonnell engineers on the two-man spacecraft, eventually serving as the astronaut office's representative on the project. Schirra noted that Gemini was essentially his friend's spacecraft. "He practically had it to himself," said Schirra. Grissom spent many hours in a mock-up of the Gemini spacecraft at McDonnell's St. Louis plant reviewing every aspect of the capsule's cockpit layout. "All I had to do was say, 'No, I don't like it,' or 'Yeah, it's okay.' If I had a suggestion of my own, I'd sometimes give it," Grissom said. He did add that he tried not to stifle debate on any particular part of the spacecraft, because an engineer might be able to analyze a system and devise a method to make it work better.[9]

What came off the McDonnell production line for the two-man Gemini missions was a craft that measured nineteen feet long, ten feet in diameter, and weighed 8,400 pounds. The spacecraft itself consisted of two main sections: an adapter module, which contained the equipment section supplying the craft with its oxygen and power and the retrograde package with the retro-rockets for reentry, and the reentry module, which included the cabin section with the heat shield, crew compartment, and the rendezvous and recovery section with its radar equipment and drogue and main parachutes. In Project Mercury, the spacecraft's systems were in the crew cabin, installed in a "layer cake" fashion that caused headaches when a number of systems had to be removed to fix technical problems. "Now in the Gemini capsule there's very little equipment inside the pressurized cabin itself," noted Grissom, "and nothing is buried. Most of the systems are installed in separate packages on the outside of the cabin or in the adapter section behind us." The hardware for the spacecraft came in modular packages that could easily be swapped out when glitches occurred. "If one [system] goes haywire," Grissom pointed out, "you take it out and plug in a new one."[10]

There were other differences between the Mercury capsule and the more advanced Gemini spacecraft. Because the Titan 2 launch vehicle used storable hypergolic propellant, which would merely burn in case of an accident rather than cause a massive fireball as would an Atlas rocket malfunction, Gemini had individual ejection seats similar to the ones used on jet aircraft instead of an escape tower to pull the capsule clear from danger. If all worked as planned, the ejection seats could be used on the launchpad and during reentry at low altitudes. Evaluating the seats produced some darkly comic moments for the astronauts. During one test, the hatch failed to open and the ejection seat blasted its way through the obstruction. "One hell of a headache—but a short one!"

Young noted later. Also, instead of swinging down on parachutes to a splashdown in the ocean, Gemini initially had
been scheduled to glide to a ground landing on a paraglider
developed by Francis Rogallo, an engineer at the Langley
Research Center. Onboard the spacecraft, a sophisticated
(for its time) shoebox-size computer aided astronauts in com-
putations for rendezvous and docking, while power and water
for the longer duration flights came from fuel cells manufactured by General Electric (batteries had been used for
Mercury missions). Gemini also came with an offset center of
gravity, which gave it enough lift so that an astronaut could
"steer" his ship during the reentry phase for more accurate
splashdowns.[11]

The black-and-white spacecraft reminded Grissom of
Oliver J. Dragon, a character from the *Kukla, Fran and Ollie*
children's television show popular in the late 1950s. "Viewed
directly from the front, the Gemini's two hatch windows
seem to give it an expression of ineffable melancholy," said
Grissom, "and the drooping nose could belong to nothing but
Oliver J. Viewed from the side, it looks like a Mercury capsule that threw the diet rules away," as the capsule had 50
percent more space for its crew compartment (about the size
of the interior of a Volkswagon). Its unusual looks, however,
could not hide one fact from Grissom and the other astronauts—Gemini was a true spacecraft. In some ways, Gemini
was a "throwback to airplanes," said Grissom, as an astronaut
could use the controls to change the craft's orbital path—a

NASA

The Paresev 1-A stands ready for use at the Rogers Dry Lakebed at the NASA Flight Research Center, Edwards, California. Grissom is at left and NASA test pilot Milton Thompson is at right. The Paresev evaluated a potential replacement for parachutes used on spacecraft.

necessity in any rendezvous operation—through its Orbital Attitude and Maneuvering System (OAMS). "And in Gemini," he said, "a man, not a machine, is the boss. We Astronauts have always felt that man ought to be an integral part of the system rather than merely a backup for automatic systems as in Mercury."[12]

Grissom became so identified with the Gemini spacecraft that fellow astronauts nicknamed it the Gusmobile. The astronauts appreciated Grissom's attempts to give them true control over their craft (Schirra called Gemini "magnificent to fly"). Slayton noted that in Gemini there existed no way for the ship "to be flown without pilots at the controls. How did the astronauts feel about it? You could hear the applause a mile down the beach." The cockpit's interior arrangement, however, owed much to Grissom's compact frame, causing problems for some of the taller astronauts, including rookie Stafford. "Gus was about five foot, six inches, 160 pounds; I was six feet, 175, and I was jammed in, especially when I had to wear a pressure suit and helmet," Stafford noted. "The top of my helmet nearly kept the hatch from closing. It was also painful." McDonnell engineers solved the problem by removing some of the insulation from the hatch's interior, creating a small space for the taller astronauts' helmets. "The bump was first installed on Gemini 6," said Stafford, "so they called it the Stafford Bump."[13]

In spite of his efforts working on Gemini's behalf, Grissom did not know if he would be one of the first to fly the

President John F. Kennedy examines a Gemini spacecraft with astronauts Gordon Cooper and Grissom during a tour of Cape Canaveral in 1963.

spacecraft. Early on, nobody knew if Gemini would ever get off the ground, as the program endured numerous delays and escalating costs. There were difficulties with such new equipment as the fuel cells and with preparing the Titan 2 to carry its human cargo. NASA responded in March 1963 by replacing Chamberlin with Charles W. Mathews, who had served as chief of the operations division for Mercury. At the time Mathews took over, the Gemini operation had its headquarters in an old government building in Houston (work on the Manned Spacecraft Center had just started). Mathews visited the various subcontractors on the project, adjusted Gemini's schedule to more realistic goals, and canceled the paraglider concept for the tried-and-true parachute recovery system. "When I came on board," said Mathews, "I was never very sympathetic with the paraglider in the first place, because I really didn't see the land-landing requirement as anything that was needed in the immediate future, certainly not for Apollo." Mathews also instituted a "rigorous change control system, where no change could be made . . . until it was not only reviewed by the contractors, but was brought up to the program office and could only happen if I personally signed [off] on it." Soon, Gemini was back on track, with the first un-manned mission set for December 1963 and the inaugural manned mission tentatively scheduled for October 1964.[14]

On November 16, 1963, President Kennedy visited the expanded facilities at Cape Canaveral and received a briefing from von Braun on the new Saturn 1 rocket with its 1.3 mil-lion pounds of thrust to boost payloads into Earth orbit. The massive Saturn 5 rocket under development would be capa-ble of launching astronauts on a voyage to the moon. In addi-tion to visiting with von Braun, the president toured the com-plex by helicopter with Grissom and fellow Mercury veteran Gordon Cooper. As Kennedy left Florida for a trip to Dallas, Texas, Grissom and his family prepared to fly to Indiana to attend the Old Oaken Bucket football game between Indiana University and Purdue University on November 22. At a refueling stop in Little Rock, Arkansas, the Grissoms learned that Kennedy had been killed by an assassin as his motorcade made its way through the streets of Dallas. The Grissoms traveled the rest of the way to Indiana via a commercial flight, but the game, like many in the country, had been canceled. Just a week later, the new president, Lyndon B. Johnson, issued an executive order renaming Cape Canaveral as the John F. Kennedy Space Center.[15]

As the nation continued to grieve for its fallen leader in early 1964, Slayton worked to make Kennedy's dream of landing a man on the moon by decade's end a reality by selecting crews not only for the ten planned Gemini missions, but also astronauts for NASA's next effort—the three-man Apollo moon program. "We were trying to get an experience base in Gemini to get us into the front end of the Apollo program," he said. "Our motivation there was not only to do the operational things that were necessary . . . but to get as many guys experienced as we could in flight also." With these requirements in mind, the grounded astronaut devised guidelines for selecting crews for future flights. Slayton considered anyone hired by NASA as an astronaut to be qualified for any mission, but some—those with command, management, or test-pilot backgrounds—were more likely to be picked for challenging assignments. "I would try to match people in a crew based on individual talents and, when possible, personal compatibility," he said. Of course, Slayton added, because everyone in the astronaut corps was both "talented and motivated" they were likely to get along together no matter what. When assigning flights, Slayton also kept in mind future requirements—for example, how a Gemini flight might effect any future Apollo missions—and planned for an annual attrition rate of 10 percent, due to resignations or accidents. Crew assignments for missions were passed along by Slayton to Gilruth, his direct supervisor. "I don't know whether he [Gilruth] had to get any approval or not from higher authority," said Slayton, "but nobody ever told me, 'you can't do that; you've got the wrong guys.'"[16]

To man the Gemini flights, Slayton had at his disposal the new group of Gemini astronauts and a portion of the Mercury seven, including Alan Shepard, Grissom, and Schirra. Glenn intended to retire to pursue a political career, Carpenter had become persona non grata at NASA following his flight, and Gorden Cooper "was a question mark," noted Slayton. For the first manned Gemini mission, scheduled to last eighteen orbits (Gemini-Titan 3, or GT-3), Slayton turned to the first American in space, Shepard, with Stafford serving as the second member of the crew as pilot. (Since no astronaut would be caught dead being known as a copilot, the crews for Gemini had a commander and a pilot as titles.) Serving as backup for the flight would be Grissom, slated for a future fourteen-day mission aboard GT-6 with Borman. Schirra received the first rendezvous flight, GT-5, with Young as his pilot. Slayton informed the astronauts of his decision at a July 1963 meeting in the astronaut office.[17]

Slayton's careful plans were derailed by events outside of

The prime and backup crews for the Gemini 3 *mission. Wally Schirra and Tom Stafford (top row, left to right) served as the backups for (bottom row, left to right) Grissom and John Young.*

his control involving Shepard, who awoke one day to nausea and dizziness. Although the feeling passed, it returned days later, subsided, and returned again. "He developed these symptoms . . . and he came to the flight surgeon's office, and said, 'I'm having a problem,' and it's got to be a problem if he's going to come in and say something about it," noted Dr. Charles Berry, chief of the Manned Spacecraft Center's medical operations office. "And it was a problem. It was a big problem, and it got worse. We tried medical therapy . . . but there is no great therapy that does something for this." Shepard had developed Ménière's syndrome, a disease affecting highly competitive individuals that resulted in periods of disorientation, dizziness, and nausea. With no known cure, the illness grounded Shepard, who later worked for Slayton as head of the astronaut office. (Both Slayton and Shepard would beat their illnesses and fly in space; Shepard, on *Apollo 14*, and Slayton on the *Apollo-Soyuz* mission between the United States and the Soviet Union).[18]

The loss of Shepard caused Slayton to shuffle his crew assignment for Gemini. He assigned Grissom to take over as commander of *Gemini 3*, but moved Stafford to serve as pilot with Schirra on *Gemini 6* (Schirra and Stafford acted as backups to the *Gemini 3* mission). There were other changes as well. Initially, Borman had been slated to fly with Grissom on *Gemini 3*, and the senior astronaut called him and invited Borman to come to his home and talk about the assignment. "I did, and we talked for about an hour," Borman remembered. "I haven't the slightest idea what went wrong, but he apparently wasn't too impressed with me." According to astronaut Gene Cernan, the last man to walk on the moon, the answer was simple—the two men's egos were too large to fit inside the snug interior of a spacecraft. Instead of Borman, the low-key Young would serve as pilot with Grissom. According to Slayton, Young was a "better personality match" for his friend.[19]

On April 13, 1964, only five days after a successful unmanned test of the Gemini-Titan configuration, Gilruth announced to members of the press at the Manned Spacecraft Center's auditorium the prime and backup crews for the first manned mission, which he hoped would get off the ground before the end of the year. Most observers were surprised at Young, the thirty-three-year-old rookie, being paired with the thirty-eight-year-old Grissom, who expressed his pleasure at receiving the assignment. "I have been following the program since its inception," he told the media. "And it is a real honor to be picked on the first crew." Schirra and Stafford were also introduced to the media as backups for the flight (Grissom and Young would turn around and serve as backups for their *Gemini 6* rendezvous mission). News of Grissom's selection received banner headlines in Mitchell, Indiana, with the astronaut's parents expressing pride and worry about their son's new assignment. "This is what he has worked so hard for, and what he wants to do," said Dennis and Cecile Grissom, "so we can't do anything but go along with him." The couple also relayed to their hometown newspaper that their grandsons, Scott and Mark Grissom, seemed to take the news in stride. "They are so used to him being in that kind of work that they don't think much about it and don't seem to get any more excited than they would if he had an ordinary job," said Cecile.[20]

With the Gemini decision made, Betty expected not to see much of her husband during the next several months, as he immersed himself in training for the mission. She was right; her husband and Young became familiar presences at McDonnell, working together on the flight simulator located there. The simulator closely reflected what the astronauts would experience on an actual mission, from liftoff to splashdown. The duo spent so much time checking out the spacecraft's systems that they rented a two-bedroom apartment in St. Louis at the Chase-Plaza Park Hotel (Schirra and Stafford also shared quarters there). According to Stafford, the astronauts usually flew into St. Louis on Sunday night or Monday morning, spent days at the McDonnell facility at Lambert Field, then returned to Houston on Thursday or Friday. "The days seemed to have forty-eight hours, the weeks fourteen days, and still there was never enough time," said Grissom. "We saw our families just enough to reassure our youngsters they still had fathers." A look at the training schedule for Grissom alone buttresses his statement. The astronaut spent 200 hours in briefings in Houston, St. Louis, and Cape Kennedy; spun 9.5 hours in the centrifuge at the Naval Air

Development Center in Johnsville, Pennsylvania; practiced exiting the spacecraft at Ellington Air Force Base's flotation tank; and endured 225 aborted missions in a moving-base abort simulator created by Ling-Temco-Vought Inc. "In those simulators," Grissom noted, "Murphy's Law really got a workout. Every conceivable abort situation appears on your instruments, and you've got to react properly."[21]

Working together as a team, Grissom and Young came to know one another quite well. When involved in a simulator, the duo would jot down any problem areas in a notebook and discuss what to do about them later that night in their apartment. The two men were both seen by NASA colleagues as doers rather than talkers, but also as possessing good senses of humor on occasion. Michael Collins, who flew in both the Gemini and Apollo programs, called the two men "a matched pair" as they were both "good engineers who understood their machines and liked fooling with them." He added that Grissom and Young were also ill at ease with the media attention thrust upon them and their families "and tried as hard as they could to deflect questions from themselves to their beloved machines." Although some considered it "colorful for a test pilot to blow his own horn," Young observed, he and Grissom aimed on their *Gemini 3* flight to "lay low and not say a word. I recall times in test flight work when things might have turned out better if people hadn't talked too much." The two also shared an aversion for anything that might interfere with checking out their new spacecraft, including medical

Young and Grissom relax during a visit to the McDonnell Aircraft Corporation in St. Louis where the Gemini spacecrafts were built.

procedures. Dr. Fred Kelly, a NASA flight surgeon, recalled that during Gemini doctors had to depend on the crew's cooperation to collect blood pressure readings—something they could not expect from Grissom, who probably viewed such measurements with suspicion following the questions raised about his increased heart rate during his Mercury mission. The grounding of his friend Slayton also did not improve Grissom's view of the medical profession. Young followed Grissom's lead. "It may be imagination," said Kelly, "but he [Young] seems to walk like Gus, talk like Gus, and sometimes, he can be just as obstinate as Gus. I think they named this program right when they called it Gemini and selected these two for the first flight."[22]

As they had with the Mercury program, NASA gave its astronauts the privilege of naming the spacecraft they would fly into space. Initially, Grissom had wanted to use a Native American name, and he asked research people at *Life* and *World Book Encyclopedia* for suggestions. The researchers unearthed the name Wapashas, after which the Wabash River had been named. "Great, John and I agreed," said Grissom. "We'd go into space aboard the *Wapasha*, a truly American name." Unfortunately, someone pointed out to Grissom that people would more than likely start calling the spacecraft *The Wabash Cannon Ball*. Such a designation might not be appreciated by Grissom's father and his coworkers at the Baltimore and Ohio Railroad. At about the time Grissom pondered renaming his spacecraft, the musical comedy *The Unsinkable Molly Brown* had recently closed a successful run on Broadway. "I'd been accused of being more than a little sensitive about the loss of my *Liberty Bell 7*," he said, "and it struck me that the best way to squelch this idea would be to kid it." Young and Grissom agreed on *Molly Brown*. Some in NASA management, however, believed the name lacked dignity and asked Grissom to make another choice. The astronaut had another one in mind: *Titanic*. "Well, compared to that, *Molly Brown* sounded great," Slayton noted. NASA officials in Washington, D.C., who disapproved of *Molly Brown*, had the final say for subsequent missions, which would go by numbers alone. Grissom joked that the space agency feared what practical-joker Schirra "might come up with when it came time to name *his* spacecraft." Individual names for spacecraft did not return until March 1969 with the *Apollo 9* mission that involved a command module and lunar lander, necessitating separate call signs to ease radio communications between ground controllers and the astronauts.[23]

Although NASA had hoped to launch *Gemini 3* sometime in December 1964, there were delays with the second unmanned mission as three separate hurricanes swept through Cape Kennedy. There also was some debate about the duration of the first manned Gemini flight, with the astronauts, backed by Slayton, seeking an open-ended mission where the crew could decide how long to keep the spacecraft in orbit. Because its tracking network at that time could only cover a three-orbit flight, NASA nixed the astronauts' request. In addition to reviewing the new spacecraft's systems and the capability of the worldwide tracking network, the *Gemini 3* mission, set for launch on March 23, 1965, had as

McDonnell test flight engineer N. R. Shyken explains to Young and Grissom the operation of an adapter ring that will attach their Gemini capsule to the Titan booster. The Gemini 3 *spacecraft sits in the background.*

its main goals testing the spacecraft's OAMS (a key to any future rendezvous and docking missions) and using the onboard computer to make a controlled reentry. The flight also included three science experiments: an examination of the effects of radiation and zero gravity on human blood samples, an assessment of low gravity's effect on the growth of fertilized sea urchin eggs, and a test of reentry communications. In addition, NASA charged Young with checking out some of the food to be used on future long-duration flights. He also had a rare opportunity to fly the spacecraft.

Practicing the mission one day with Grissom in the simulator, the rookie astronaut noted, "Well, here's where I get my chance to touch the controls." Young noted that his partner laughed and said, "I guess we'll have to take that part out of the [flight] plan." Although Young described the mission as "a piece of cake" compared with the trips to come, Grissom noted that he experienced the same "odd feeling" every test pilot had before taking "a new aircraft up for the very first time; the knowledge that if something goes to worms, it won't be you heading back to the old drawing board."[24]

On March 15, 1965, Grissom, Young, Schirra, and Stafford moved into the new astronaut quarters at the Manned Spacecraft Operations Building, located on Merritt Island next to Cape Kennedy, so they could familiarize themselves with the Pad 19 launch complex. The accommodations were a far cry from the ones the astronauts were used to at Hangar S in their Mercury days. "These quarters are quiet, comfortably furnished, and you might think you were in some brand new hotel," said Grissom. The astronauts also had access to the building's gymnasium, complete with punching bags and exercise bicycles. Just three days after the Americans had settled into their pleasant surroundings, however, the Soviet Union shocked the world again with another space triumph when cosmonaut Alexei Leonov floated out of his *Voskhod 2* spacecraft and made the first extravehicular activity (EVA), a space walk lasting approximately ten minutes. The risky maneuver—Leonov almost could not make it back into the capsule when his space suit overinflated—seemed to be a way for the Russians to grab the world's attention from the upcoming Gemini mission, noted Kraft, who would be monitoring the flight of the *Molly Brown* from the Cape (the new control center in Houston would handle subsequent American space ventures). "They had the advantage of knowing exactly what we were going to do, and when, simply by reading the newspapers," he said, terming the EVA a "stunt."[25]

Except for a few choice "four-letter words" from Grissom about the Russian surprise, *Gemini 3* proceeded on schedule, with Grissom and Young successfully passing a physical just two days before the March 23 liftoff. The night before the launch, the men enjoyed a "quiet dinner" with fellow astronauts Shepard, Slayton, Ed White, Jim McDivitt, and attorney and adviser Leo DeOrsey at the operations building. After dinner, Grissom and Young exercised in the gymnasium, watched television, and went to bed at 9:00 p.m. At 4:40 a.m. the next morning, Slayton, as he would for twenty-four manned space missions, woke the crew in time for their physical exams. "These took only ten minutes; they were feeling us to see if we were still warm and breathing, I guess," said Grissom. Along with twelve guests, including Gilruth and James "Mr. Mac" McDonnell, the head of McDonnell Aircraft, the astronauts ate a breakfast consisting of tomato juice, half a cantaloupe, scrambled eggs, two-pound porterhouse steaks, and toast and jelly (Grissom also had a glass of milk). During the gathering, Young received a sixty-foot-long good-luck telegram signed by 2,400 residents of Orlando, Florida, from where he had graduated from high school, and the men discussed the recent success of the unmanned Ranger probe of the moon.[26]

At 5:53 a.m. the astronauts left the operations building and entered a waiting automobile for the six-mile trip to the medical trailer parked near Pad 16, where they had biomedical sensors attached to their skin, slipped on their "long john" undergarments, and donned their space suits for the flight. "I saw that John Young, who isn't particularly fond of long underwear, had chopped the arms off his," Grissom remembered. When the two astronauts passed along their urine samples to nurse Dee O'Hara, Young was particularly careful, remembering an earlier incident when he had stored such a sample to give to O'Hara in his briefcase. When he reached in to give the sample to the nurse, he discovered that the cap had come loose and soaked the flight papers stored inside. Meanwhile, at Pad 19, the site of the launch, backups Schirra and Stafford were busy setting switches inside the *Molly Brown* as the countdown for the mission continued. The backups had also prepared a couple of surprises for the prime crew. The day before, Schirra and Stafford had stopped at Wolfie's Deli on North Atlantic Avenue in Cocoa Beach. "We were both irked by the fact that Gus and John weren't going to have real food on their flight, so Wally had a corned beef sandwich [with pickles] made up. (Gus loved those sandwiches at Wolfie's)," said Stafford. As Grissom and Young finished suiting up for their trip in their immaculate white G3C pressure suits, Young had stowed the corned beef sandwich in the leg pocket of his suit. The astronauts were greeted by Schirra clad in his tattered old Mercury training suit and wearing approximately twenty assorted security badges around his neck. "If you're not feeling up to it," Schirra told a laughing Grissom, "I'll be happy to take this one."[27]

At 7:06 a.m., the astronauts left the medical trailer in an air-conditioned van headed to Pad 19 on a road that became known as the Barton FREEway, made possible by an air force warrant officer named Gunner Barton, who reminded the astronauts of television's schemer Sergeant Bilko. During preflight tests, the astronauts had complained about the roundabout and rough ride they took on the existing roadway between Pad 16 and Pad 19, but were told by NASA officials there were no funds for any improvements. A few days before the launch, a new "straight-as-an-arrow road" magically appeared. "The Gunner was looking particularly innocent," Grissom noted, "so we knew he'd wrangled it. But we weren't about to ask embarrassing questions." Instead, the astronauts painted signs saying "Barton FREEway" and snuck out of their quarters one night to post them along the new road. Grissom and Young arrived at Pad 19 at 7:09 a.m., took the elevator for the hundred-foot ride up to the white room, and entered the *Molly Brown*, Young first followed by Grissom. "There were plenty of smiles, but not much of the joking that we had on some of the Mercury flights," said

Young leads the way with Grissom following as the astronauts prepare to take the gantry elevator at Launch Complex 19 to board their Gemini spacecraft on the morning of their flight.

Guenter Wendt, pad leader. "Gus and John were serious about the flight and had little room for levity."[28]

After his team of technicians completed a test to see if the crew's space suits had any leaks, Wendt removed the seven safety pins on each of the ejection seats, reported his action to the blockhouse, and closed the hatches at 7:34 a.m. "This was always a sobering time for me," Wendt noted, "seeing my friends being locked inside their machine." Following a check of the spacecraft for any leaks from the cabin, Wendt and his team cleared the area. The countdown ran like clockwork until 8:20 a.m., when mission control called a hold to check on a possible leak in an oxidizer line in the Titan 2's first stage. Pad technicians solved the problem and the countdown proceeded smoothly until liftoff at 9:24 a.m. Grissom reported to Cooper, serving as capsule communicator (CapCom) at the control center, that the clock had started and the Gemini-Titan configuration had entered its roll program. "There was not a distinct feeling when lift-off occurred," Grissom reported. "It was a gentle, smooth lift-off with no jolt or disturbance." As the craft entered its pitch program, Cooper called out: "You're on your way, *Molly Brown*."[29]

For the first fifty seconds of the mission, Grissom had both hands on the ring triggering the ejection seats in case of an emergency. Young also had a ring, but when Grissom glanced over at his partner he noticed his hands resting in his lap. He may have seemed casual, Young later said, but he watched Grissom carefully and if the commander had expe-

A Titan rocket boosts the Gemini 3 *spacecraft into orbit on March 23, 1965. Grissom and Young tested the new ship and its systems during their three-orbit flight.*

PHOTOGRAPH BY NASA, INDIANA HISTORICAL SOCIETY, C9169

Young snapped these two photographs during the second orbit as the Molly Brown *passed over Mexico at a ninety-mile altitude. At the center of the photo is the California-Mexico border. The large, clear area to the right of the nose of the spacecraft is the Sonoran Desert.*

rienced any problems with his ejection ring he planned on yanking his with dispatch. "During this time we didn't say a word to each other because there was so much to do so fast," Young noted, "but once we got into orbit we could relax just a little." The Titan 2 booster had exceeded its estimated thrust, placing the astronauts into a higher-than-expected orbit, with an 87-mile perigee and a 125-mile apogee. As the spacecraft reached a speed of 16,600 miles per hour, the astronauts enjoyed an incredible view of the planet they had left behind. The scenery fascinated space rookie Young. "You can't take your eyes away from that window at first," he noted after the flight. "It is incredible. There aren't words in the English language to describe it. It was beautiful." As the spacecraft streaked above the Earth, Young grabbed a Hasselblad camera to snap photographs of Bermuda. "But we were going so damned fast that by the time Gus had lined up the spacecraft for my shot, Bermuda was almost gone," said Young. "We were really hauling the mail."[30]

As they left the Canary Islands behind on their first orbit, the astronauts experienced a moment of alarm when they noticed the pressure in the oxygen system, supplying air to the cabin and to their suits, suddenly drop, and other instrument readings also registering oddly. Grissom acted quickly, snapping the visor down on his helmet. "If the oxygen pressure is really gone," he thought to himself, "it won't make any difference. You've had it already." With the experience he had gained through hours of work in the Gemini simulator,

Young, in just forty-five seconds, diagnosed the problem—
the primary electrical converter system had malfunctioned—
and switched to the backup system. Another problem arose
with the planned sea urchin egg experiment. For the procedure, Grissom had to turn a knob that would activate a device
to fertilize the eggs, which would later be studied to see how
their cells had been affected by weightlessness. "Maybe, after
our oxygen scare, I had too much adrenalin pumping, but I
twisted the handle so hard that I broke it," Grissom said.
(After their flight, the astronauts learned that a controller on
the ground, duplicating the experiment, had also broken the
handle.) Although he discovered that the clearance between
the hatch and radiation experiment proved to be "much
smaller than on the mission simulator," Young managed to
complete the task.[31]

The evaluation of meals undertaken by Young for future
long-duration flights on Gemini proved to be one of the high
spots for Grissom during the mission. Sealed in plastic bags,
the dehydrated food had to be reconstituted using a water
gun. Young reconstituted packages of applesauce and grapefruit juice, and opened a package of chicken bits, which
"were not very tasty and were rather difficult to get out of the
package while wearing pressure-suit gloves," he said. The
brownies provided for dessert proved to be the "best-tasting
thing on the flight," according to Young. The astronaut also
had another item, not on NASA's official menu, to sample. As
Grissom monitored *Molly Brown*'s performance, he was sur-

prised to hear Young nonchalantly inquire: "You care for a corned beef sandwich, skipper?" Grissom, who noted that if he could have fallen out of his couch he would have, thanked his crewmate for the treat and took a bite. Crumbs from the rye bread, however, started floating around the cabin, and the overpowering aroma of kosher corned beef proved too much for the spacecraft's life-support system to handle, so Grissom put the sandwich away. (According to Wendt, Young later told him Grissom had jokingly complained that the sandwich had no mustard.) For an additional taste treat, he also sampled a bit of Young's applesauce.[32]

Experiments with sea urchin eggs and a chance to eat the first corned beef sandwich in space paled in comparison with the opportunity the astronauts had to investigate the worthiness of America's new space vehicle. One hour and thirty-three minutes after liftoff, Grissom achieved a space first when he fired the OAMS to slow the spacecraft's speed to fifty feet per second, changing its path into nearly a circular orbit. Over the Indian Ocean on *Molly Brown*'s second orbit, the commander tested the ship's translational movement, using the forward and aft thrusters to change its orbital path by one-fiftieth of a degree, paving the way for future Gemini rendezvous and docking missions. Finally, four hours and twenty-one minutes into the flight, Grissom again activated the OAMS in a preretrofire maneuver to ensure reentry in case of a problem with the retro-rockets. "Gus felt so good about all this that he even let me fly the *Molly Brown* for a few minutes," said Young. "I thought I'd have to break his arm to take over even for that long."[33]

The final maneuver proved to be unnecessary as the spacecraft's retro-rockets fired on schedule and the astronauts were pushed back into their couches by the g forces caused by reentry. "It was some sight—very impressive," Grissom said. "We could see the whole retro pack burning up as it came in right behind us." Both astronauts reported that the view they had of reentry matched the simulations they had gone through during training, including the color pictures taken from the unmanned *Gemini 2* mission. *Molly Brown's* onboard computer indicated to the astronauts they would land short of the expected splashdown point near the recovery carrier, the USS *Intrepid*. Grissom performed two banking maneuvers to correct the error, but discovered that the lift predicted in wind-tunnel tests did not match real-world results. The crew experienced another surprise when the spacecraft's main parachute deployed. The parachute's harness was designed to change from a vertical position to a forty-five degree landing attitude. "John and I were both thrown against our windows, and I banged into a knob that punctured my face plate," Grissom noted. "John's face plate was scratched." The severe jolt caused Grissom to believe the astronauts had lost their main parachute, but the water landing proved to be "quite soft compared to the single-point release."[34]

At 2:17 p.m., four hours and fifty-three minutes after

liftoff, *Molly Brown* splashed down near Grand Turk Island in the Bahamas about nine-and-a-half miles from the Coast Guard cutter *Diligence*, stationed fifty miles up range from the *Intrepid*. Grissom's first thought when the spacecraft hit the water flashed back to his experience in Mercury: "Oh my God, here we go again!" Gemini had been designed so that the left window, the one Grissom looked out of, would be above the water after landing. Instead of looking at blue sky, however, the astronaut saw nothing but seawater. Grissom soon realized he had not yet cut loose the main parachute that had been catching the twenty-knot wind, dragging the spacecraft "underneath like a submarine." With the memory of his *Liberty Bell 7* mission still fresh in his mind, Grissom mustered his nerve, reached out, and triggered the parachute-release switch. "But with the parachute gone," he said, "we bobbed to the surface like a cork in the position we were supposed to take." As Grissom and Young breathed easier, an Air Rescue Service C-54 aircraft dropped a pararescue team near the spacecraft to render assistance if needed. Five minutes later, a navy helicopter dropped another team that secured a flotation collar around the spacecraft.[35]

An early communication to the astronauts had indicated the *Intrepid* only five miles away from the spacecraft, prompting Grissom and Young to remain in *Molly Brown* until the carrier's arrival. Twenty minutes later, however, they learned of the carrier's true position, approximately fifty-five miles away, and that the ship would take almost two hours to

Flanked by John C. Stonsifer (left), landing and recovery division, Manned Spacecraft Center, and Dr. Howard Minners, MSC medical office, Grissom and Young walk on the flight deck of the recovery aircraft carrier USS Intrepid.

reach their position. "We were getting extremely uncomfortable in our suits; so we elected to take the suits off, egress, and be picked up by helicopter," said Grissom, who kept the hatches closed so as to not repeat his Mercury misadventure. (The astronaut said if the Gemini spacecraft had sunk, he would have "jumped right off that carrier.") The hot temperatures in the closed cabin, combined with five-foot swells, caused both astronauts to become seasick. Navy veteran Young barely held onto his meal, but Grissom vomited into a plastic bag stowed for just such an emergency. "It's a wonderful spacecraft, but it's not much of a boat," said Young. "It's got pitch, heave, and roll." Navy frogmen Gilbert A. Timone and Raymond C. Blanche assisted Grissom in opening his three-hundred-pound hatch—the one out of the water—first and exiting the capsule. "That's the first time I ever heard of a skipper leaving the ship first," Young said. Grissom responded by joking that he made his partner captain when he left the spacecraft. With his new title, Young renamed the spacecraft the USS *Molly Brown*.[36]

PHOTOGRAPH BY NASA, INDIANA HISTORICAL SOCIETY, C7878

As Young looks on, Grissom talks to President Lyndon B. Johnson, who congratulated the astronauts for their successful Gemini mission.

Safely aboard the recovery helicopter, Grissom and Young donned regulation navy bathrobes to cover their space long johns. The outfits gave the duo the "appearance of a couple of guys waking up after a big night at a convention," Grissom noted as they landed on the carrier and underwent a postflight medical examination and debriefing. The *Intrepid* hoisted the Gemini capsule onto its deck at 5:01 p.m. The astronauts received a congratulatory ship-to-shore telephone call from President Johnson, who had watched the mission on a television in his office. After expressing his and the nation's pride in their accomplishment, Johnson told Grissom, first on the phone, that "apparently the Molly Brown was as unsinkable as her namesake and we are all mighty happy about it." The only problem with the flight was that it did not last long enough, Young told the president, who responded by telling the astronaut he'd try to work something out in the days ahead. Johnson also invited both men to visit him at the White House—quite an honor for two men whose pay for the day, according to Associated Press figures, totaled just seventy dollars ($37.25 for Grissom and $32.75 for Young).[37]

As they had done during Grissom's Mercury flight, the residents of Mitchell, Indiana, stopped what they were doing and breathlessly waited for their native son to make his second trip into space. Before the launch, the ABC television network set up its cameras and a microwave relay tower directly across the street from the home of the astronaut's parents to provide live coverage from the small community. The day before the flight, Claude Moore, Gus's father-in-law, indicated family members were "jittery" about the mission, but had faith in the astronaut's poise and determination to complete the mission. On the morning of the blastoff, businesses in Mitchell either closed for the day so their employees could watch the proceedings at home or provided television sets in their establishments to follow every step of the *Gemini 3* mission. In addition, several television sets were brought in to local schools so students could monitor the flight. Joining Dennis and Cecile Grissom inside their home for the launch were a representative from NASA's Washington, D.C., headquarters, Fred Asselin; the couple's minister, Roy VanTassel, and his wife; their son Norman Grissom; and several friends of the family. An additional fifty friends and relatives, including Moore and his wife, watched the launch via a closed-circuit television in the First Baptist Church, located just northeast of the Grissom residence.[38]

With liftoff accomplished, Norman Grissom, speaking for his parents, told newsmen they were confident that the mission would proceed to a successful conclusion. At the First Baptist Church, Moore told a reporter: "I feel better. Better is a word of comparison you know. I felt good before the flight. I feel better now, but I will feel the best when they are back down safely." After the *Molly Brown*'s splashdown, Grissom's parents met with reporters on the front porch of their home. Both expressed relief over their son's safe return.

PHOTOGRAPH BY NASA, INDIANA HISTORICAL SOCIETY, C9167

Grissom and Young pinpoint their landing site on a map before being examined by a group of physicians at Cape Kennedy. MSC physicians are (left center, moving clockwise): Dr. Charles Berry, Dr. Gordon Bensond, Dr. Eugene Tubbs, Dr. John Ziegleschmid, and Dr. Howard Minners.

As sirens wailed throughout the town and a parade of well-wishers approached the house, Cecile told the media: "We are happy and very proud of him. We were worried some, but not too worried." The couple beamed as they reported they would be traveling to Cape Kennedy to greet their son on his return from the *Intrepid*.[39]

Joining Grissom's parents at the Cape Kennedy welcome for the returning astronauts were Betty, Mark, and Scott, who had the opportunity to tour mission control in Houston during the Gemini flight. Betty, who told newsmen she planned on pasting trading stamps into booklets to "while away the hours" until her husband landed safely, had received a telephone call from an official at the Manned Spacecraft Center inviting her to visit mission control, which in this flight served as backup to the controllers at Cape Kennedy. When Betty asked if her sons could also come, the official at first turned down her request, saying it was against NASA policy. When she said she would not attend without her children and hung up the telephone, the space agency reconsidered, called her back, and extended an invitation to the boys as well. "I thought, 'My kids are old enough not to disturb anyone,'" Betty recalled. "If my children can't go, then I'm too good to go. After that all the astronauts' children were permitted to go in." Scott remembered the excitement of listening in to his father and Young as they made their second orbit aboard *Molly Brown*. "That was really fantastic!" Scott said.[40]

Upon their return to Cape Kennedy from the *Intrepid* via a navy S2 aircraft, Grissom and Young were greeted by their family members and an air force band playing the theme song from the musical *The Unsinkable Molly Brown* before being whisked away to undergo additional physical examinations. After the medical probing, the astronauts were upbeat and talkative during a press conference about their mission. Evert Clark, covering the event for the *New York Times*, noted that the reticent spacemen "turned out to be two of the funniest on the ground," joking and feeding each other "straight lines like two comedians." Asked about the change in their demeanor, Young explained: "I think Zero-G flight could make an extrovert out of anybody." He became particularly verbose when talking about the tremendous view from space, drawing applause from the gathered reporters and space officials, prompting Grissom to reply dryly, "Well, to carry on with the flight—." Grissom made sure to praise the Martin Company, the manufacturer of the Titan 2 rocket, and had nothing but high marks for the McDonnell Aircraft–produced Gemini. "The spacecraft performed so well that we really didn't expect it to be so good," he said. "It felt terrific. The launch went great. The booster runs smooth. There isn't a jiggle or a bump in it on the whole flight."[41]

On March 26, Grissom, Young, and their families journeyed to Washington, D.C., for a ceremony with President Johnson in the East Room of the White House (cloudy weather had forced the proceedings inside from the Rose Garden). Calling the duo "two brave, patriotic, gallant, exceptional young Americans," Johnson presented each with NASA's Exceptional Service Award, with Grissom receiving another citation for becoming the first person to fly in space twice. The astronaut accepted the honors as "tokens of affection of this nation" for the entire space effort. Young became so wrapped up in the proceedings that he forgot to shake the president's hand until prompted to by the crowd. "I didn't have this kind of heart beat before the launch," joked Young.

In addition to honoring the Gemini astronauts, Johnson handed out NASA's medal for exceptional scientific achievement to Harris M. Schurmeier, project manager for the Ranger program that photographed the moon. The honors continued in the next few days as Grissom and Young were treated to ticker-tape parades in New York City and Chicago. Grissom attributed the outpouring of goodwill the astronauts received to the public's relief at having America "back in the manned-space-flight business with probably the most sophisticated spacecraft in the world, or out of it."[42]

Despite the tributes paid to the astronauts, controversy soon developed after the flight concerning the corned beef sandwich briefly enjoyed by Grissom on *Molly Brown*. At first, the astronauts had no inkling that the nonregulation food might cause any fuss, as they joked about it while discussing the flight in *Life* magazine just a week after the mission's conclusion. Some members of Congress, however, failed to see any humor in the situation, with NASA administrator James Webb being peppered with complaints at an appropriations subcommittee hearing that the space agency "had lost control of its astronauts." Kraft noted that some congressmen and doctors had the mistaken idea the astronauts had compromised medical tests by ingesting the sandwich, which they had not. The complaints eventually made their way to Slayton, who had given Young permission to take the sandwich on the flight. Slayton officially informed the astronauts they could not take "unauthorized items, especially

Grissom, joined by Vice President Hubert Humphrey (left) and President Johnson (right), listens as NASA administrator James Webb speaks at a ceremony honoring the Gemini 3 *astronauts at the White House.*

food, aboard the spacecraft. I even had to give poor John a formal reprimand . . . not that it affected his career."[43]

In addition to the textbook flight of *Molly Brown*, the year 1965 saw NASA launch four more Gemini missions, achieving several triumphs in the process, including White's space walk on *Gemini 4* and the first true rendezvous in space with *Gemini 6*, crewed by Stafford and Schirra, meeting up and flying with *Gemini 7*'s crew of Borman and Lovell. As the Gemini program continued, Slayton turned his attention to

PHOTOGRAPH BY NASA, INDIANA HISTORICAL SOCIETY, C6411

Grissom and Young wave to the crowd during a ticker-tape parade for the astronauts in Chicago.

the future Apollo missions, scheduled for Earth-orbital flights before the end of 1966. With Shepard still out of commission due to his medical condition, Slayton again turned to Grissom to take command of the new space program's first mission. Because the flight would take place without a lunar module, the remainder of Grissom's crew included astronauts with little experience, including rookies Donn F. Eisele and Roger Chaffee. Eisele injured his shoulder in a zero-g flight in a KC-135 aircraft and had to be replaced. "He was going to be behind the training curve right from the start, so I simply swapped him with Ed White, who I'd originally had down as senior pilot of the next crew, Apollo 2," said Slayton, who called Grissom, Chaffee, and White into his office to inform them privately of their selection for the mission.[44]

Gaining the plum Apollo assignment caused Grissom to begin thinking about the dream of every astronaut—becoming the first man to walk on the moon. Jim Rathmann remembered sharing many flights in his airplane with Grissom where the astronaut often talked about the possibility. "We'd all talk about it quite a bit," said Rathmann, who along with Grissom and Cooper twice sponsored a car at the Indianapolis 500. "He wanted to be the first man on the moon and I thought he was the logical guy because of his attitude, his motivation and everything." In the backs of everyone's minds, however, lurked the dangers involved with space travel, especially the approximately 239,000-mile trip to the moon. Rathmann and Grissom were returning home one day from Milwaukee aboard Rathmann's aircraft when the astronaut realized they were not far from Mitchell. "You know," said Grissom, "they're going to name that airfield down there after me. Man, I don't like that. They just name those airports after dead people." He even confided to his wife that if NASA ever had a serious accident, it would likely involve him because of his long service with America's space program. Grissom's foreboding about the future, however, would be shunted to the background for a time as he became absorbed in training for the next step on the way to the moon: Project Apollo.[45]

7

Apollo

WHEN ALAN SHEPARD BECAME THE FIRST AMERICAN IN SPACE in May 1961, he accomplished his suborbital flight onboard a tiny capsule powered by the 78,000 pounds of thrust provided by the Redstone missile's single S-7 engine. A trip to the moon, however, involved technology that dwarfed Project Mercury's tentative early explorations. To launch a three-man crew on a moon-landing mission for Project Apollo, the National Aeronautics and Space Administration turned to Wernher von Braun and his team at the Marshall Space Flight Center. What the rocket men eventually designed for the moon flights—the Saturn 5, the first launch vehicle developed solely for spaceflight—had three stages, stood 363 feet tall (higher than the Statue of Liberty), and weighed 6.2 million pounds fully loaded with the command and lunar modules. The five F-1 engines on the rocket's first stage burned their kerosene fuel to produce 7.5 million pounds of thrust at liftoff as the launch vehicle strained to reach a target (the moon) traveling in space at 2,000 miles per hour in its orbit around the Earth. NASA accepted bids from three different companies to construct the rocket's separate stages, with the Boeing Company working on the first stage, North American Aviation the second stage, and Douglas Aircraft the third stage.[1]

During its history, Project Apollo involved more than five hundred contractors from across the country building everything from the massive thirty-six-story Vehicle Assembly Building at the John F. Kennedy Space Center where the Saturn rocket came together to the dehydrated food eaten by the crew. One study even estimated that one in fifty Americans had, in one way or another, worked to help NASA reach its goal of a moon landing by the end of the decade. The contractor that most interested the astronauts, however, was the one to be selected by NASA to build the command and service module. On October 9, 1961, five contractors presented bids to build the spacecraft at a meeting at the Chamberlain Hotel in Old Point Comfort, Virginia. A source evaluation board from the space agency scrutinized the submissions for the contract for several weeks before selecting the Martin Company as the "outstanding source for the Apollo prime contractor," with North American Aviation ranked by the board as the best alternative, calling the firm "well qualified" to carry out the assignment. Although Martin employees learned they had received the highest score, and celebrated their good fortune accordingly, NASA officials

A small group of NASA officials is dwarfed by the gigantic size of the Saturn 5's first stage as it sits in the shipping area of the Manufacturing Engineering Laboratory at the Marshall Space Flight Center in Huntsville, Alabama.

awarded the contract to North American Aviation and its hard-charging chief engineer Harrison Storms. On November 28 North American workers in Downey, California, learned they would be responsible for building the moonship. Almost a year later, the space agency selected Grumman Aircraft Corporation in Bethpage, Maryland, to build the lunar module.[2]

Rumors abounded that politics, and not technical competence, won North American the contract. Wally Schirra believed that North American received the pact because companies in California had yet to receive their fair share of the space business. Others pointed to North American's Washington, D.C., lobbyist Fred Black, who had developed a close relationship with Capitol Hill insider Bobby Gene Baker, a protégé of President Lyndon B. Johnson. Before the contract had been awarded, Black had told North American officials their bid might receive a more favorable response if the company agreed to have Serv-U Corporation, a firm Black owned with Baker, stock the vending machines in its various facilities. North American agreed to the arrangement and, when it received NASA's approval as the builder of the Apollo spacecraft, Black claimed credit for the success.[3]

Despite the gossip, the choice of North American over Martin reflected the opinions of those associated with flying. During World War II, Martin had built the B-26 Marauder medium bomber, which earned for itself from pilots the nicknames "Widow Maker" and "The Flying Prostitute" (no visible means of support thanks to its short, small wings). North American Aviation, however, became beloved by fliers for producing such legendary craft as the P-51 Mustang fighter and the B-25 Mitchell medium bomber used by Col. Jimmy Doolittle for his surprise attack on Japan from the aircraft carrier USS *Hornet*. Plaudits continued for the company after the war with the development of the sleek F-86 Sabre jet used in Korea by pilots such as Grissom, the advanced XB-70 Valkyrie bomber, and the spectacular X-15 rocket research aircraft. NASA astronauts, joined by officials such as

Robert Gilruth, Manned Spacecraft Center director, pushed for the firm that had a solid reputation for building reliable flying machines. Although concerned that North American's resources might become stretched with both a contract for Saturn 5's second stage and the command and service module, James Webb, NASA administrator, acquiesced to the decision.[4]

With the successful conclusions of the Mercury and Gemini programs, NASA's attention turned more and more to achieving Kennedy's goal, which it distilled into a three-word mantra: man, moon, decade. As envisioned by North American and NASA, the craft taking the astronauts on their two-week voyage had a cone-shaped command module constructed out of titanium, stainless steel, and aluminum alloy. The module would serve as the vehicle to survive the 25,000-mile-per-hour reentry and to safely splash down via three parachutes, each eighty-eight feet in diameter. Attached to the command module would be a cylindrical service module containing the fuel cells providing power and water to the spacecraft, the attitude control system to adjust the flight path, and the service propulsion system used to blast the ship out of lunar orbit for the return to Earth. Instead of the ejection seats provided for Gemini, the Apollo spacecraft returned to its Mercury roots with a solid rocket escape tower in case of emergency on the launchpad or early in the flight. Because design work had been started before NASA had made a final determination on how to get to the moon, the

NASA

*The prime crew for the first flight of the new Apollo spacecraft pose
in front of Launch Complex 34. Left to right: Grissom,
Ed White, and Roger Chaffee.*

original command module had no docking mechanism for
mating with a lunar module. These Block 1 spacecrafts, as
they came to be called, would be used for the early Earth-
orbit Apollo missions launched on Saturn 1B rockets, while
North American developed a more advanced Block 2 lunar
version to be shot into space by the Saturn 5.[5]

On March 21, 1966, just a few days after *Gemini 8* had
been forced to cut its time in space short after a stuck thruster
caused it to tumble out of control, NASA announced the
crew members for the first Apollo mission, dubbed Apollo-

Saturn 204 (flights on Saturn 1B rockets were designated as the 200 series with Saturn 5 trips the 500 series). Joining the nearly forty-year-old Grissom, who was now a lieutenant colonel in the air force thanks to a promotion from President Johnson, were Ed White, another air force veteran and the first American to walk in space, and Roger Chaffee, a Purdue University graduate and navy pilot who had flown U-2 surveillance missions during the Cuban Missile Crisis. Named as backup crew for the mission were James McDivitt, David Scott, and Russell Schweickart. In the Houston press conference introducing the crew, Gilruth noted it was "very important to have the coolest heads in the business" for Apollo's first trip, an open-ended mission that could last as long as fourteen days in Earth orbit and had been slated to be launched by October or November. Joseph Shea, Apollo project manager, said the primary goal for the mission would be to "exercise the spacecraft and crew." In addition, the space agency indicated it was considering having the Apollo craft rendezvous with *Gemini 12*. "A study is still going on," Shea told reporters, "but it's much too early to say."[6]

The news of Grissom's third potential trip into space touched off the usual media attention in Indiana, with the announcement receiving front-page treatment in such newspapers as the astronaut's hometown *Mitchell Tribune*, the nearby *Bedford Daily Times-Mail*, as well as the capital city's *Indianapolis Star*. According to newspaper reports, Grissom's parents had learned their son would be named for the Apollo crew in late February while watching a taped television program featuring the astronaut and other Purdue alumni. Grissom called from his home in Seabrook, Texas, to inform his parents that he had been selected as commander of the first Apollo flight. "This is a pretty big trip, this Apollo," said Dennis Grissom, whose home now sat on a street named in the astronaut's honor. "But I think they have it pretty well in hand." Cecile Grissom, who had been apprehensive about her son's previous space adventures, told reporters she was not quite as worried as she had been before. "That's what he wants," she said of her son. "That's his work and I'll go along with him."[7]

His role in the inaugural Apollo mission—the second time he had been called upon by NASA to test a new spacecraft—came at an opportune time for Grissom, as he had been somewhat out of sorts following his Gemini experience. With American involvement in Vietnam escalating, Grissom even considered taking a leave of absence from the space program to volunteer to fly combat missions with the air force. "I said, That's all I need!" remembered Betty Grissom. "If he didn't have anything to do for awhile, why not stay home?" After talking to another pilot who had flown in Vietnam, who advised Grissom that this conflict had nothing in common with Korea, the astronaut remained in the program. Even with his new Apollo assignment, Grissom continued to think about life after his NASA career ended. Republican party officials back in Indiana had even asked him to consider entering politics in the Hoosier State. Virgil D. Scheidt, Bartholomew County GOP chairman, wrote Grissom in the fall of 1965 and asked him to run for Congress from the Ninth District against Democrat officeholder Lee H. Hamilton—an offer the astronaut declined. "He gave me to understand his time would be up in the space program in less than three years and he might be interested in politics then," Scheidt said. He added that there were rumors other Republican officials hoped Grissom could be convinced to run against incumbent U.S. senator Birch Bayh, a Democrat, in 1968.[8]

Retirement from the space program might have been in the back of Grissom's mind due to the numerous problems associated with developing the Apollo command and service module. At a December 1966 press briefing on the project, Shea noted there had been twenty thousand failures during the spacecraft's six years of development, with the environmental control system alone logging more than two hundred failures. But Shea indicated such problems were part of the expected "maturation process" for the new vehicle. "It is kind of like watching children grow up," he said. "My feeling is we are somewhere in the middle of adolescence." Privately, NASA officials and astronauts were uneasy about the attitude displayed by North American managers and workers. Years later, Shea told the story that when North American won the contract for the spaceship, managers there threw a party and had hats with NASA printed on them, with the letter "S" replaced with a dollar sign. Michael Collins, fresh off a successful mission on *Gemini 10*, was impressed by the machine being built by the company but believed those involved in putting it together were ignoring lessons learned by the smaller Gemini program. Tom Stafford, another Gemini veteran, agreed with Collins's assessment, noting that in Gemini NASA had learned much about such key areas as "quality control in manufacturing, about organizing a factory shop floor for the intricate business of building a spacecraft, as well as basic nuts and bolts issues involved in laying out a cockpit or designing environmental systems." Both Stafford and Deke Slayton expressed concern about the workers at North American's Downey plant being more worried about what they were going to do with their leisure time than in making sure the job of building the Apollo moonship was done right.[9]

NASA's frustrations about the spacecraft were shared by the crew for the first Apollo flight, particularly its commander, Grissom. In both the Mercury and Gemini programs, he had the opportunity to use his engineering skills to improve the spacecraft, pointing out any problems and ensuring they were fixed. If McDonnell Aircraft Company engineers on the plant floor refused to listen to him, the astronaut—one of the original seven—had the cachet to appeal directly to the firm's director, James "Mr. Mac" McDonnell, to have the matter resolved, noted Betty. The same situation did not exist at North American with the Apollo program. "It was too

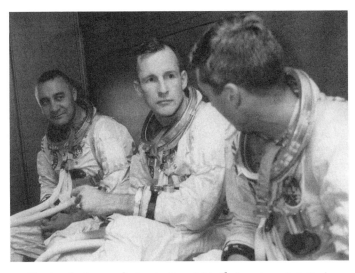

NASA

The Apollo 1 *crew during testing at North American Aviation's Downey, California, facility.*

damned big: you couldn't have an astronaut ramming some little change through without fitting it into the overall system," Slayton observed. "At least that's what we thought in 1966." In Mercury and Gemini, noted Guenter Wendt, who had been monitoring the program in hopes of McDonnell becoming involved with the space business again, there were hundreds of people involved and a number of contractors, but with Apollo there were tens of thousands of people involved and countless numbers of contractors. "The program was mammoth, much bigger than I had ever imagined," he said. The troubles were not just with the spacecraft, but also with the simulators used by the astronauts to train for the upcoming mission. Technicians could not keep up with the vast number of changes being made with Spacecraft 012—the machine the Grissom crew would take into space. Riley McCafferty, the person responsible for updating the simulator, noted that at one time there were more than a hundred modifications waiting to be made on the machine. Consequently, the simulator used by the astronauts at Cape Kennedy never matched what was being constructed at the Downey plant. To express his feelings on the matter, a frustrated Grissom cut a large Texas lemon, the size of a grapefruit, off a tree in his backyard and hung it on the simulator.[10]

For North American's part, it had problems with some of the decisions made by NASA about the spacecraft's design. In its original specifications for the command module, the company had called for a complicated two-gas system of oxygen and nitrogen, similar to what people breathe every day, for the cabin. The space agency, however, insisted on the pure-oxygen environment it had used successfully on its previous voyages. Disagreements also cropped up over the design of the spacecraft's hatch, with North American urging the installation of a heavier one with explosive bolts that could be blown off quickly in case of an emergency. NASA technicians and designers such as Max Faget, however, were more concerned about having the hatch fire prematurely during a flight to the moon, dooming the astronauts inside. Also, such a hatch meant that there could be no extravehicular activities from the command module. Although North American officials were dubious of his claim of innocence, Grissom stood as an example of what could happen when an explosive hatch fired prematurely. The final design included a hatch opening into the cabin that could be sealed tightly into place by the pressure from the spacecraft's interior. "Hindsight is wonderful," Faget said years later. Although the pure oxygen atmosphere had worked flawlessly in Mercury and Gemini, Faget said he had failed to realize the major difference between the Mercury and Apollo programs, with "one Apollo experience . . . probably equivalent to maybe twenty or thirty Mercurys, simply because there's so much more volume in Apollo and there's so much more stuff in Apollo, so that it's going to burn just as badly."[11]

In addition to delays with Grissom's *Apollo 1* spacecraft, there were problems with the second Block 1 ship, intended for Earth orbit with a crew of Schirra, Donn F. Eisele, and Walt Cunningham. The astronauts for the second Apollo mission began to see their voyage as superfluous, about as useful, Cunningham said, as "windshield wipers on a submarine." The only difference between the two missions came when Grissom, who wanted to ensure "an engineering test flight," Cunningham noted, began to transfer any scientific experiments to the *Apollo 2* mission. Both Grissom and Schirra viewed the science tests with disdain and Schirra and his crew members wrote a memo to NASA management outlining their frustrations. "I saw this as a very *dumb* flight," Schirra said. "I said, 'Why should we duplicate two Block I flights, neither of which prove a thing about Block II and the capability of going to the Moon and back?'" Slayton and other space agency officials agreed with the assessment that *Apollo 2* seemed redundant and canceled the mission in November 1966. The original backup team for the first Apollo flight (McDivitt, Scott, and Schweickart) were moved to a new *Apollo 2* mission on a Block 2 spacecraft, while Schirra's crew became backups to the Grissom mission. "It was a comedown to be backing up Gus again," Schirra noted, "a real ego douser. Nothing personal, for Gus and I were the best of friends and next-door neighbors. But it was like Gemini again, with Gus in the prime slot and me as the substitute." In fact, both Slayton and Grissom had to make personal appeals to their friend in order to have him accept the assignment.[12]

The problems with the Apollo program spilled over into Gus's personal life, at home with his family where such matters had never intruded before, and with his dealings with the press. Betty noticed more and more telephone calls to her husband involving trouble with the spacecraft. "I really didn't know quite what was going on," she said. "When he was at home he normally did not want to be with the space program. He would rather be just messing around with the kids. But now he was uptight about it." One incident stuck out in her mind. It seems that a worker at North American's Downey facility had made the comment, not knowing Gus could hear him, that the spacecraft would leave the plant by a certain date whether it was ready or not. "He was furious," said Betty. "It seemed like there was nothing that he could do."[13]

Grissom had always been reticent, at best, when dealing with the media, but the lax attitude displayed by some of the people involved in the spacecraft's construction, and the craft's imperfections, grew to be so trying that the astronaut expressed his growing worries to reporters. He admitted he had been displaying a "pretty hard-nosed" attitude about the space vehicle, but stressed that everything connected with it had "to be exactly right . . . or somebody's going to get it." Grissom's irritation finally reached the boiling point, and he frankly told another reporter that with the problems coming "in bushelfuls" he believed the mission had "a pretty damn slim chance of flying its full fourteen days." Asked by one reporter what he might consider a successful flight, the astronaut joked: "As far as we're concerned, it's a success if all three of us get back."[14]

North American had been scheduled to send Spacecraft 012 to Cape Kennedy in early August 1966, but problems with a water glycol pump in the command module's environmental control unit delayed shipment until August 25. Upon further inspection at the Cape, NASA technicians discovered that more than half of the engineering work on the spacecraft, which should have been done by North American, had not been completed. Other deficiencies were also outlined by space-agency engineers, including a leak in the service module's main engine and more difficulties with the environmental control system. All of these troubles caused NASA to delay the first Apollo flight from late 1966 to February 1967, but officials were still hopeful of reaching the moon before the end of the decade. "Time was getting short and schedule was considered God," Cunningham said of the atmosphere at NASA. "So, anything that would slow things down, it was really tough to get through. They didn't ignore it, but it just didn't have the same weight as it did before. The managers had 'go' fever." That fever, and a bit of hubris, also infected the astronauts. Although they knew the spacecraft "was in poor shape relative to what it ought to be," said Cunningham, he and his cohorts were confident in their abilities to whip the vehicle into shape. "We also had such big egos that we felt that we could fly the crates they shipped these things in," he noted. "We honestly felt that, with things that were wrong, we always had a mental workaround on them." Gemini veteran Eugene Cernan agreed that as a test pilot he believed "the bird simply wasn't ready," but pressured by the idea that the Russians might possibly beat America in the race to the moon, NASA would do everything it could, including bending "mechanical and physical laws through sheer willpower," to make the spacecraft fly.[15]

On Friday morning January 27, 1967, the crew for *Apollo 1* prepared to participate in another test of its balky spacecraft, a "plugs-out" procedure in which the vehicle, with its hatch closed and pressured with 100 percent oxygen, underwent a simulated countdown at Cape Kennedy's Launch

NASA

The command and service module of Apollo spacecraft 012 is moved to NASA's Operations Building.

Complex 34 to check to see if the booster (unfueled) and the command and service module could operate on internal power alone. Lola Morrow, a NASA secretary who had nicknamed the program "Project Appalling," recalled that the astronauts were unusually subdued and quiet, an attitude quite unlike what she had seen before. "The test was something they didn't want to do," Morrow noted. The night before, the backup crew of Schirra, Cunningham, and Eisele had completed a "plugs-in" test, with power provided from outside of the spacecraft and the hatch open so the astronauts breathed normal Florida air. At a debriefing after the test in the ready room at the Cape's crew quarters, Schirra, who likened the attempt to stay on schedule as "riding a locomotive down a track with ten more locomotives bearing down behind," expressed some apprehension about the next day's procedure. "I said to Gus about the test, if it doesn't check out well, if you have a glitch or an anomaly, get the hell out of there," Schirra recalled. With their role complete for now, the backup crew members planned on taking off in their T-38 jets for a trip home to Houston for a visit with their families after the prime crew had finished its test.[16]

As the *Apollo 1* crew ate breakfast before the test, scheduled to start at 11:00 a.m., communication problems between the spacecraft and controllers became a key bone of contention, especially with Grissom. The astronaut even called upon Shea to "get his ass in there" with the rest of the crew to witness firsthand how bad things were going with commu-

NASA

A technician makes adjustments to Grissom's Apollo pressure suit before a test of the spacecraft at Cape Kennedy. Note the Apollo 1 mission patch on Grissom's shoulder.

nications by crouching in the lower equipment bay. With the command module closed and pressurized, however, there seemed to be no way for engineers to wire a fourth communication system for Shea. "You think I'm going to sit at your feet for four hours and not be able to communicate?" Shea remembered saying. "You are nuts—you go through the test; I'll go back to Houston and I'll come back Monday and do it in the simulator with you instead of doing it in this particular test." For a time, Slayton considered taking Shea's place, but decided instead to remain in the blockhouse and monitor communications from there with capsule communicator Stu Roosa, a rookie astronaut. "I can tell from there [the block-house] how bad it is without being in the spacecraft; it would be crowded enough with three guys in there," said Slayton.[17]

Donning their space suits, the *Apollo 1* crew arrived at Pad 34, rode the elevator to the top of the 310-foot-tall service tower, strode into the White Room surrounding the entrance to their spacecraft, and finally entered the cabin at 1:00 p.m. with Grissom, as commander, slipping into the left-hand seat. Almost immediately, there were problems. When he hooked into the oxygen supply from the spacecraft, Grissom reported an odd odor, which he described as smelling like sour buttermilk. Technicians arrived to take air samples but could find nothing of a serious nature and the test continued with Chaffee taking his place in the right-hand seat, where he would monitor communications during the test, and White sliding into the center couch. Once the astro-

The crew for the first manned Apollo mission prepares to enter its spacecraft inside the altitude chamber at the Kennedy Space Center. Entering the hatch is Grissom. Behind him is Chaffee. Standing at left with chamber technicians is White.

nauts were securely in place, technicians sealed the command module's pressure vessel inner hatch, an outer crew access hatch, and secured the boost protective cover that shielded the capsule from the launch escape rocket attached at the top. With the hatches sealed, pure oxygen began to be pumped into the cabin until it reached a pressure of 16.7 pounds per square inch (two pounds higher than the atmosphere outside the spacecraft), the pressure it would be during a normal launch. Once in space, the pressure would be reduced to five pounds per square inch.[18]

The test dragged on and on into the early evening as the astronauts encountered problems with a high oxygen flow indicator that periodically triggered the spacecraft's master alarm and glitches with communications. "The overall communications problem was so bad at times that we could not even understand what the crew was saying," said Clarence Chauvin, NASA spacecraft test conductor. An upset Grissom questioned how the space agency could get to the moon if those on the ground could not even communicate between two or three buildings. Communication difficulties caused a hold to be placed on the countdown at 5:40 p.m. "Everything was pretty quiet; wasn't anything going on really," Slayton remembered, noting everyone involved with the test were "sitting there, waiting to pick things up." Controllers were ready to resume the test when biomedical sensors indicated an increased oxygen flow in the astronauts' space suits and some movement in the cabin. Other sensors recorded a brief power surge. At 6:31 p.m. those involved with the test were stunned to hear a report from Grissom of a fire in the spacecraft, which investigators later determined most likely started in the lower forward portion of the left-hand equipment bay below the commander's seat. About two seconds later, another voice, probably that of Chaffee, called out, "We've got a fire in the cockpit." The final garbled transmission from Chaffee was heard by some as three different phrases—"We've got a bad fire . . . Let's get out . . . We're burning up"—followed by a scream of pain.[19]

Once sparked, the fire fed greedily on the pure-oxygen atmosphere under more than sixteen pounds of pressure inside the cabin. At such pressure, and bathed by pure oxygen, a cigarette could be reduced to ashes in seconds and even metal could burn. There also existed plenty of material in the cabin on which the fire could feed, including numerous strips of Velcro patches applied by the astronauts, netting used to keep objects from falling to the spacecraft's floor, padding, and the paperwork that went along with any space mission. As the flames spread, the astronauts started the complicated and time-consuming process of escaping the spacecraft. The procedure took at a minimum ninety seconds, but during training the astronauts had never accomplished the task in that amount of time. Gary W. Propst, an RCA technician located on the first floor of Pad 34 working with a closed-circuit television monitoring the test, heard the cry of "fire in the cockpit" and could see on his screen what appeared to be White's arm reaching above his head toward the hatch. "There followed a great deal of motion as his arms seemed to fumble with something and then quickly reach back for it," Propst said. He also saw another pair of arms—probably Grissom's—come in from the left to assist White with his frantic efforts. As flames blocked his view, Propst anxiously asked others gathered around the monitor: "Blow the hatch, why don't they blow the hatch?"[20]

Propst did not know that no way existed for the astronauts to "blow the hatch." Instead, White had to grab a special ratchet to release the six bolts securing the inner hatch. The astronaut valiantly attempted to follow the emergency procedure, but pressure inside the spacecraft's cabin rose considerably, dooming the effort. There was an oxygen relief valve to Grissom's left, which could have vented the pressure, but the growing flames prevented him from reaching the device. Even if Grissom had been able to activate the relief valve, it would not have extinguished the fire. As White and Grissom struggled with the hatch, Chaffee remained in his position and followed emergency procedures, turning up the cabin's lights to aid vision and switching on the internal batteries. Finally, the pressure inside exceeded the spacecraft's design and the command module ruptured, filling the White Room with thick, black smoke and flames. As the oxygen feeding the inferno became exhausted, poisonous smoke rolled through the cabin, overcoming the astronauts' supply of oxygen, and asphyxiating them.[21]

Stationed at his desk on the south side of gantry level eight about twelve feet from the spacecraft, Donald O. Babbitt, pad leader for North American during the test, heard on his headset about the fire and immediately turned to Jim Gleaves, his lead technician, and shouted at him to get the crew out of the spacecraft. Babbitt turned to his left to call to the blockhouse via the communications system when a blast of heat and pressure from the ruptured command module hit him and slammed him against his desk. The intense heat charred the papers scattered on his desk. Despite the smoke and flames that filled the White Room, Babbitt managed to make his way to the umbilical access arm where he gasped for fresh air and told a telephone technician there to notify the blockhouse about the fire. Although the fire could have set off the escape rocket attached to the top of the command module, Babbitt, joined by Gleaves, Stephen Clemmons, Jerry Hawkins, and L. D. Reece, returned to the scene of the disaster. "As we proceeded into the White Room, the smoke was extremely heavy," Babbitt recalled. "It appeared to me to be a heavy thick grey smoke, very billowing but very thick, we couldn't, as we went in the first time, see the hatches well to work." Gleaves, who told investigators the visibility in the room was so bad a person could not see six inches from his face, had to run his hands around the outside of the boost protective cover hatch to find the hole into which a special tool had to be inserted for removal.[22]

The technicians frantically working to remove the three

hatches had inadequate emergency equipment to do the job—the gas masks on hand were suitable for fumes from toxic fuels from rockets, but not for smoke—and had to leave the White Room several times to recover from the choking smoke (approximately twenty-seven technicians were eventually treated for smoke inhalation at Cape Kennedy's dispensary). Babbitt had to order Gleaves out of the White Room as he had come close to passing out, as did many of those who worked to free the astronauts from the capsule. As Babbitt approached the spacecraft again, Reece, who had help from Hawkins, removed the middle hatch. Additional technicians, including firefighters, arrived on the scene and the desperate men were finally able to remove the inner hatch. "We could see the whole hatch well enough to work on it," said Babbitt, "the handles on the hatch, on the outer side of it, were cool enough to hold on to but the face of the hatch itself was extremely hot." Fireman Jim Burch, who finally wrestled the inner hatch loose after several attempts, took a flashlight and peered into the spacecraft but could not see anything but burnt wires. "People were hollering for me to get them [the astronauts] out and I was confused," Burch said. "I couldn't see anybody; it didn't seem real. Where were they? I backed off with my light. Then I could see the bodies. I told the test conductor, 'They're all dead—there's no fire inside.'" With all the hatches opened, Babbitt left the White Room and reported over his headset of this fact and added: "I cannot describe what I saw." His report came five minutes and twenty-seven seconds after the first report of a fire in the spacecraft.[23]

That Friday of the plugs-out test on Spacecraft 012 happened to be the last day Grissom's friend Sam Beddingfield served as chief of the mechanical engineering division before moving on to the space agency's program office. "Gus said there was really something he really wanted to tell me about," said Beddingfield. "And Gus didn't get a chance to do that." In a day filled with ironies—from a disaster befalling a supposedly safe test on the ground to Grissom's continued ill fortune with hatches—Beddingfield's perhaps topped the list. When the fire broke out in the spacecraft, he had been on his way to the Cape to supervise a simulation involving an emergency egress by the astronauts from the spacecraft. Although a traumatic time for Beddingfield, he used his talents to assist in finding out what happened. As an expert in pyrotechnics, he worked at Pad 34 to remove the unpredictable escape tower and assisted with the command module's disassembly, finally returning home to change clothes on Tuesday evening at nine o'clock. "That's how busy I was," Beddingfield said. "I lost track of days and nights."[24]

At the blockhouse, a stunned Slayton tracked down flight surgeon Fred Kelly and told him he had better make his way to the spacecraft. "You know what I'll find," Kelly responded. When he finally arrived at the White Room and looked inside the cabin, Kelly made a quick check and confirmed his fears; the astronauts were dead. Talking, he said, to "no one in particular," the doctor observed that it would take hours to free the bodies as the heat had caused everything to melt and fuse together. He called Slayton and told him what he had found, advised him to clear the pad because of the danger from the escape rocket, and asked for photographers to record the spacecraft's interior before removing Grissom, White, and Chaffee. After agreeing with Kelly's suggestions, Slayton went to the crew quarters and telephoned flight directors in Houston and NASA officials in Washington, D.C., about the tragedy. He also made arrangements for telling the astronauts' families the terrible news, with astronauts Michael Collins telling Martha Chaffee and Pete Conrad informing Pat White. Dr. Charles Berry broke the tragic news to Betty. "It was a bad day," said Slayton. "Worst I ever had."[25]

Betty had been busy preparing dinner for her two sons at her home in Seabrook, Texas, when she heard a knock on her door. When she opened the door, she found on her doorstep Adelin Hammack, wife of a NASA engineer. She told Betty her husband Jerry had called her and told her to make the visit. "I'm here, but I don't know why I'm here," Betty remembered Adelin as saying. The next person to appear was Jo Schirra, wife of astronaut Wally Schirra and Betty's next-door neighbor, who told her there had been an accident at Cape Kennedy involving Gus. "She had a ghastly look on her face and I pretty much knew, right there, when she walked into the door," said Scott, who had just returned home from school. Betty finally received the news of her husband's death from Berry, who had been preceded in the Grissom home by his wife. "Not one of the big guys [at NASA] ever came to offer to explain to us how this fire started," Betty said years later. "I would like for them to do it."[26]

Although Berry offered to inform Gus's parents about his death, Betty declined the offer and made the awful telephone call to Mitchell, Indiana, herself. "She [Betty] didn't want us to hear about it on the news," Cecile remembered. A physician called to the Grissom home gave Cecile a sedative to help her sleep, but the grief-stricken mother failed to fall asleep until 8:30 the next morning. Only ten days before the accident, Cecile and Dennis had visited their son at Cape Kennedy, touring the facility and eating lunch with the *Apollo 1* crew. Norman Grissom, Gus's younger brother, had gone to cover Mitchell High School's basketball game at Salem for the *Mitchell Tribune* when he heard the news of his brother's death. "A family friend called and told me that there had been—you know, I forget how he phrased it. A tragedy," said Norman. He noted that the entire community descended into "sadness and shock" upon learning about his brother's death. "None of us thought anything would happen to him," said Norman. He added that he and other family members were particularly unprepared for an accident to occur on the ground during a test instead of in space during a mission. Mitchell mayor James Fortner had a city policeman stand guard over the Mitchell home, noting "this is not the time for them [Grissom's parents] to be bothered."[27]

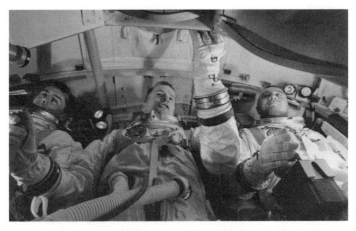

NASA

Interior view of the Apollo command module showing the locations of the astronauts in the spacecraft.

Lowell Grissom, Gus's younger brother, arrived in Mitchell during the night from his home in Cincinnati, where he worked in the personnel department at General Electric, and Wilma Beavers, the astronaut's sister, joined him there from her home in West Virginia just before dawn. Speaking to reporters from the steps of the family home at 715 Grissom Avenue, Lowell asked the media not to let "crackpots" halt the American space effort because of the accident. "It was an experimental program, a test. We all knew an accident was going to happen someday," he said. "And as it turned out Gus was in it. We feel badly but the space program was Gus' life. Please don't let the people who don't understand destroy the program." Lowell said his parents took the news of their son's death very hard and did not believe they could talk to the press about their loss. He did say his parents repeatedly expressed the opinion "they didn't realize how many good people there were until this happened."[28]

It took NASA technicians at Pad 34 until one in the morning to remove the deceased astronauts from the spacecraft. Workers discovered that Grissom had detached his harness and hoses and left his position, probably to help White with the hatch and to escape the growing flames. He was found with his feet on his couch and his body underneath White's position. White's body lay perpendicular to the astronauts' couches and under the hatch. Chaffee remained strapped in his seat with the various hoses supplying oxygen and other life support still attached. Once removed from the spacecraft—a laborious process—the bodies were taken to a temporary morgue established at the Bioastronautic Operational Support Unit at the nearby air force base. Upon a request from NASA, the Armed Forces Institute of Pathology in Washington, D.C., sent a team of three pathologists and a medical photographer to Cape Kennedy to perform the autopsies on the astronauts. The team, assisted by Kelly and others, started its work at 11:00 a.m. on January 28 and completed the task at 1:00 a.m. on January 29. "I worked automatically and methodically, ensuring that the suit technicians, the photographers, and the other necessary personnel were available; supporting the pathologists; insisting on detailed notes; rechecking every item," Kelly remembered.

"It helped to be busy with the work at hand, but it was impossible to completely detach myself from the reality of the situation. I had worked with these three men too long. I knew them too well."[29]

In spite of the wide media speculation that the astronauts had burned to death in the blaze that engulfed Spacecraft 012, the medical examination by the pathologists discovered the cause of death for all three to be asphyxia due to the inhalation of toxic gases released by the fire. Thermal burns were listed as contributing causes of death for all three men, but the burns were survivable. Because he had been closest to the fire's outbreak, Grissom received the most injuries, thermal burns estimated at 60 percent of his total body surface (36 percent were third-degree—the most severe—burns). White suffered burns to 48 percent of his body surface and Chaffee, the farthest from the fire, had burns to only 6 percent of his body surface. Some of the damage to the astronauts could also have been incurred after death, according to the pathologists.[30]

NASA acted quickly to convene a review board, which eventually numbered eight members, to investigate the accident. At the time of the fire, a number of high-ranking space-agency officials were at the White House as a number of nations, including the United States and the Soviet Union, signed the Outer Space Treaty pledging the peaceful use of space. The NASA officials left the White House ceremony to attend a dinner at the International Club with contractors, including North American's Lee Atwood, to discuss the American space effort. Before the dinner could start, Webb received word about the disastrous fire at Pad 34. The administrator met at NASA headquarters with his top officials, including deputy administrator Robert Seamans Jr. and associate administrator George Mueller, who became responsible for selecting review board members. By midnight, Seamans and Mueller had cobbled together a list of people, including selecting Floyd "Tommy" Thompson, director of the Langley Research Center, as chairman, and deciding that the panel should also include a representative from the astronaut corps, agreeing upon Gemini veteran Frank Borman. "The effect of the fire on me was that we had to find out what happened and fix it and move ahead," Webb later observed, "that we had to do that expeditiously and we had to maintain our support while we were doing it, and particularly we had to be very careful not to destroy the system that gave us success." Webb used his considerable political and personal skills to cut off any independent investigation, convincing President Johnson to allow NASA to probe the *Apollo 1* fire and delaying for a time any hearings by the Senate and House space committees. "We will go ahead with the spacecraft program," Webb told reporters. "Although everyone realized that some day space pilots would die, who would have thought the first tragedy should be on the ground?"[31]

Although the media clamored for answers, NASA remained tight-lipped in the days following the disaster. With approximately 150 reporters at the Cape's press center calling for access to the spacecraft, NASA agreed to have a still photographer and a newsreel cameraman shoot the command module and share their work with other members of the media. The press, however, insisted on having a reporter accompany the photographers, and the space agency agreed on George Alexander, a respected journalist from *Aviation Week and Space Technology* magazine. In his report distributed to all members of the media, Alexander, who NASA officials forbade to touch anything or ask anyone questions, likened the spacecraft to the interior of a furnace, with its walls "covered with a slate-gray deposit of smoke and soot; its floor and couch frame . . . covered with ashes and debris—most of it indeterminate." The spacecraft's exterior had been blackened by the fire, its paint blistered and flaking off "like old paint on a house," Alexander noted. Peering into the cabin, the reporter could see a flight plan book "turned to ancient parchment by the intense heat" and tangles of electrical cables with melted insulation leaving the copper wiring exposed. "The acrid smell of an electrical fire is still there," said Alexander. Ashes and unrecognizable debris littered the floor of *Apollo 1*. "It looks like the basement of a fire-gutted house," he said, "into which the rubble has dropped." Both the American flag and the words "United States" painted on the command module's exterior were stained by smoke. After his tour, Alexander told his fellow reporters that the cabin resembled "a gutted shell. It looked like a bunker from World

*Closeup view of the exterior of the Apollo command module at Pad
34 showing the effects of the intense heat of the flash fire
that killed astronauts Grissom, White, and Chaffee.*

NASA

NASA

The charred interior of the Apollo 1 *spacecraft.*

War Two or the Korean War that had taken a direct hit."[32]

On January 30, after a memorial service for Grissom and White at the Seabrook Methodist Church (a memorial for Chaffee had been held the day before at the Webster Methodist Church), the bodies of the three fallen astronauts were taken from the Bioastronautics Support Unit for a flight to Andrews Air Force Base in Washington, D.C. An air force band played Chopin's Funeral March, "Abide with Me," and "Faith of Our Fathers" as the bodies were loaded onto a military Boeing 707 for the journey north. On a clear, breezy, and cold afternoon, the three pine boxes containing the silver-gray, steel, GI-issue coffins with the astronauts' remains were met at Andrews by air force and navy honor guards and representatives from NASA and the Johnson administration. "It was an almost silent scene," noted a reporter at Andrews, one of several hundred spectators on hand for the arrival. As Grissom and Chaffee's bodies were placed in two civilian hearses, the only sounds heard "were those of the wind whipping the flags, the click of the still cameras, and the whir of the television cameras." From the air base, the bodies of Grissom and Chaffee were taken for burial at Arlington National Cemetery, about a half mile south of the Tomb of the Unknown Soldier and near the grave of army Lieutenant Thomas Selfridge, the first member of the armed forces to be killed in a plane crash. (Selfridge died in a September 17, 1908, accident at Fort Myer, Virginia, in a plane flown by Orville Wright.) White's body was taken to a Highland Falls, New York, funeral home for eventual interment at the U.S. Military Academy cemetery at West Point.[33]

The January 31 services for Grissom at Arlington were held at 9:00 a.m., with those for Chaffee following at 1:00 p.m. President Johnson joined Grissom's wife and sons, the astronaut's parents and other relatives, politicians from Indiana, friends from Mitchell, and a large crowd of onlookers at the approximately half-hour-long ceremony. Reporters estimated that despite the freezing weather the burial service drew the largest number of spectators at Arlington since the one held

AP/WIDE WORLD PHOTOS

Three astronauts, wearing their military uniforms, stand beside the caisson bearing Grissom's casket at Arlington National Cemetery. From left are: John Glenn, Gordon Cooper, and John Young.

for President John F. Kennedy in 1963. Six black horses pulled the caisson carrying the silver-gray casket containing Grissom's body. Accompanying the caisson were Grissom's pallbearers—five of the six remaining Mercury astronauts plus John Young (Schirra served as the Grissom family's official escort). Roy Van Tassel, pastor of the Mitchell Church of Christ, offered a short graveside sermon, eulogizing Grissom as having a "wonderful life, filled with wonderful experiences—a life of service to his country and his fellow men. He was one of the great heroes of the space age." After a twenty-one-gun salute and the playing of "Taps," three F-101 fighter jets streaked over the gravesite in the classic "missing man" formation. As Betty cradled the flag that had draped her husband's coffin, Johnson shook her hand and consoled her two sons before comforting the astronaut's parents as well. Returning to her home in Texas after the funeral, Betty thought to herself: "Well, I'm going to miss the phone calls. That's mostly what I had of him. The phone calls."[34]

Mitchell resembled a ghost town the day Grissom received his hero's funeral at Arlington, with special memorial services conducted at both Mitchell High School and Burris Elementary School. With Mayor Fortner declaring an official day of mourning, flags flew at half-mast throughout the community and businesses were closed until noon. Many downtown storefronts displayed photographs of Grissom draped in black. "Main Street was quiet and deserted all morning," according to an account in the *Mitchell Tribune*, "as friends and acquaintances mourned along with the family." To honor the astronaut's memory, local business leaders proposed the building of a memorial to Grissom and state legislators introduced a bill in the Indiana General Assembly calling for the establishment of a visitors' center named for the astronaut at Spring Mill State Park, located near Mitchell.[35]

The shock and disbelief expressed by the citizens of Mitchell about the death of their favorite son were echoed by NASA employees, who were desolate at the loss of three astronauts during a supposedly innocuous ground test. As investigators worked painstakingly to disassemble the space-craft piece by piece to uncover what had gone wrong, ground controllers pored over data impounded after the disaster to see if they could spot any telltale glitches. The relentless effort to find answers to why the tragedy occurred resulted in sleepless nights for many. "Everybody at NASA was feeling the strain," noted Seamans. "The trouble was not that our people didn't care enough about the fire; they cared too much." The pressure even took its toll on those on the review board. Borman had been one of the first to view the charred spacecraft, which he described as a "fire-blackened charnel house." Seeing the damage firsthand upset Borman so much that he went out with Slayton and Faget that evening to a nightclub to get drunk, drinking toast after toast to the three departed astronauts. "We closed the evening by throwing glasses against a wall—it was right out of a World War I movie," said Borman. "But then, sorrow ended and work began." According to Schirra, the astronauts, as test pilots used to losing friends in the line of duty, were more accustomed to death than the civilian employees at the space agency. The pilots wore black armbands for awhile to mourn a loss, but then returned to their jobs. "NASA, unfortunately, as a bunch of civilians, didn't know how to take off the black armband," said Schirra. "And we kept saying, 'Look, take the band off! We've got to get back to work.' Gus would be the first person to say, 'Let's get on with it. Do good work.'" Borman noted that some people at the space agency were so depressed they had to take "downers to ease the pain of guilt and uppers so they could face the next day." Not surprisingly, the pharmaceutical mixture led to breakdowns for at least two engineers, according to Borman.[36]

One NASA official—Shea—was particularly haunted by the fire, wondering if he might have been able to physically prevent the catastrophe from happening. In an oral history interview with reporter and writer Robert Sherrod, Shea, who would eventually be moved from his job with the Apollo program to a position at NASA headquarters, indicated he might have been able to snuff out the fire if he had decided to take Grissom's suggestion to join the astronauts in the capsule for the plugs-out test. "I'm probably 70 percent convinced . . . that had I been down there I probably would have seen it [the fire start], I think I could have grabbed it; I probably would have burned my hands or something—and I could have smothered it enough, so that it never would have spread," Shea told Sherrod. For awhile, the NASA official told the reporter, he had even wished he had been in the spacecraft and "gone with those guys."[37]

One of the first tasks undertaken by the review board, which had the direct support of fifteen hundred technical experts (six hundred from government and nine hundred from contractors and universities), involved establishing procedures for taking apart the burned spacecraft piece by piece. After the launch escape system and other pyrotechnics had been safely removed, two people at a time were allowed into the spacecraft to remove components, after which photographs were taken of the exposed areas. With the couches removed, workers constructed a transparent false floor that gave investigators access to the command module's interior without the worry of disturbing any of the evidence. On February 1, North American shipped Spacecraft 014 to Cape Kennedy to assist in developing techniques for taking apart individual parts in *Apollo 1*. Those involved in dismantling the spacecraft at first operated on a three-shift, seven-day-a-week schedule, which switched to two eight-hour shifts after NASA moved the capsule from Pad 34 to the Pyrotechnics Installation Building. As components were removed, investigators studied each part and the exposed portions to help pinpoint the source of the fire. Wire bundles proved to be of considerable interest to the review board, and these items were studied under seven-power magnification. By March 27, the work on disassembling the command module had been completed.[38]

Delivered to Webb on April 9, the review board's final report—the result of an investigation that cost $4 million—could not positively identify the equipment failure responsible for the *Apollo 1* catastrophe. "We never did determine definitely what had caused the spark," Borman said, "although we would have bet our combined bank accounts that it originated in a bundle of electrical wiring in front of Grissom's feet." The board, however, did identify the conditions that helped lead to the disaster, including: a sealed, pure-oxygen atmosphere under pressure; the existence of a considerable amount of combustible materials throughout the cabin; weak wiring carrying power to the spacecraft; inadequate plumbing carrying corrosive coolant; insufficient provisions for crew escape; and limited means for providing rescue or medical assistance. In considering how these conditions came about, the board concluded that the Apollo team, looking ahead to reaching the moon before Kennedy's deadline, had failed to "give adequate attention to certain mundane but equally vital questions of crew safety." The report blasted management at both NASA and North American for allowing deficiencies to exist in the command module's design, workmanship, and quality control. One particularly damning incident cited by the board, reported again and again in the media, involved some North American worker carelessly leaving a socket wrench tangled in the spacecraft's electrical wiring. To help remedy matters, the board called for the development of a new, easily opened hatch; the replacement wherever possible of combustible with nonflammable materials; and rewriting emergency procedures to plan for possible future fires.[39]

The more than two-thousand-page report fueled sharp questions to NASA and North American officials by committees investigating the Apollo fire in both the House and Senate. Asked for his response to the review board's report, Representative Olin E. Teague, a Texas Democrat who chaired a House subcommittee investigating the accident, said the material represented "a broad indictment of NASA and North American and the whole program." Even before the review board's report had been issued, members of the Senate space committee had raked NASA managers over the coals for the spacecraft fire. Future vice president and Democratic presidential candidate Walter F. Mondale, then a senator from Minnesota, blindsided space-agency officials during one hearing when he asked about a document called the Phillips Report, the existence of which had been told to him by Jules Bergman, an NBC television reporter. The Phillips Report was prompted by NASA's unhappiness with schedule delays by North American on both the command module and the Saturn 5's second stage. In late 1965 Mueller had called upon Samuel C. Phillips, Apollo program manager at NASA headquarters, to assemble a team of specialists to review the firm's performance. Phillips's team found much to be improved upon at North American, and his report blistered the firm for its inadequacies and recommended a host of changes to get the program back on schedule. The existence of such a document, and Mondale's insistent questions about North American's faults, irritated Webb, who told Mondale that as a fellow Democrat it was inappropriate for him to bring up such matters. "I said, I don't agree with that at all," said Mondale. "I am a United States Senator. I've got a duty . . . to explore these things."[40]

The charges against the company in the Phillips Report, and claims of negligence by some of its own employees,

Seated at the witness table before the Senate Committee on Aeronautical and Space Services on the Apollo 1 *accident are (left to right): Robert C. Seamans Jr., NASA deputy administrator; James E. Webb, NASA administrator; George E. Mueller, associate administrator for manned space flight; and Samuel C. Phillips, Apollo program director.*

placed North American on the defensive. Appearing before the House's oversight subcommittee, Atwood, North American president, testified that his company's design philosophy had been aimed at achieving safety and reliability. "North American has what I consider an outstanding program to train employees to these high requirements and to foster pride of individual accomplishment," Atwood said. Still, John F. McCarthy Jr., the firm's vice president for research and engineering, said top engineers at NASA and North American had made a "grave error" in not designing the Apollo spacecraft to guard against a fire on the ground. In public, company officials indicated they agreed in large part with the findings and recommendations from the review board's report. "I want to make it very clear," Atwood said, "that we at North American will do everything in our power, in conjunction with NASA, to evaluate and, as appropriate, implement the board's recommendations." He told the House subcommittee that standards might have been relaxed due to "overconfidence" about previous successes in space. Privately, however, North American managers were incensed about being blamed for the fire by some in NASA, pointing instead to the space agency's insistence upon using the pure oxygen atmosphere and decision against using an explosive hatch. (An oxygen fire at Brooks Air Force Base in Texas that killed two airmen shortly after the *Apollo 1* fire reiterated the danger of such an environment.) "I do feel quite strongly that the allegation that poor workmanship caused the Apollo fire is completely wrong," Atwood later told an interviewer. "I think it's demonstrated that the fire could not have started in a reasonable cabin atmosphere." In 1987 he wrote Schirra and noted that if the question had been put properly—did people realize the astronauts were being shut in a machine loaded with electrical components and inflated at high pressure in a pure-oxygen environment—"a whistle would have been blown."[41]

North American, however, did not help its case with an American public still mourning the astronauts' deaths when one of its engineers theorized during testimony before the House subcommittee that Grissom was to blame for the *Apollo 1* fire. The testimony came at the end of a long day of questioning about the disaster when a number of congressmen probed North American's reaction to the review board's findings that faulty wiring had contributed to the fire's outbreak. Asked to give alternate scenarios for the blaze, McCarthy hypothesized that the command pilot—Grissom—had kicked or scuffed an energized wire lead that had been attached to an air-sampling unit, which had been removed for modification before the plugs-out test. Such a circumstance had been considered by NASA, who rejected it, noting that to accomplish such a feat while lying in his couch meant that Grissom "would have had to be a contortionist," according to one investigator. "Given Gus's history with the Mercury hatch, of course," noted Slayton, "this just played right into the image of Gus as some sort of screwup. It really pissed me off, and I wasn't the only one, especially because there were no grounds for the story . . . and because Gus wasn't around to defend himself the way he was on the *Liberty Bell* incident." After McCarthy made his statement, representatives, including William F. Ryan, a Democrat from New York; James Fulton, a Republican from Pennsylvania; and Earle Cabell, a Democrat from Texas, forcefully refuted speculation that Grissom was to blame for the inferno on the spacecraft. "In my opinion as an attorney of some years' experience," said Fulton, "there is no scintilla of evidence based upon any physical condition noted after the fire upon which to base a prima facie presumption that Astronaut Gus Grissom in any movement kicked or disturbed with his foot any equipment that had any bearing upon, or contributed to the cause of the accident." An ill at ease McCarthy, prompted by a note passed to him by a North American publicist, attempted to stem the tide of protest by telling the subcommittee: "I wish to make it clear that this is strictly hypothesis and there was no reason to give this as a probable cause."[42]

Whatever its private feelings about the Apollo tragedy, both NASA and North American made major changes to their management staff. At NASA, George Low replaced Shea as head of the Apollo program at the Manned Spacecraft Center. At North American, Atwood replaced Storms with William B. Bergen, a former executive with the Martin Company, an original bidder on the command module. (Bergen made himself popular with the astronauts by bringing back Guenter Wendt to run the White Room operations for North American.) NASA instituted a Configuration Control Board, which met every Friday at noon, to evaluate design changes to the spacecraft. "Arguments sometimes got pretty hot as technical alternatives were explored," said Low. "In the end I would decide, usually on the spot, always explaining my decisions openly and in front of those who liked it the least. To me, this was the true test of a decision—

to look straight into the eyes of the person most affected by it, knowing full well that months later, on the morning of a flight, I would look into the eyes of the men whose lives would depend on that decision. One could not make any mistakes." Over the next two years, the board evaluated 1,697 changes, approving 1,341. Major revisions included the addition of a unified hatch that could be opened in a matter of seconds, the development of new flame-proof material (Beta cloth, a woven glass fiber) for the astronauts' space suits, improved wiring throughout the cabin, and increased attention to safety on the launchpad. In addition, instead of pure oxygen permeating the cabin prior to launch, the atmosphere in the command module consisted of a mixture of 60 percent oxygen and 40 percent nitrogen (to be replaced by 100 percent oxygen in space).[43]

Perhaps the biggest irony of the disaster was the fact that the fire, as great a tragedy as it was, enabled the American space program to put a man on the moon before the decade's end. Because the accident happened on the ground, instead of in space, investigators could determine what areas needed the most attention to ensure the safety of future missions. If the fire had occurred in space, noted Rocco Petrone, director of launch operations at Cape Kennedy, it would have been "a mystery hanging over the whole program," causing untold delays or perhaps even the cancellation of Apollo. The delay in the program caused by the fire gave a number of problem areas, including the development of the lunar module, the needed time to work out any kinks. "I hesitate to say this," legendary NASA flight director Chris Kraft told an interviewer for a program on the Apollo program, "but I have to say it. I don't think we would have gotten to the moon in the sixties if we had not had the fire. That's a terrible thing to say but I think it is true."[44]

On October 11, 1968, from the same launchpad that had claimed the lives of Grissom, White, and Chaffee twenty-one months before, *Apollo 7* blasted off from Cape Kennedy via a Saturn 1B rocket for an eleven-day mission to evaluate the revamped command and service module. Spacecraft 101 flown by the crew of Schirra, Cunningham, and Eisele had been delivered to the Cape from the North American plant at Downey with the message: "We care enough to send the very best." Although the spacecraft performed impeccably, the flight proved to be a tense one, as everyone at NASA, and at North American, had much riding on a successful mission. "I had fun with Mercury," Schirra recalled. "I had fun with Gemini. I lose a buddy, my next-door neighbor Gus. . . . I lose two other guys I thought the world of. And I began to realize this was no longer fun. I was now assigned a mission where I had to put it [the space program] back on track, like Humpty Dumpty." Matters were not helped much when first Schirra, and then his fellow crewmates, came down with colds— another first for NASA. "From then on we sneezed and sniffed up a storm," said Schirra, "and we used the contents of nine of the ten Kleenex tissue containers we had on

NASA

The prime crew for the Apollo 7 *mission from left to right are: Donn F. Eisele, Schirra, and Walter Cunningham. The photograph shows the newly designed hatch for the spacecraft.*

board." The colds may have helped account for the sometimes testy exchanges between mission control and the astronauts, who were determined to achieve a perfect engineering flight and were not shy about complaining to those who wanted to add new experiments and tests to the flight schedule. Schirra, who had announced his retirement before the mission, had vowed that the flight would not "be jeopardized by the influence of special interests—scientific, political, whatever." Glenn Lunney, the lead flight director for the mission, became "pissed off" about the astronauts' attitude, calling them "frankly insubordinate" and the only flight crew during his long career "difficult to deal with and hostile to what we were trying to do." The bickering between mission control and the astronauts had no effect on the machine provided by North American. The spacecraft worked to perfection on the 163-orbit flight, making the moon seem once again to be within the grasp of the American space program.[45]

AT APPROXIMATELY FOUR O'CLOCK IN THE AFTERNOON ON JULY 20, 1969, Neil Armstrong, commander of the *Apollo 11* mission, hovered above the surface of the moon onboard the lunar module—nicknamed *Eagle*—seeking a suitable landing site in the Sea of Tranquility. Taking over for the automatic-targeting system that had been maneuvering him and his fellow astronaut Buzz Aldrin into a crater strewn with rocks and boulders, Armstrong had only thirty seconds left of fuel in the descent engine before he finally found a spot to his liking and eased the lunar module in for touchdown. Back in Houston, Charles Duke, serving as capsule communicator, radioed the crew, "We copy you down, Eagle." Armstrong responded with the words everyone in Houston, and the world, had been waiting to hear: "Houston, Tranquility Base here. The Eagle has landed." Hours later, at 10:56 p.m. Eastern Daylight Time, Armstrong planted his historic footprint on the moon's surface. For the next two hours and twenty-one minutes,

Armstrong, soon joined by Aldrin, collected rocks and soil, set up scientific experiments, and received a congratulatory call from President Richard Nixon.[1]

As Armstrong and Aldrin blasted off at 1:54 p.m. on July 21 to rendezvous with Michael Collins, orbiting above in the command module *Columbia*, left behind on the moon's surface were such items as an American flag and a plaque on the lunar module's leg reading: "Here Men From the Planet Earth First Set Foot Upon the Moon July 1969, A.D. We came in peace for all mankind." The astronauts also left on the moon a medallion depicting a patch from a mission that never flew: *Apollo 1*. The astronauts who gave their lives for America's space program—Gus Grissom, Ed White, and Roger Chaffee—had large moon craters named in their honor as well. For Scott Grissom, these memorials paled in comparison to his father's true legacy. "If it hadn't been for my father, Ed White, and Roger Chaffee they would have never gotten to the moon," said Scott. "There wouldn't have been anything else!"[2]

Grissom's accomplishments received wide recognition in Indiana, with Purdue University's engineering school naming one of its buildings for the astronaut and in 1968 the Bunker Hill Air Force Base in Miami County had its designation changed to Grissom Air Force Base. Those who grew up with Grissom in Mitchell also ensured their community's fallen hero would not soon be forgotten by building a memorial to the astronaut at Spring Mill State Park. Formally dedicated on

Astronaut Buzz Aldrin salutes the American flag planted on the moon by himself and Neil Armstrong during the Apollo 11 *mission.*

July 21, 1971, the tenth anniversary of the astronaut's Mercury flight, the memorial featured Grissom's *Gemini 3* spacecraft, the *Molly Brown*, and other items from the astronaut's career. John Young, Grissom's crewmate on the Gemini mission, described Grissom for the crowd of thousands gathered for the ceremony as a "very rare individual in this day and age." Indiana governor Edgar Whitcomb, who served as master of ceremonies when television personality and former baseball player Joe Garagiola ran late, said if Grissom were present for the occasion he would have been "terribly happy and proud, and his greatest thrill would be seeing the young boys walk up to the Molly Brown space capsule and dream and have visions

INDIANAPOLIS STAR

Lee Keith (left) and Kevin Allec install signposts around the Virgil I. Grissom Memorial in preparation for dedication ceremonies in July 1971 at the memorial in Spring Mill State Park in Mitchell, Indiana.

of the future and go on to accept the challenge of space."[3]

Seven months before the Grissom memorial opened in Mitchell, Betty Grissom filed a $10 million lawsuit in Florida charging North American and its subsidiaries with negligence in the death of her husband. Although dismissed because the statute of limitations had expired, Betty's attorneys moved the case to the California courts (where the spacecraft had been built) on behalf of Scott and Mark Grissom. Eventually, the parties reached an out-of-court settlement totaling $350,000, with Betty receiving $60,000 and her two sons $75,000 each. (The widows of White and Chaffee also received settlements from North American.) By 1974, the year she published an account of her life with Gus called *Starfall*, Betty had moved from her Seabrook residence to a townhouse in Houston. Scott and Mark both graduated from their father's alma mater, Purdue, which had given them a free education, and also pursued careers in aviation—Scott as a pilot for Federal Express and Mark as an air-traffic controller and later a pilot.[4]

Over the years, the Grissom family has maintained a troubled, at best, relationship with NASA. When disasters took the lives of the crews of the shuttles *Challenger* and *Columbia*, the media turned its attention for a time to another tragedy, the *Apollo 1* fire. In interviews Betty said that after her husband's burial at Arlington National Cemetery, her family had been "cut off" by the space agency. It seemed as if, she said, NASA officials hoped everyone would simply forget about the fire. Matters were not helped in 1999 when Scott charged in an interview with the weekly tabloid *The Star* that the space agency had been conspiring to cover up the fact that his father had been deliberately murdered through sabotage of *Apollo 1* in order to prevent him from being the first man on the moon. The most recent disagreement between the Grissom family and NASA erupted in November 2002 and involved the ownership of Gus's Mercury space suit and other items from his career that were on display at the failed U.S. Astronaut Hall of Fame, a private facility near the John F. Kennedy Space Center. After the Hall of Fame went bankrupt, its operation was turned over to Delaware North Park Services, the company that is in charge of the Kennedy Space Center Visitors Complex.[5]

The sometimes bitter sparing between the Grissom family and NASA has failed to quash the public's curiosity about the astronaut, particularly his problem with the hatch on the *Liberty Bell 7* mission. The debate on the question of whether or not Grissom was to blame for the hatch's firing seemed about to be put to rest for good in May 1999 when Curt Newport—whose twin passions as a child had been spaceflight and undersea exploration—found the long-abandoned spacecraft on the bottom of the Atlantic Ocean. Even this spectacular achievement, however, engendered controversy. As Newport prepared to set sail to find the lost capsule in an expedition financed by the Discovery Channel, Betty expressed her disgust to the media that she and her family

*Crowds waited for hours to view the interior of the Grissom
Memorial upon its opening. In the background is the* Molly
Brown *spacecraft the astronaut flew during his
Gemini mission.*

had not been consulted about the salvage operation. "I hope
that they do not find it," she said. Betty's negative view of the
attempt may have been prompted by the spacecraft's intended final destination—display at the Kansas Cosmosphere and
Space Center in Hutchinson, Kansas. Betty charged that the
center had earlier unsuccessfully attempted to have her husband's *Gemini 3* capsule moved from its home in Mitchell to
the Kansas museum. Guenter Wendt, who offered advice to
Newport on his search, expressed puzzlement at Betty's
opposition, noting the Cosmosphere already had a Gemini
spacecraft in its collection and had made no attempt to obtain
the *Molly Brown*.[6]

After Newport's team found the *Liberty Bell 7* spacecraft on May 1 approximately 300 miles southeast of Cape Canaveral at a depth of more than 15,000 feet (deeper than the wreck of the *Titanic*), the astronaut's widow called it "a sad day," adding the discovery "brings back memories and there's nothing good." Rough seas, however, resulted in the loss of the expedition's robotic rover, putting an end to any recovery. (The troublesome hatch remained lost somewhere on the ocean floor.) In July, Newport, joined by Wendt and Jim Lewis, the helicopter pilot on the original *Liberty Bell 7* recovery, returned to the site and, at 2:15 a.m. July 20—thirty-eight years almost to the day it had been blasted into space—hoisted the capsule off of the ocean floor and onto the deck of the ship *Ocean Project*. "In a moment of resignation to the finality of our accomplishment," said Newport about the capsule's return, "my body hunched over until I heard behind me the cheers and clapping of the entire ship. I rotated around with excitement and started clapping in acknowledgement of their enthusiasm and thrust both arms into the air in a moment of triumph. It was finally done." When the ship returned to Port Canaveral the next day, a large crowd had gathered to welcome the spacecraft home. Wendt noted one member of the crowd, a "quiet gentleman with a curiously familiar smile," walk up to the capsule to touch it. "I think Gus would be really pleased to see the Liberty Bell back home," said Lowell Grissom, the astronaut's brother.[7]

Guenter Wendt addresses the media upon the return of the Liberty Bell 7 *spacecraft to Florida. At right is Curt Newport who led the expedition to recover the capsule from the bottom of the Atlantic Ocean.*

As the restoration team at the Cosmosphere cleaned and reassembled the spacecraft's 27,000 separate parts, they discovered some intriguing material to help the case that Grissom had not panicked on his flight and prematurely blown the hatch. The museum team, which completed its work in March 2000, discovered Grissom's waterlogged checklist, which had been about a third of the way completed before the hatch blew. "As far as I'm concerned, that checklist pretty much cleared Grissom of any wrongdoing in connection to what happened," said John Glass, who supervised the capsule's restoration at the Cosmosphere. In addition, Greg "Buck" Buckingham, a key figure in the restoration effort, pointed out that there were no burn marks from the explosive cord that had been intended to trigger the hatch's release. If the explosive cord never detonated, Buckingham theorized that the spacecraft had slammed hatch-down into the ocean when it returned to Earth, causing a titanium strip along the hatch sill to buckle and the seventy explosive bolts to fire one by one. "Most telltale to me are the lack of burn marks," said Buckingham.[8]

In October 2000, the craft piloted by Grissom as the third man in space made its way to Indiana as part of a traveling exhibition from the Cosmosphere hosted by the Children's Museum of Indianapolis. Both Betty and her son Scott attended a special preview at the museum for fifth-grade students at Spring Mill Elementary School and seemed pleased with what she saw. "It really doesn't seem that long ago," Betty

Closeup view of the Liberty Bell 7 *capsule. Despite its long exposure to seawater, the lettering "United States" is still clearly visible on its side.*

said of her husband's Mercury spaceflight. The thousands who visited the exhibition, including this author, were transported back to 1961, complete with a television set in a typical American living room giving details of Grissom's historic mission. Visitors could hear the sounds of the flight in a mock-up of mission control, see what it was like inside the helicopter trying to save the spacecraft from sinking, and take a ride on a centrifuge to experience g-forces endured by the astronauts.[9]

The focal point of the exhibition, however, came at the end. In a darkened room sat the recovered *Liberty Bell 7*. Peering inside the spacecraft on a visit to the exhibition together with my wife, Megan, I wondered how anyone could fit inside the tiny cockpit and began to realize how Grissom's small physical stature—a liability when it came to making his high school basketball team—proved to be an asset for his career as an astronaut. For anyone who has marveled at American and Russian achievements in space, nothing can match the feeling of being next to, and surreptitiously, touching a craft that has taken a man out of his earthly bounds and into the heavens. In that moment, all the controversy and questions about Grissom's life melted away and what was left was admiration for the modest beginnings he had come from and what he had accomplished during his brief life on this planet. It's a legacy that continues to inspire.

THE FOLLOWING IS THE MISSION TRANSCRIPT FOR GUS GRISSOM'S *LIBERTY Bell 7* flight. The spacecraft is identified as "Bell 7." The astronaut communicator in the blockhouse is identified as "Stony." The "Cap Com" is the astronaut communicator in Mercury Mission Control. "Chase" is an astronaut flying chase in an F-106 aircraft. "ATS" stands for the Atlantic Ocean Ship, a Mercury range station that had been moved in close to the landing area for the flight. "Hunt Club" is the designation given to the recovery helicopters. "Card File" is the radio-relay airplane that relayed spacecraft communication to mission control.

Stony: Lift-off.

Bell 7: Ah, Roger. This is Liberty Bell 7. The clock is operating.

Cap Com: Loud and clear, José, don't cry too much.

Bell 7: Oke-doke.

Bell 7: OK, it's a nice ride up to now.

Cap Com: Loud and clear.

Bell 7: Roger.

Bell 7: OK. The fuel is go; about 1 ½ g's; cabin pressure is just coming off the peg; the O_2 is go; we have 26 amps.

Cap Com: Roger. Pitch [attitude] 88 [degrees], the trajectory is good.

Bell 7: Roger, looks good here.

Bell 7: OK, there. We're starting to pick up a little bit of the noise and vibration; not bad, though, at all. 50 secs, more vibration.

Bell 7: OK. The fuel is go; 1 ½ g's; cabin is 8 [psi]; the O₂ is go; 27 amps.

Bell 7: And [Rest of communication not received.]

Cap Com: Pitch is [Rest of communication not received.]

Bell 7: 4 [g], 5 [g] [Rest of communication not received.]

Cap Com: Pitch [attitude] is 77 [degrees]; trajectory is go.

Bell 7: Roger. Cabin pressure is still about 6 [psi] and dropping slightly. Looks like she's going to hold about 5.5 [psi].

Bell 7: Eh [Rest of communication not received.]

Cap Com: Cabin [Rest of communication not received.]

Bell 7: Believe me, O₂, is go.

Cap Com: Cabin pressure holding 5.5 [psi].

Bell 7: Roger, roger.

Bell 7: This is Liberty-Bell 7. Fuel is go; 2 ½ g's; cabin pressure 5.5; O₂ is go; main [bus] 25 [volts], isolated—ah, isolated [bus] is 28 [volts]. We are go.

Cap Com: Roger. Pitch [attitude] is 62 [degrees]; trajectory is go.

Bell 7: Roger. It looks good in here.

Bell 7: Everything is good; cabin pressure is holding; suit pressure is OK; 2 minutes and we got 4 g's; fuel is go; ah, feel the hand controller move just a hair there; cabin pressure is holding, O₂ is go; 25 amps.

Cap Com: Roger, we have go here.

Bell 7: And I see a star!

Cap Com: Stand by for cutoff.

Bell 7: There went the tower.

Chase: Roger, there went the tower, affirmative. Chase.

Bell 7: Roger, squibs are off.

Cap Com: Roger.

Bell 7: There went posigrades, capsule has separated. We are at zero g and turning around and the sun is really bright.

Cap Com: Roger, cap. sep. [capsule separation light] is green; turnaround has started, manual handle out.

Bell 7: Oh boy! Manual handle is out; the sky is very black; the capsule is coming around into orbit attitude; the roll is a little bit slow.

Cap Com: Roger.

Bell 7: I haven't seen a booster anyplace. OK, rate command is coming on. I'm in orbit attitude, I'm pitching up. OK, 40 [Rest of communication not received.] Wait, I've lost some roll here someplace.

Cap Com: Roger, rate command is coming on. You're trying manual pitch.

Bell 7: OK, I got roll back. OK, I'm at 24 [degrees] in pitch.

Bell 7: Roger, your IP [impact point] is right on, Gus, right on.

Bell 7: OK. I'm having a little trouble with rate, ah, with the manual control.

Cap Com: Roger.

Bell 7: If I can get her stabilized here, all axes are working all right.

Cap Com: Roger. Understand manual control is good.

Bell 7: Roger, it's—it's sort of sluggish, more than I expected.

Bell 7: OK, I'm yawing.

Cap Com: Roger, yaw.

Bell 7: Left, ah.

Bell 7: OK, coming back in yaw. I'm a little bit late there.

Cap Com: Roger. Reading you loud and clear, Gus.

Bell 7: Lot of stuff—there's a lot of stuff floating around up here.

Bell 7: OK, I'm going to skip the yaw [maneuver], ah, or [rather the] roll [maneuver] because I'm a little bit late and I'm going to try this rough yaw maneuver. About all I can really see is clouds. I haven't seen any land anyplace yet.

Cap Com: Roger, you're on the window. Are you trying a yaw maneuver?

Bell 7: I'm trying the yaw maneuver and I'm on the window. It's such a fascinating view out the window you just can't help but look out that way.

Cap Com: I understand.

Bell 7: You su, ah, really. There I see the coast, I see.

Cap Com: 4+30 [elapsed time since launch] Gus.
4+30 [elapsed time since launch] he's looking out the window, A - OK.

Bell 7: I can see the coast but I can't identify anything.

Cap Com: Roger, 4+30 [elapsed time since launch] Gus.

Bell 7: OK, let me get back here to retro attitude, retro sequence has started.

Cap Com: Roger, retro sequence has started. Go to retro attitude.

Bell 7: Right, we'll see if I'm in bad, not in very good shape here.

Cap Com: Got 15 seconds, plenty of time, I'll give you a mark at 5:10 [elapsed time since launch].

Bell 7: OK, retro attitude [light] is still green.

Cap Com: Retros on my mark, 3, 2, 1, mark.

Communicator unidentified: He's in limits. [Falls in the middle of last Cap Com communication.]

Bell 7: OK, there's 1 firing, there's 1 firing.

Communicator unidentified: Retro 1. [Cuts out Bell 7.]

Cap Com: Roger, retro 1.

Bell 7: There's 2 firing, nice little boost. There went 3.

Cap Com: Roger, 3, all retros are fired.

Bell 7: Roger, roger.

Bell 7: OK, yeh, they're fired out right there.

Cap Com: Roger, retrojettison armed.

Bell 7: Retrojettison is armed, retrojettison is armed, going to rate command.

Bell 7: OK, I'm going to switch.

Cap Com: Roger. Understand manual fuel handle is in.

Bell 7: Manual fuel handle is in, mark, going to HF.

Cap Com: Roger, HF.

Cap Com: Liberty Bell 7, this is Cap Com on HF, 1, 2, 3, 4, 5. How do you read [Bell] 7?

Communicator unidentified: I got you.

Bell 7: . . . here, do you read me, do you read me on HF? . . . Going back to U [UHF] . . . [received by ATS ship]. Boy is that . . . Retro, I'm back on UHF and, ah, and the jett—the retros have jettisoned. Now I can see the Cape any, oh boy, that's some sight. I can't see too much.

Cap Com: This is Cap Com on HF, 1, 2, 3, 4, 5. How do you read, [Bell] 7?

Bell 7: Roger, I am on UHF high, do you read me?

Cap Com: Roger, reading you loud and clear UHF high, can you confirm retrojettison?

Bell 7: OK, periscope is retracting, going to reentry attitude.

Cap Com: Roger. Retros have jettisoned, scope has retracted, you're going to reentry attitude.

Bell 7: Affirmative.

Cap Com: Bell 7 from Cap Com, your IP [impact point] is right on.

Bell 7: Roger. I'm in reentry attitude.

Bell 7: Ah.

Cap Com: Roger, how does it look out the window now?

Bell 7: Ah, the sun is coming in and so all I can see really is just, ah, just darkness, the sky is very black.

Cap Com: Roger, you have some more time to look if you like.

Cap Com: [Bell] 7 from Cap Com, how do you feel up there?

Bell 7: I feel very good, auto fuel is 90 [percent], manual is 50 [percent].

Cap Com: Roger, 0.05 g in 10 [seconds].

Bell 7: OK.

Bell 7: OK, everything is very good, ah.

Bell 7: I got 0.05 g [light] and roll rate has started.

Cap Com: Roger.

Bell 7: Got a pitch rate in here, OK, g's are starting to build.

Cap Com: Roger, reading you loud and clear.

Bell 7: Roger, g's are building, we're up to 6 [g].

Bell 7: There's 9 [g].

Bell 7: There's about 10 [g]; the handle is out from under it; here I got a little pitch rate coming back down through 7 [g].

Cap Com: Roger, still sound good.

Bell 7: Oh, the altimeter is active at 65 [thousand feet]. There's 60 [thousand feet].

Cap Com: Roger, 65,000.

Bell 7: OK, I'm getting some contrails, evidently shock wave, 50,000 feet; I'm feeling good. I'm very good, everything is fine.

Cap Com: Roger, 50,000.

Bell 7: 45,000, do you still read?

Cap Com: Affirmative. Still reading you. You sound good.

Bell 7: OK, 40,000 feet, do you read?

Bell 7: 35,000 feet, if you read me.

Bell 7: 30,000 feet, everything is good, everything is good.

Cap Com: Bell 7, this is Cap Com. How [Rest of communication not received.]

Communicator unidentified: Cape, do you read?

Bell 7: 25,000 feet.

Bell 7: Approaching drogue chute attitude.

Bell 7: There's the drogue chute. The periscope has extended.

Cap Com: This is . . . we have a green drogue [light] here, 7 how do you read?

Bell 7: OK, we're coming down to 15,000 feet, if anyone reads. We're on emergency flow rate, can see out the periscope OK. The drogue chute is good.

Cap Com: Roger, understand drogue is good, the periscope is out.

Bell 7: There's 13,000 feet.

Cap Com: Roger.

Bell 7: There goes the main chute; it's reefed; main chute is good; main chute is good; rate of descent coming down, coming down to—there's 40 feet per second, 30 feet per, 32 feet per second on the main chute, and the landing bag is out green.

Bell 7: Ah, it's better than it was, Chuck.

Bell 7: Hello, does anybody read Liberty Bell, main chute is good, landing bag [light] is on green.

Cap Com: And the landing bag [light] is on green.

ATS: Liberty Bell 7, Liberty Bell 7, this is Atlantic Ship Cap Com. Read you loud and clear. Our telemetry confirms your events. Over.

Bell 7: Ah, roger, is anyone reading Liberty Bell 7? Over.

Card File 23: Roger, Liberty Bell 7, reading you loud and clear. This is Card File 23. Over.

Bell 7: Atlantic Ship Cap Com, this is Liberty Bell 7, how do you read me? Over.

ATS: Read you loud and clear, loud and clear. Over. Liberty Bell 7, Liberty Bell 7, this is Atlantic Ship Cap Com. How do you read me? Over.

Bell 7: Atlantic Ship Cap Com, this is Liberty Bell 7, I read you loud and clear. How me? Over.

ATS: Roger, Bell 7, read you loud and clear, your status looks good, your systems look good, we confirm your events. Over.

Bell 7: Ah, Roger, and confirm the fuel has dumped. Over.

ATS: Roger, confirm again, confirm again, has your auto fuel dumped? Over.

Bell 7: Auto fuel and manual fuel has dumped.

ATS: Roger, roger.

Bell 7: And I'm in the process of putting the pins back in the door at this time.

Bell 7: OK, I'm passing down through 6,000 feet, everything is good, ah.

Bell 7: I'm going to open my face plate.

Bell 7: Hello, I can't get one; I can't get one door pin back in. I've tried and tried and I can't get it back in. And I'm coming, ATS, I'm passing through 5,000 feet and I don't think I have one of the door pins in.

ATS: Roger, Bell 7, Roger.

Bell 7: Do you have any word from the recovery troops?

Card File 23: Liberty Bell 7, this is Card File 23; we are heading directly toward you.

Bell 7: ATS, this is Cap—this is Liberty Bell 7. Do you have any word from the recovery troops?

ATS: Negative, Bell 7, negative. Do you have any transmission to MCC [Mercury Control Center]? Over.

Bell 7: Ah, Roger, you might make a note that there is one small hole in my chute. It looks like it's about 6 inches by 6 inches—it's a sort of a— actually it's a triangular rip, I guess.

ATS: Ah, roger, roger.

Bell 7: I'm passing through 3,000 feet, and all the fuses are in flight conditions; ASCS is normal, auto; we're on rate command; gyros are normal; auto retrojettison is armed; squibs are armed also. Four fuel handles are in; decompress and recompress are in; retro delay is normal; retroheat is off, cabin lights are both. TM [telemeter] is on. Rescue aids is auto; landing bag is auto; retract scope is auto; retroattitude is auto. All the three, five pull rings are in. Going down through some clouds to 2,000 feet. ATS, I'm at 2,000 feet; everything is normal.

ATS: Roger, Bell 7, what is your rate of descent again? Over.

Bell 7: The rate of descent is varying between 28 and 30 feet per second.

ATS: Ah, roger, roger, and once again verify your fuel has dumped. Over.

Communicator unidentified: Seven ahead at bearing 020. Over.

Bell 7: OK. My max g was about 10.2; altimeter is 1,000 [feet]; cabin pressure is coming toward 15 [psi].

Communicator unidentified: We'll make up.

Bell 7: Temperature is 90 [degrees Fahrenheit].

Communicator unidentified: We'll make an eye rep.

Bell 7: Coolant quantity is 30 [percent]; temperature is 68 [degrees Fahrenheit]; pressure is 14 [psi]; main O_2 is 60 [percent]; normal is, main is 60 [percent]; emergency is 100 [percent]; suit fan is normal; cabin fan is normal. We have 21 amps, and I'm getting ready for impact here.

Bell 7: Can see the water coming right on up.

ATS: Liberty Bell 7, Liberty Bell 7, this is Atlantic Cap Com, do you read me? Over.

Bell 7: OK, does anyone read Liberty Bell 7? Over.

Hunt Club 1: Liberty Bell 7, Hunt Club 1 is now 2 miles southwest you.

Card File 9: Liberty Bell 7 this 9 Card File. We have your entry into the water. Will be over you in just about 30 seconds.

Bell 7: Roger, my condition is good; OK the capsule is floating, slowly coming vertical, have actuated the rescue aids. The reserve chute has jettisoned, in fact I can see it in the water, and the whip antenna should be up.

Communicator unidentified: Hunt Club, did you copy?

Communicator unidentified: OK, Hunt Club, this is . . . Don't forget the antenna.

Hunt Club 1: This is Hunt Club, say again.

Bell 7: Hunt Club, this is Liberty Bell 7. My antenna should be up.

Hunt Club 1: This is Hunt Club 1 . . . your antenna is erected.

Bell 7: Ah, roger.

Bell 7: OK, give me how much longer it'll be before you get here.

Hunt Club 1: This is Hunt Club 1, we are in orbit now at this time, around the capsule.

Bell 7: Roger, give me about another 5 minutes here, to mark these switch positions here, before I give you a call to come in and hook on. Are you ready to come in and hook on anytime?

Hunt Club 1: Hunt Club 1, roger we are ready anytime you are.

Bell 7: OK, give me about another 3 or 4 minutes here to take these switch positions, then I'll be ready for you.

Hunt Club 1: 1, wilco.

Card File 9: Hey Hunt Clubs, Card File, Card File 9, I'll stand by to escort you back as soon as you lift out. I keep other aircraft at at least 2,000 feet.

Hunt Club 1: Ah, Bell 7 this is Hunt Club 1.

Bell 7: Go, go ahead Hunt Club 1.

Hunt Club 1: Roger, this is 1, observe something, possibly the canister in the water along side capsule. Will we be interfering with any TM [telemetry] if we come down and take a look at it?

Bell 7: Negative, not at all, I'm just going to put the rest of this stuff on tape and then I'll be ready for you, in just about 2 more minutes, I would say.

Hunt Club 1: 1 Roger.

Cap Com: Liberty Bell 7, Cap Com at the Cape on a test count. Over.

Cap Com: Liberty Bell 7, Cape Cap Com on a test count. Over.

Card File 9: Any Hunt Club, this is 9 Card File.

Hunt Club 1: Station calling Hunt Club, say again.

Card File 9: This is Niner Cardfile, there's an object on a line in the water, ah, just about 160 degrees. The NASA people suspect it's the dye marker that didn't activate; ah, say it's about, ah, ¾ of a mile out from the capsule. Ah, after the lift out, will you take a check on it? Over.

Hunt Club 1: All, this is Hunt Club 1, Roger, will have Hunt Club 3 check at this time, you copy 3.

Hunt Club 3: Hunt Club 1, believe he said ¾ of a mile?

Card File 9: This is 9 Card, that is affirmative.

Bell 7: OK, Hunt Club. This is Liberty Bell 7. Are you ready for the pick-up?

Hunt Club 1: This is Hunt Club 1; this is affirmative.

Bell 7: OK, latch on, then give me a call and I'll power down and blow the hatch, OK?

Hunt Club 1: This is Hunt Club 1, roger, will give you a call when we're ready for you to blow.

Bell 7: Roger, I've unplugged my suit so I'm kinda warm now so.

Hunt Club 1: 1, Roger.

Bell 7: Now—if you tell me to, ah, you're ready for me to blow, I'll have to take my helmet off, power down, and then blow the hatch.

Hunt Club 1: 1, Roger, and when you blow the hatch, the collar will already be down there waiting for you, and we're turning back at this time.

Bell 7: Ah, Roger.

Chapter 1

1. Tom Wolfe, *The Right Stuff* (New York: Farrar, Straus, and Giroux, 1979), 288–89.

2. John J. Shaughnessy, "Grissom in Film not Right Stuff in Mitchell," *Indianapolis Star*, November 20, 1983.

3. Bill Head, interview with the author, May 14, 2003, Mitchell, Indiana, and Wolfe, *Right Stuff*, 112.

4. Mary G. Johnson, "Grissom Regarded as First-Rate Pilot," *Bedford Times-Mail*, January 25, 1997.

5. Ibid. See also Charles Murray and Catherine Bly Cox, *Apollo: Race to the Moon* (New York: Simon and Schuster, 1989), 221–22, and Sam Beddingfield, interview with the author, February 19, 2003, Titusville, Florida.

6. Glen E. Swanson, "*Liberty Bell 7* This Is *Hunt Club 1*," *Quest: The History of Spaceflight Quarterly* 7 (Spring 2000): 14.

7. David Mannweiler, "Wolfe Off Mark," *Indianapolis News*, October 21, 1983.

8. D. C. Agle, "Flying the Gusmobile," *Air & Space Magazine* (August/September 1998).

9. Donald K. "Deke" Slayton, *Deke! U.S. Manned Space: From Mercury to the Shuttle* (New York: Tom Doherty Associates, 1994), 191.

10. Michael Okuda, Denise Okuda, and Debbie Mirek, *The Star Trek Encyclopedia: A Reference Guide for the Future* (New York: Pocket

Books, 1994), 118; Madalyn Russell, "Tales from Innerspace: Recovering NASA's Liberty Bell 7," *Underwater Magazine* (Summer 1999); "Grissom's Widow Protests Mission to Recover Capsule," *Indianapolis Star*, April 17, 1999; "Finding Mercury Capsule 'A Sad Day,' Widow Says," *Indianapolis Star*, May 4, 1999; Discovery Online, "Liberating the Liberty Bell 7," http://www.discovery.com/exp/libertybell7/story.html; and "CSI: Crime Scene Investigation," Internet Movie Database, http://www.IMDb.com/.

11. Nelson Price, "The Century's Ten Greatest Hoosiers," *Indianapolis Star*, December 19, 1999.

12. Diana Wires, "Grissom Family Helps Dedicate Boyhood Home," *Hoosier Times*, September 28, 2003; Scott McGregor, "Indiana Is Launch Pad for Astronauts," *Indianapolis Star*, July 15, 2001; and "Martian Hills Named for Crew of Apollo 1," *Indianapolis Star*, February 1, 2004.

13. William Manchester, *The Glory and the Dream: A Narrative History of America, 1932–1972* (New York: Bantam Books, 1990), 785.

14. Sherman Adams, *Firsthand Report: The Story of the Eisenhower Administration* (New York: Harper and Brothers, 1961), 415.

15. Howard E. McCurdy, *Space and the American Imagination* (Washington, D.C.: Smithsonian Institution Press, 1997), 74–75.

16. Adams, *Firsthand Report*, 415.

17. Richard Hirsch and Joseph John Trento, *The National Aeronautics and Space Administration* (New York: Praeger Publishers, 1973), 13, and Loyd S. Swenson Jr., James M. Grimwood, and Charles C. Alexander, *This New Ocean: A History of Project Mercury* (Washington, D.C.: National Aeronautics and Space Administration, 1966), 28–29.

18. Paul Dickson, *Sputnik: The Shock of the Century* (New York: Walker and Company, 2001), 156.

19. Alan Shepard and Deke Slayton, *Moon Shot: The Inside Story of America's Race to the Moon* (Atlanta: Turner Publishing, 1994), 45.

20. William B. Breuer, *Race to the Moon: America's Duel with the Soviets* (Westport, Conn.: Praeger Publishers, 1993), 150; William E. Burrows, *This New Ocean: The Story of the First Space Age* (New York: Random House, 1998), 204–5; T. A. Heppenheimer, *Countdown: A History of Space Flight* (New York: John Wiley and Sons, 1997), 127–28; and Dickson, *Sputnik*, 158–59.

21. Gordon Cooper, Walter Schirra Jr., Alan Shepard Jr., John Glenn Jr., Scott Carpenter, Donald Slayton, Virgil Grissom, with Loudon

Wainwright, *The Astronauts: Pioneers in Space* (New York: Golden Press, 1961), 9, and Slayton, *Deke!* 74.

22. Shepard and Slayton, *Moon Shot*, 70.

23. James Schefter, *The Race: The Complete True Story of How America Beat Russia to the Moon* (New York: Anchor Books, 1999), 84–85.

24. Slayton, *Deke!*, 88.

25. Scott Carpenter et al., *We Seven* (New York: Simon and Schuster, 1962), 12, and Carl L. Chappell, *Seven Minus One: The Story of Gus Grissom* (Madison, Ind.: New Frontier Publishing, 1968), v.

26. Loudon Wainwright, *The Great American Magazine: An Inside History of* Life (New York: Alfred A. Knopf, 1986), 262–63, 274.

27. Walter Cunningham, *The All-American Boys* (New York: Macmillan Publishing Company, 1977), ix.

28. Burrows, *This New Ocean*, 441–43.

29. Wolfe, *Right Stuff*, 163, 168.

30. Cunningham, *All-American Boys*, 183.

31. William Goldman, *Adventures in the Screen Trade: A Personal View of Hollywood and Screenwriting* (New York: Warner Books, 1983), 238, 241.

32. Ibid., 241, and "20th Anniversary Retrospective Documentaries," *The Right Stuff*, DVD, Special Edition directed by Philip Kaufman, Warner Brothers, 2003. Also in the commentary, Barbara Hershey, who plays Chuck Yeager's wife Glennis, noted that the film served as the test pilot's "parade," because he never got one for breaking the sound barrier.

33. *The Right Stuff*, VHS, directed by Philip Kaufman, 193 min., Warner Brothers, 1983.

34. Slayton, *Deke!* 82. See also Swenson, Grimwood, and Alexander, *This New Ocean*, 131.

35. For details on the careers of Slayton and Shepard, see Slayton, *Deke!*, and Shepard and Slayton, *Moon Shot*.

36. Virgil Grissom, "You Just Don't Have Time to Get Frightened," *Life*, September 14, 1959.

37. Betty Grissom and Henry Still, *Starfall* (New York: Thomas Y. Crowell Company, 1974).

Chapter 2

1. Virgil I. Grissom, "Proud to Help Out," in Scott Carpenter et al., *We Seven* (New York: Simon and Schuster, 1962), 69.

2. Virgil Grissom, *Gemini: A Personal Account of Man's Venture into Space* (New York: Macmillan Company, 1968), 21.

3. Betty Grissom and Henry Still, *Starfall* (New York: Thomas Y. Crowell Company, 1974), 45.

4. Grissom, *Gemini*, 22.

5. Joseph D. Atkinson Jr. and Jay M. Shafritz, *The Real Stuff: A History of NASA's Astronaut Recruitment Program* (New York: Praeger Publishers, 1985), 38–43.

6. Grissom, *Gemini*, 17.

7. Joseph A. Batchelor, *An Economic History of the Indiana Oolitic Limestone Industry* (Bloomington: School of Business, Indiana University, 1944), 8, and Bill McDonald, *A Short History of Indiana Limestone* (Bedford, Ind.: Lawrence County Tourism Commission, 1995), 2, 7.

8. Batchelor, *Economic History of the Indiana Oolitic Limestone Industry*, 14, and Robert M. Taylor Jr., Errol Wayne Stevens, Mary Ann Ponder, and Paul Brockman, eds., *Indiana: A New Historical Guide* (Indianapolis: Indiana Historical Society, 1989), 314.

9. For Mitchell's early history, see *History of Lawrence County, Indiana* (Paoli, Ind.: Stout's Print Shop, 1884), 155; James W. Edwards, *History of Mitchell and Marion Township, Indiana* (Mitchell, Ind.: Mitchell Tribune, 1916), 119–20; Taylor et al., eds., *Indiana*, 335; and "Mitchell Historical Walking & Driving Tour," Lawrence County, Indiana, Web site, http://www.limestonecountry.com/MitchellTour.html.

10. Edwards, *History of Mitchell and Marion Township*, 146–47, and Taylor et al., eds., *Indiana*, 335.

11. Norman Grissom, interview with the author, August 30, 2001, Mitchell, Indiana.

12. Ibid.

13. Grissom and Still, *Starfall*, 9, and Carl L. Chappell, *Seven Minus One: The Story of Gus Grissom* (Mitchell, Ind.: New Fronter Publishing, 1968), 1–5.

14. Grissom, *Gemini*, 17, and Norman Grissom interview.

15. Grissom, *Gemini*, 17–18.

16. Jackie Schjeckler, "One of the First in Space," *Bloomington*

Herald-Times, July 21, 1991, and Nancy Lowe, "Hoosier Astronaut Traded BB Gun for 1st Air Jaunt," *Indianapolis Times*, April 12, 1959.

17. "Virgil I. Grissom: From Boy Scout to Astronaut," *Mitchell Tribune*, June 14, 1962.

18. Grissom and Still, *Starfall*, 8, 12, and "Virgil I. Grissom."

19. Grissom, *Gemini*, 17, and Chappell, *Seven Minus One*, 18–19.

20. "Virgil I. Grissom."

21. George Gill, "Space Man," *Louisville Courier-Journal Magazine*, March 12, 1961.

22. "Teen Topics," *Indianapolis Star Magazine*, September 14, 1969.

23. Betty Grissom, interview with the author, April 20, 2002, Houston, Texas.

24. Grissom, *Gemini*, 18, and Grissom and Still, *Starfall*, 13.

25. Betty Grissom interview.

26. Lori Beshears, "Mitchell Residents Remember a Real Hometown Hero—Virgil I. Grissom," *Bedford Times-Mail*, newspaper clipping file, Indiana Historical Society library, Indianapolis, Indiana.

27. Bill Head, interview with the author, May 14, 2003, Mitchell, Indiana.

28. See Betty Grissom interview; Grissom and Still, *Starfall*, 15; and Gill, "Space Man," 22.

29. Grissom, *Gemini*, 18.

30. Lowe, "Hoosier Astronaut Traded BB Gun for 1st Air Jaunt"; "Virgil I. Grissom"; and Betty Grissom interview.

31. Grissom and Still, *Starfall*, 18–19.

32. *Mitchell Tribune*, July 12, 1945.

33. See Betty Grissom interview, and Grissom and Still, *Starfall*, 23.

34. Grissom, *Gemini*, 18.

35. Betty Grissom interview, and Chappell, *Seven Minus One*, 30–31.

36. Robert W. Topping, *A Century and Beyond: The History of Purdue University* (West Lafayette, Ind.: Purdue University Press, 1988), 255, 258–59.

37. Betty Grissom interview; Chappell, *Seven Minus One*, 32; and "Virgil I. Grissom."

38. Grissom and Still, *Starfall*, 26; Betty Grissom interview; and Betty Grissom, "I Guess I Will Worry," *Life*, September 21, 1959.

39. Chappell, *Seven Minus One*, 33–34.

40. "Virgil I. Grissom"; Grissom, *Gemini*, 19; and Grissom and Still, *Starfall*, 28.

41. John Darrell Sherwood, *Officers in Flight Suits: The Story of American Air Force Fighter Pilots in the Korean War* (New York: New York University Press, 1996), 11–13.

42. "Virgil I. Grissom to Ride Mercury Capsule Tuesday," *Indianapolis Star*, July 16, 1961, and Grissom and Still, *Starfall*, 29–30.

43. Grissom and Still, *Starfall*, 30.

44. Grissom, *Gemini*, 19.

45. Betty Grissom interview. For the history of the Presque Isle Air Force Base, see Paul Freeman, "Abandoned and Little-Known Airfields: Maine," http://members.tripod.com/airfields_freeman/ME/Airfields_ME.htm.

46. Randy K. Mills, "Unexpected Journey: Evansville's Marine Corps Reserve and the Korean War," *Traces of Indiana and Midwestern History* 12, no. 3 (Summer 2000): 9.

47. Jennie Ethell Chancel and William R. Forstchen, eds., *Hot Shots: An Oral History of the Air Force Combat Pilots of the Korean War* (New York: William Morrow, 2000), 13–14; Walter J. Boyne, *Beyond the Wild Blue: A History of the United States Air Force, 1947–1997* (New York: St. Martin's Press, 1997), 59–60; and Judy C. Endicott, ed., *The U.S. Air Force in Korea: Campaigns, Units, and Stations, 1950–1953* (Washington, D.C.: Air Force History and Museums Program, 2001), 7–8.

48. Sherwood, *Officers in Flight Suits*, 74–75; Endicott, ed., *U.S. Air Force in Korea*, 16; and Wayne Thompson and Bernard C. Nalty, *Within Limits: The U.S. Air Force and the Korean War* (Washington, D.C.: Air Force History and Museums Program, 1996), 32.

49. Grissom and Still, *Starfall*, 36.

50. Sherwood, *Officers in Flight Suits*, 117, 121–22.

51. Grissom, "Proud to Help Out," 70, and Tom Wolfe, *The Right Stuff* (New York: Farrar, Straus, and Giroux, 1979), 41–42.

52. Grissom and Still, *Starfall*, 38, and Betty Grissom interview.

53. Betty Grissom interview.

54. Sherwood, *Officers in Flight Suits*, 78, and Grissom, "Proud to Help Out," 70–71.

55. "Our Men in Service," *Mitchell Tribune*, February 19, 1953.

56. Grissom and Still, *Starfall*, 39, and Betty Grissom interview.

57. Grissom, "Proud to Help Out," 71–72.

58. Betty Grissom interview, and Grissom and Still, *Starfall*, 40–41.

59. Sanders A. Laubenthal, "The Air Force Institute of Technology," in Lois E. Walker and Shelby E. Wickam, *From Huffman Prairie to the Moon: The History of Wright-Patterson Air Force Base* (Washington, D.C.: Air Force Logistics Command, 1986), 399, 412–13.

60. Gordon Cooper, *Leap of Faith: An Astronaut's Journey into the Unknown* (New York: HarperCollins, 2000), 22.

61. Grissom and Still, *Starfall*, 42, and Betty Grissom interview.

62. For a history of Edwards Air Force Base and the first supersonic flight, see "Edwards before the Military," Edwards Air Force Base Web site, http://www.edwards.af.mil/history/docs_html/center/premilitary_history.html; Chuck Yeager, *Yeager: An Autobiography* (New York: Bantam Books, 1985), 130; and Chuck Yeager, Bob Cardenas, Bob Hoover, Jack Russell, and James Young, *The Quest for Mach One: A First-Person Account of Breaking the Sound Barrier* (New York: Penguin Studio, 1997), 99–109. The XS-1 Yeager flew to supersonic speed is today at the Smithsonian Institution's National Air and Space Museum in Washington, D.C.

63. "U.S. Air Force Test Pilot School," Edwards Air Force Base Web site, http://www.edwards.af.mil/history.docs_html/center/test_pilot_school.html.

64. Rick Boos, "Life without Dad: An Interview with Scott Grissom," *Quest: The Magazine of Spaceflight* 5, no. 2 (1996): 58.

65. Betty Grissom interview.

66. Ibid.

67. Ibid. See also Paul Dickson, *Sputnik: The Shock of the Century* (New York: Walker and Company, 2001), 9; Rex Hall and David J. Shayler, *The Rocket Men: Vostok and Voskhod, The First Soviet Manned Spaceflights* (New York: Springer; Chichester [England]: Published in association with Praxis, 2001), 63; and David S. F. Portree, *NASA's Origins and the Dawn of the Space Age*, NASA History Division, September 1998, http://www.hq.nasa.gov/ office/pao/History/monograph10/.

Chapter 3

1. Milton Lehman, *This High Man: The Life of Robert H. Goddard* (New York: Farrar, Straus and Company, 1963), 34.

2. Jeffrey Kluger, "Rocket Scientist: Robert Goddard," *Time 100: Scientists and Thinkers*, http://www.time.com/time/time100/scientists/profile/goddard.html, and "Frequently Asked Questions about Dr. Robert H. Goddard," Dr. Robert H. Goddard Web site, Clark University, http://www.clarku.edu/offices/library/archives/Goddard FAQ.htm.

3. T. A. Heppenheimer, *Countdown: A History of Space Flight* (New York: John Wiley and Sons, 1997), 6–7; Roger D. Launius, *Frontiers of Space Exploration* (Westport, Conn.: Greenwood Press, 1998), 91–92; and "The Life of Konstantin Eduardovitch Tsiolkovsky," Konstantin E. Tsiolkovsky State Museum of the History of Cosmonautics, http://www.infomatics.org/museum/tsiol.html.

4. Asif A. Siddiqi, "Korolev, Sputnik, and the International Geophysical Year," NASA History Office Web site, http:// www.hq.nasa.gov/office/pao/History/sputnik/siddiqi.html.

5. William E. Burrows, *This New Ocean: The Story of the First Space Age* (New York: Random House, 1998), 187–88; Howard E. McCurdy, *Space and the American Imagination* (Washington, D.C.: Smithsonian Institution Press, 1997), 62; and Heppenheimer, *Countdown*, 124.

6. Roger D. Launius, *NASA: A History of the U.S. Civil Space Program* (Malabar, Fla.: Krieger Publishing Company, 1994), 25–26, and Heppenheimer, *Countdown*, 149.

7. Launius, *NASA*, 29–35. For NASA's beginnings, see also Richard Hirsch and Joseph John Trento, *The National Aeronautics and Space Administration* (New York: Praeger Publishers, 1973), 21–29.

8. Dr. Robert Gilruth, interview, February 27, 1987, National Air and Space Museum Oral History Project, http://www.nasm.si.edu/ TRANSCPT/GILRUTH5.HTM/research/dsh.

9. Allen O. Gamble, "Personal Recollections of the Selection of the First Seven Astronauts," speech given March 10, 1971, to the Men's Club of the Bethesda United Methodist Church, Bethesda, Maryland, http://geocities.com/mingomae/index.html.

10. Loyd S. Swenson Jr., James M. Grimwood, and Charles C. Alexander, *This New Ocean: A History of Project Mercury* (Washington, D.C.: National Aeronautics and Space Administration, 1966), 129–30.

11. Gamble, "Personal Recollections of the Selection of the First Seven Astronauts."

12. Joseph D. Atkinson Jr. and Jay M. Shafritz, *The Real Stuff: A*

History of NASA's Astronaut Recruitment Program (New York: Praeger Publishers, 1985), 36–37; Swenson, Grimwood, and Alexander, *This New Ocean*, 131; and Gamble, "Personal Recollections of the Selection of the First Seven Astronauts."

13. Gamble, "Personal Recollections of the Selection of the First Seven Astronauts."

14. Dr. Robert B. Voas, interview, May 19, 2002, NASA Johnson Space Center Oral History Collection, University of Houston–Clear Lake, Houston, Texas.

15. Atkinson and Shafritz, *Real Stuff*, 39–40, and Voas interview.

16. Chuck Yeager, *Yeager: An Autobiography* (New York: Bantam Books, 1985), 268, and Gordon Cooper, *Leap of Faith: An Astronaut's Journey into the Unknown* (New York: HarperCollins, 2000), 8.

17. Virgil I. Grissom, "Proud to Help Out," in Scott Carpenter et al., *We Seven* (New York: Simon and Schuster, 1962), 69–70.

18. Voas interview.

19. Atkinson and Shafritz, *Real Stuff*, 40–42; "Sample Questions from the Project Mercury Tests," NASA Release No. 59-136, May 12, 1959, NASA History Office Web site, http://history.nasa.gov/40thmerc7/ sample-questions.pdf; and Gamble, "Personal Recollections of the Selection of the First Seven Astronauts."

20. Betty Grissom, "I Guess I Will Worry," *Life*, September 21, 1959, p. 152, and Betty Grissom and Henry Still, *Starfall* (New York: Thomas Y. Crowell Company, 1974), 55–56.

21. Donald K. "Deke" Slayton, *Deke! U.S. Manned Space: From Mercury to the Shuttle* (New York: Thomas Doherty Associates, 1994), 71.

22. Martin Caidin, *The Astronauts: The Story of Project Mercury, America's Man-in-Space Program* (New York: E. P. Dutton and Company, 1960), 83; John Catchpole, *Project Mercury: NASA's First Manned Space Programme* (Chichester, England: Springer-Praxis Books in Astronomy and Space Sciences, 2001), 93; Walter M. Schirra Jr., *Schirra's Space* (Boston: Quinlan Press, 1988), 60; Atkinson and Shafritz, *Real Stuff*, 43; and Slayton, *Deke!*, 72.

23. Scott Carpenter and Kris Stoever, *For Spacious Skies: The Uncommon Journey of a Mercury Astronaut* (Orlando, Fla.: Harcourt, 2002), 187–88.

24. Caidin, *Astronauts*, 84–87, and Patricia A. Santy, *Choosing the*

Right Stuff: The Psychological Selection of Astronauts and Cosmonauts (Westport, Conn.: Praeger Publishing, 1994), 17.

25. Grissom, "Proud to Help Out," 72–73.

26. Ibid., 73.

27. Charles J. Donlan, interview, April 27, 1998, NASA Johnson Space Center Oral History Collection; Swenson, Grimwood, and Alexander, *This New Ocean*, 163; Atkinson and Shafritz, *Real Stuff*, 46; and Grissom, "Proud to Help Out," 73.

28. Santy, *Choosing the Right Stuff*, 19, 246, and Carpenter et al., *We Seven*, 8.

29. Tom Wolfe, *The Right Stuff* (New York: Farrar, Straus, and Giroux, 1979), 141, and John Glenn, *John Glenn: A Memoir* (New York: Bantam Books, 1999), 193–96.

30. Transcript of Press Conference, Mercury Astronaut Team, April 9, 1959, NASA History Office Web site, http://history.nasa.gov/40thmerc7/presscon.pdf, and Slayton, *Deke!*, 74.

31. Transcript of Press Conference.

32. Grissom and Still, *Starfall*, 60–61, and Betty Grissom, interview with the author, April 20, 2002, Houston, Texas.

33. Rick Boos, "Life without Dad: An Interview with Scott Grissom," *Quest: The Magazine of Spaceflight* 5, no. 2 (1996): 56, and Betty Grissom, "During Shot, Gus's Wife to Paste Trading Stamps," *Indianapolis Star*, March 21, 1965.

34. "Capt. Grissom One of 7 Spacemen," *Mitchell Tribune*, April 9, 1959; Norman Grissom, interview with the author, August 30, 2001, Mitchell, Indiana; "Grissom Always Liked Airplanes," *Bedford Daily Times-Mail*, April 10, 1959; and Nancy Lowe, "Hoosier Astronaut Traded BB Gun for 1st Air Jaunt," *Indianapolis Times*, April 12, 1959.

35. Bill Head, interview with the author, May 14, 2003, Mitchell, Indiana. See also Lori Beshears, "Mitchell Residents Remember a Real Hometown Hero—Virgil I. Grissom," *Bedford Times-Mail*, newspaper clipping file, Indiana Historical Society library, Indianapolis, Indiana.

36. Loudon Wainwright, *The Great American Magazine: An Inside History of* Life (New York: Alfred Knopf, 1986), 254–56.

37. Robert Sherrod, "The Selling of the Astronauts," *Columbia Journalism Review* (May/June 1973): 17; Wainwright, *Great American Magazine*, 262–63; and James L. Kauffman, *Selling Outer Space: Kennedy,*

the Media, and Funding for Project Apollo, 1961–1963 (Tuscaloosa: University of Alabama Press, 1994), 72.

38. Associated Press, *Footprints on the Moon* (New York: American Book—Stratford Press, 1969), 33; Glenn, *John Glenn*, 200–201; and Sherrod, "Selling of the Astronauts," 17.

39. Wainwright, *Great American Magazine*, 261–62, and Sherrod, "Selling of the Astronauts," 18.

40. Wainwright, *Great American Magazine*, 264, and Grissom and Still, *Starfall*, 66.

41. Wainwright, *Great American Magazine*, 269–71.

42. Virgil Grissom, "You Just Don't Have Time to Get Frightened," *Life*, September 14, 1959, p. 39.

43. Grissom, "I Guess I Will Worry."

44. Carpenter and Stoever, *For Spacious Skies*, 205.

45. Catchpole, *Project Mercury,* 249.

Chapter 4

1. Gordon Cooper, *Leap of Faith: An Astronaut's Journey into the Unknown* (New York: HarperCollins Publishers, 2000), 20.

2. Alan Shepard, interview, February 20, 1998, NASA Johnson Space Center Oral History Collection, University of Houston–Clear Lake, Houston, Texas.

3. Donald K. "Deke" Slayton, *Deke! U.S. Manned Space: From Mercury to the Shuttle* (New York: Tom Doherty Associates, 1994), 75.

4. Chris Gainor, *Arrows to the Moon: Avro's Engineers and the Space Race* (Burlington, Ontario: Apogee Books, 2001), 37.

5. Sam Beddingfield, interview with the author, February 19, 2003, Titusville, Florida.

6. Ibid. See also Mary T. Schmich, "The Other Stuff," *Orlando Sentinel*, November 6, 1983.

7. John Catchpole, *Project Mercury: NASA's First Manned Space Programme* (Chichester, England: Springer-Praxis Books in Astronomy and Space Sciences, 2001), 101–3, and Walter M. Schirra Jr., *Schirra's Space* (Boston: Quinlan Press, 1988), 70.

8. Chris Kraft, *Flight: My Life in Mission Control* (New York: Dutton, 2001), 91–94.

9. Cooper, *Leap of Faith*, 24, and Slayton, *Deke!* 80.

10. Slayton, *Deke!* 80–81, 98–99.

11. Dr. Robert B. Voas, interview, May 19, 2002, NASA Johnson Space Center Oral History Collection.

12. Walter Schirra, "Some Séances in the Room," in Scott Carpenter et al., *We Seven* (New York: Simon and Schuster, 1962), 121; Slayton, "A Job for Everybody," in ibid., 97–98; Schirra, *Schirra's Space*, 65; and Walter M. Schirra Jr., interview, December 1, 1998, NASA Johnson Space Center Oral History Collection.

13. Schirra, "Some Séances in the Room," 118–19, 122, and *Schirra's Space*, 66.

14. John Glenn, *John Glenn: A Memoir* (New York: Bantam Books, 1999), 215; Catchpole, *Project Mercury*, 98–99; Loyd S. Swenson Jr., James M. Grimwood, and Charles C. Alexander, *This New Ocean: A History of Project Mercury* (Washington, D.C.: National Aeronautics and Space Administration, 1966), 237; and Douglas J. Ingells, *The McDonnell Douglas Story* (Fallbrook Calif.: Aero Publishers, 1979), 232.

15. Schirra interview.

16. Michael Collins, *Liftoff: The Story of America's Adventure in Space* (New York: Grove Press, 1988), 47.

17. For quote, see "The Astronauts—Ready to Make History," *Life*, September 14, 1959, p. 26.

18. Glenn, *John Glenn*, 220.

19. Ibid.

20. Tom Wolfe, *The Right Stuff* (New York: Farrar, Straus, and Giroux, 1979), 170–75, and Glenn, *John Glenn*, 221.

21. Malcom Scott Carpenter, "The One Unknown," in Carpenter et al., *We Seven*, 189–91.

22. Swenson, Grimwood, and Alexander, *This New Ocean*, 238–39, and William K. Douglas, interview, February 13, 1986, NASA Johnson Space Center Oral History Collection. Douglas noted that only one of the original seven astronauts "didn't accept my presence" and came up to him early in the program and told him he would have chosen another man to serve as flight surgeon. A year later, however, the astronaut came to him and admitted he had been wrong and expressed appreciation for Douglas's efforts. Douglas interview.

23. Gus Grissom, "The Three-Way Spin," in Carpenter et al., *We*

Seven, 195–99, and Glenn, *John Glenn*, 217.

24. Schirra, *Schirra's Space*, 67–68, and Catchpole, *Project Mercury*, 108.

25. Deke Slayton, "A Standing Start," in Carpenter et al.,*We Seven*, 175.

26. Betty Grissom and Henry Still, *Starfall* (New York: Thomas Y. Crowell Company, 1974), 71, 73, and Rick Boos, "Life without Dad: An Interview with Scott Grissom," *Quest: The Magazine of Spaceflight* 5, no. 2 (1996): 56.

27. Grissom and Still, *Starfall*, 135–36.

28. Guenter Wendt and Russell Still, *The Unbroken Chain* (Burlington, Ontario: Apogee Books, 2001), 27, and William Barnaby Faherty, *Florida's Space Coast: The Impact of NASA on the Sunshine State* (Gainesville: University Press of Florida, 2002), 2, 15.

29. Wendt and Still, *Unbroken Chain*, 27, and Henri Landwirth, *Gift of Life* (n.p., 1996), 97.

30. Wendt and Still, *Unbroken Chain*, 12. See also Alan Shepard and Deke Slayton, *Moon Shot: The Inside Story of America's Race to the Moon* (Atlanta: Turner Publishing, 1994), 86–87, and Landwirth, *Gift of Life*, 103, 119.

31. Landwirth, *Gift of Life*, 119, and Douglas interview.

32. Schirra, *Schirra's Space*, 74.

33. Jim Rathmann, interview with the author, February 18, 2003, Melbourne, Florida. See also Schirra, *Schirra's Space*, 139, and Grissom and Still, *Starfall*, 138. Schirra explained that the astronauts' affinity for racecar drivers came from sharing a "high-risk profession. They put their lives on the line doing what we called their low-altitude orbits." See Schirra, *Schirra's Space*, 142.

34. Wendt and Still, *Unbroken Chain*, 28.

35. Shepard and Slayton, *Moon Shot*, 84–85.

36. Wendt and Still, *Unbroken Chain*, 28.

37. Rathmann interview.

38. See Kraft, *Flight*, 118–20, and Schirra, *Schirra's Space*, 72–73.

39. Catchpole, *Project Mercury*, 251, and John Glenn, "Glitches in Time Save Trouble," in Carpenter et al., *We Seven*, 216.

40. Schmich, "Other Stuff," and Joe W. Schmitt, interview, July 1997, NASA Johnson Space Center Oral History Collection.

41. Glenn, *John Glenn*, 232; Slayton, *Deke!* 93; and Kraft, *Flight*, 124.

42. Slayton, *Deke!* 93; Shepard interview; and Shepard and Slayton, *Moon Shot*, 81.

43. Betty Grissom, interview with the author, April 20, 2002, Houston, Texas.

44. Loudon Wainwright, *The Great American Magazine: An Inside History of* Life (New York: Alfred A. Knopf, 1986), 273.

45. Glenn, *John Glenn*, 233–34.

46. "Glenn: An Unswerving and a Self-Denying Man Engaged in a Stern, Dangerous Pursuit," *Life*, March 3, 1961, p. 26, and "Shepard: A Cool Customer and a Hot Pilot with an Eye for the Big Picture," ibid., 30.

47. "Grissom: A Quiet Little Fellow Who Scoffs at the Chance of Becoming a Hero," *Life*, March 3, 1961, pp. 28–29.

48. Slayton, *Deke!*, 93–94, and Schirra, *Schirra's Space*, 72.

49. Catchpole, *Project Mercury*, 249, and Slayton, *Deke!* 95. When asked to take the NASA job, Webb at first demurred, saying he did not have the necessary technical skills. Kennedy, however, responded by telling Webb he wanted him because of his experience in shaping government policy. "There are great issues of national and international policy involved in this program," said Kennedy. "I want you because you have been involved in policy at the White House level, State Department level." See W. Henry Lambright, *Powering Apollo: James E. Webb of NASA* (Baltimore: Johns Hopkins University Press, 1995), 84.

50. Rex Hall and David J. Shayler, *The Rocket Men: Vostok and Voshkod, The First Soviet Manned Spaceflights* (New York: Springer; Chichester [England]: Published in association with Praxis, 2001), 138–41.

51. Catchpole, *Project Mercury*, 259–63; Kraft, *Flight*, 127; and Shepard and Slayton, *Moon Shot*, 91.

52. Catchpole, *Project Mercury*, 271–72, and National Aeronautics and Space Administration, Launch Operations Directorate, Public Information Office, "Comment by Mercury Astronaut Virgil I. Grissom," April 12, 1961, http://www. pao.ksc.nasa.gov/kscpao/ release/1961/4-12-61b.htm.

53. Hugh Sidey, *John F. Kennedy, President* (New York: Atheneum, 1964), 114.

54. Sidey, *John F. Kennedy*, 122–23, and John M. Logsdon, *The Decision to Go to the Moon: Project Apollo and the National Interest*

(Cambridge, Mass.: Massachusetts Institute of Technology Press, 1970), 107.

55. Stephen J. Garber, "Multiple Means to an End: A Reexamination of President Kennedy's Decision to Go to the Moon," *Quest: The History of Spaceflight Quarterly* 7 (summer 1999): 5–6; Roger D. Launius, *NASA: A History of the U.S. Civil Space Program* (Malabar, Fla.: Krieger Publishing Company, 1994), 60; Logsdon, *Decision to Go to the Moon;* and Lambright, *Powering Apollo*, 95.

56. Cooper, *Leap of Faith*, 31, and Virgil Grissom, *Gemini: A Personal Account of Man's Venture into Space* (New York: Macmillan Company, 1968), 35–36.

57. Shepard and Slayton, *Moon Shot*, 102; Slayton, *Deke!* 97; and William E. Burrows, *The Infinite Journey: Eyewitness Accounts of NASA and the Age of Space* (New York: Discovery Books, 2000), 45.

58. Alan Shepard, "The First American," in Carpenter et al., *We Seven*, 240–42.

59. Catchpole, *Project Mercury*, 280–82; Swenson, Grimwood, and Alexander, *This New Ocean*, 351–52; Shepard and Slayton, *Moon Shot*, 104–8; and Slayton, *Deke!* 98.

Chapter 5

1. John M. Logsdon, *The Decision to Go to the Moon: Project Apollo and the National Interest* (Cambridge, Mass.: Massachusetts Institute of Technology Press, 1970), 125–29; Alan Shepard and Deke Slayton, *Moon Shot: The Inside Story of America's Race to the Moon* (Atlanta: Turner Publishing, 1994), 128–29; and William E. Burrows, *The Infinite Journey: Eyewitness Accounts of NASA and the Age of Space* (New York: Discovery Books, 2000), 46.

2. John F. Kennedy, "Special Message to the Congress on Urgent National Needs," http://www.cs.umb.edu/jfklibrary/ j052561.htm, and John Catchpole, *Project Mercury: NASA's First Manned Space Programme* (Chichester, England: Springer-Praxis Books in Astronomy and Space Sciences, 2001), 292–93.

3. Logsdon, *Decision to Go to the Moon*, 129, and Roger D. Launius, *NASA: A History of the U.S. Civil Space Program* (Malabar, Fla.: Krieger Publishing Company, 1994), 65.

4. W. Henry Lambright, *Powering Apollo: James E. Webb of NASA*

(Baltimore: Johns Hopkins University Press, 1995), 101.

5. Jerome B. Hammack, "Spacecraft and Flight Plan for the Mercury-Redstone 4 Flight," in *Results of the Second U.S. Manned Suborbital Space Flight, July 21, 1961* (Washington, D.C.: National Aeronautics and Space Administration, 1961), 3–4, and Loyd S. Swenson Jr., James M. Grimwood, and Charles C. Alexander, *This New Ocean: A History of Project Mercury* (Washington, D.C.: National Aeronautics and Space Administration, 1966), 365–69.

6. Swenson, Grimwood, and Alexander, *This New Ocean*, 365–69. See also Guenter Wendt and Russell Still, *The Unbroken Chain* (Burlington, Ontario: Apogee Books, 2001), 38.

7. Gus Grissom, "The Trouble with Liberty Bell," in Scott Carpenter et al., *We Seven* (New York: Simon and Schuster, 1962), 269, and Carpenter quote in *In Search of the* Liberty Bell 7, VHS, 104 min., Discovery Communications, 1999.

8. Grissom, "Trouble with Liberty Bell," 270, and Chris Kraft, *Flight: My Life in Mission Control* (New York: Dutton, 2001), 145.

9. Grissom, "Trouble with Liberty Bell," 272–73 and "It Was a Good Flight and a Great Float," *Life*, July 28, 1961, p. 27.

10. Grissom, "Trouble with Liberty Bell," 275 and "It Was a Good Flight and a Great Float," 27.

11. Grissom, "Trouble with Liberty Bell," 278.

12. Ibid., 278–79.

13. Ibid. See also Betty Grissom and Henry Still, *Starfall* (New York: Thomas Y. Crowell Company, 1974), 91.

14. Swenson, Grimwood, and Alexander, *This New Ocean*, 368; John Glenn, *John Glenn: A Memoir* (New York: Bantam Books, 1999), 239; and Grissom, "Trouble with Liberty Bell," 280.

15. Glenn, *John Glenn*, 240, and Shepard and Slayton, *Moon Shot*, 141.

16. Grissom, "Trouble with Liberty Bell," and William K. Douglas, "Flight Surgeon's Report for Mercury-Redstone Missions 3 and 4," in *Results of the Second U.S. Manned Suborbital Space Flight*, 24.

17. Grissom, "Trouble with Liberty Bell," 283–84, and William K. Douglas et al., "Results of the MR-4 Preflight and Postflight Medical Examination Conducted on Astronaut Virgil I. Grissom," in *Results of the Second U.S. Manned Suborbital Space Flight*, 9.

18. Grissom, "Trouble with Liberty Bell," 284–85.

19. Ibid., 286, and Wendt quote, *In Search of the* Liberty Bell 7.

20. Betty Grissom, "Nothing So Important as 'I Love You,'" *Life*, July 28, 1961, p. 29, and Gus Grissom, "Trouble with Liberty Bell," 287.

21. "Weather Again Delays Astronaut; Grissom Ready to Go Tomorrow," *Indianapolis Star*, July 20, 1961, and Gus Grissom, "Trouble with Liberty Bell," 287.

22. *Moon Shot: The Inside Story of the Apollo Project*, directed by Kirk Wolfinger, VHS, 192 min., Turner Home Video, 1994, and Betty Grissom, "Nothing So Important as 'I Love You.'"

23. Virgil Grissom, "A Hero Admits He Was Scared," *Life*, August 4, 1961, and "Pilot's Flight Report," in *Results of the Second U.S. Manned Suborbital Space Flight*, 51.

24. Grissom, "Trouble with Liberty Bell," 290–91 and "Pilot's Flight Report," 52.

25. Grissom, "Pilot's Flight Report," 53; *Project Mercury Postlaunch Report for Mercury-Redstone Mission 4 (MR-4 Capsule 11)*, September 22, 1961, Kennedy Space Center Archives, John F. Kennedy Space Center, Florida; and Catchpole, *Project Mercury*, 298–99.

26. Grissom, "Trouble with Liberty Bell," 293; "Air-Ground Communications for MR-4" in *Results of the Second U.S. Manned Suborbital Space Flight*, 45; Ron White, "The Right Stuff, The Wrong Story: A 'Hollywood History' Blurs the Truth Behind America's Second Manned Spaceflight," *Quest: The History of Spaceflight Magazine* 2 (Fall 1993): 18; and Kraft quote, *In Search of the* Liberty Bell 7.

27. Grissom, "Pilot's Flight Report," 54–55 and "A Hero Admits He Was Scared."

28. Glen E. Swanson, "*Liberty Bell 7*, This is *Hunt Club 1*," *Quest: The History of Spaceflight Quarterly* 7 (Spring 2000): 12–13; Swenson, Grimwood, and Alexander, *This New Ocean*, 373; and "Air-Ground Communications for MR-4," 45–46.

29. Grissom, "Trouble with Liberty Bell," 295, and *Project Mercury Postlaunch Report for Mercury-Redstone Mission 4.*

30. Swanson, "*Liberty Bell 7*," p. 13, Grissom, "Trouble with Liberty Bell," 295 and "A Hero Admits He Was Scared."

31. Swanson, "*Liberty Bell 7*," pp. 13–14. Asked what he might have done if the chip indicator warning light had not flashed on, Lewis said he

would have attempted to hover with the spacecraft underwater until the carrier arrived on the scene. "Of course," he added, "if that happened, figuring out how to bring the spacecraft aboard the carrier would have been a challenge." Ibid.

32. Curt Newport, *Lost Spacecraft: The Search for* Liberty Bell 7 (Burlington, Ontario: Apogee Books, 2002), 82; Robert F. Thompson, interview, August 29, 2000, NASA Johnson Space Center Oral History Collection, University of Houston–Clear Lake, Houston, Texas; Grissom, "Trouble with Liberty Bell," 296–97 and "A Hero Admits He Was Scared."

33. *Project Mercury Postlaunch Report for Mercury-Redstone Mission 4*; Grissom, "Trouble with Liberty Bell," 297–98 and "Hero Admits He Was Scared"; "Grissom OK Despite Swim," *Indianapolis Star*, July 22, 1961; and "Saga of the Liberty Bell," *Time*, July 28, 1961, p. 35.

34. Eugene Kranz, *Failure Is Not an Option: Mission Control from Mercury to Apollo 13 and Beyond* (New York: Simon and Schuster, 2000), 57–58, and Kraft, *Flight*, 146.

35. Grissom, "Nothing So Important as 'I Love You,'" 29, and "Capsule's Loss Almost Causes Wife to Weep," *Indianapolis Star*, July 22, 1961.

36. Don Reeder, "Grissoms Are Happy, Relieved It's All Over," *Bedford Daily Times-Mail*, July 21, 1961, and Bob Collins, "Mitchell Breathes Easier, Prouder," *Indianapolis Star*, July 22, 1961.

37. "Grissom OK Despite Swim," *Indianapolis Star*, July 22, 1961; Douglas et al., "Results of the MR-4 Preflight and Postflight Medical Examiniation," 10; and Grissom, "Trouble with Liberty Bell," 298.

38. Newport, *Lost Spacecraft*, 93; "Grissom Gets a Salute Reserved for Admirals," *New York Times*, July 22, 1961; and Douglas, "Flight Surgeon's Report," 29.

39. Grissom, "Nothing So Important as 'I Love You,'" and Grissom and Still, *Starfall*, 103–4.

40. "Grissom Reports Flight Details and Gets Medal," *Indianapolis Star*, July 23, 1961, and John W. Finney, "Grissom Receives Medal for Flight," *New York Times*, July 23, 1961.

41. John W. Finney, "Unplanned Swim Leaves Grissom 'A Little Uneasy,'" *New York Times*, July 22, 1961; "Grissom Receives Medal for Flight"; *In Search of the* Liberty Bell 7; "A-Okay—Almost All the Way," *Newsweek*, July 31, 1961; and Grissom, "A Hero Admits He Was Scared."

42. Tom Wolfe, *The Right Stuff* (New York: Farrar, Straus, and

Giroux, 1979), 292–94; *The Right Stuff*, directed by Philip Kaufman, VHS, 193 min., Warner Brothers, 1983; and Betty Grissom, interview with the author, Houston, Texas, April 20, 2002.

43. Rick Boos, "Life without Dad: An Interview with Scott Grissom," *Quest: The Magazine of Spaceflight* 5, no. 2 (1996): 57.

44. "Gus Won't Be Able to Attend Big Festival," *Bedford Daily Times-Mail*, July 25, 1961.

45. Wolfe, *Right Stuff*, 280, 289–90, and Newport, *Lost Spacecraft*, 90–91.

46. "A-Okay—Almost All the Way;" Swenson, Grimwood, and Alexander, *This New Ocean*, 376; Catchpole, *Project Mercury*, 304; and Sam Beddingfield, interview with the author, February 19, 2003, Titusville, Florida.

47. Thompson interview.

48. Kraft, *Flight*, 147; Wendt and Still, *Unbroken Chain*, 41; and Thompson interview.

49. For details on the Mercury missions from Glenn to Cooper, see Catchpole, *Project Mercury*, 320–83.

50. *In Search of the* Liberty Bell 7, and Catchpole, *Project Mercury*, 363.

51. Cece Bibby Web site, http://freepages.genealogy.rootsweb.com/~cecebibby/nasa-stories/naked-lady.htm. See also Cece Bibby, e-mail to author, May 9, 2003.

52. Walter M. Schirra Jr., *Schirra's Space* (Boston: Quinlan Press, 1988), 94.

Chapter 6

1. Roger D. Launius, *NASA: A History of the U.S. Civil Space Program* (Malabar, Fla.: Krieger Publishing Company, 1994), 75–77; Barton C. Hacker and James M. Grimwood, *On the Shoulders of Titans: A History of Project Gemini* (Washington, D.C.: National Aeronautics and Space Administration, 1977), 60–62; and David J. Shayler, *Gemini: Steps to the Moon* (Chichester, England: Springer-Praxis Books in Astronomy and Space Sciences, 2001), 13–14.

2. W. Henry Lambright, *Powering Apollo: James E. Webb of NASA* (Baltimore: Johns Hopkins University Press, 1995), 112–13.

3. Robert R. Gilruth, "I Believe We Should Go to the Moon," in *Apollo Expeditions to the Moon*, Edgar M. Cortright, ed. (Washington, D.C.: National Aeronautics and Space Administration, 1975), 33.

4. "World Spaceflight News Special Report: Gemini Program Material," National Aeronautics and Space Administration Fact Sheet #291, February 1965, Kennedy Space Center Archives, John F. Kennedy Space Center, Florida; Shayler, *Gemini*, 23–24; Hacker and Grimwood, *On the Shoulders of Titans*, 3; Lambright, *Powering Apollo*, 110.

5. Henry C. Dethloff, *Suddenly, Tomorrow Came—:A History of the Johnson Space Center* ([Houston, Tex.]: Lyndon B. Johnson Space Center; [Washington, D.C.]: National Aeronautics and Space Administration, 1993), 38–40, and Lambright, *Powering Apollo*, 106–7.

6. Dethloff, *Suddenly, Tomorrow Came*, 124.

7. "During Shot, Gus's Wife to Paste Trading Stamps," *Indianapolis Star*, March 21, 1965; Betty Grissom and Henry Still, *Starfall* (New York: Thomas Y. Crowell Company, 1974), 118, 121; and Thomas P. Stafford, *We Have Capture: Tom Stafford and the Space Race* (Washington, D.C.: Smithsonian Institution Press, 2002), 43.

8. Joseph D. Atkinson Jr. and Jay M. Shafritz, *The Real Stuff: A History of NASA's Astronaut Recruitment Program* (New York: Praeger Publishers, 1985), 10; Shayler, *Gemini*, 83–85; Donald K. "Deke" Slayton, *Deke! U.S. Manned Space: From Mercury to the Shuttle* (New York: Tom Doherty Associates, 1994), 123; Stafford, *We Have Capture*, 41–42; and *Moon Shot: The Inside Story of the Apollo Project*, directed by Kirk Wolfinger, VHS, 192 min., Turner Home Video, 1994.

9. Virgil Grissom, "If It Goes Wrong, I'll Be Responsible," *Life*, June 5, 1964, pp. 118, 121, and D. C. Agle, "Flying the Gusmobile," *Air and Space Magazine* (August/September 1998).

10. "World Spaceflight News Special Report"; Shayler, *Gemini*, 29–31; and Grissom, "If It Goes Wrong," 118.

11. "World Spaceflight News Special Report"; Virgil Grissom, *Gemini: A Personal Account of Man's Venture into Space*, (New York: Macmillian Company, 1968), 49; and Shayler, *Gemini*, 29–41.

12. Grissom, *Gemini*, 42 and "If It Goes Wrong," 118.

13. Alan Shepard and Deke Slayton, *Moon Shot: The Inside Story of America's Race to the Moon* (Atlanta: Turner Publishing, 1994), 177; Agle, "Flying the Gusmobile"; and Stafford, *We Have Capture*, 52–53.

14. Charles W. Mathews, interview, February 25, 1999, NASA Johnson Space Center Oral History Collection, University of Houston–Clear Lake, Houston, Texas, and Slayton, *Deke!* 125.

15. Shepard and Slayton, *Moon Shot*, 166–67; Grissom and Still, *Starfall*, 131; and Hacker and Grimwood, *On the Shoulders of Titans*, 182.

16. Donald K. "Deke" Slayton, interview, October 15, 1984, Apollo Spacecraft History Interviews, Johnson Space Center History Collection and *Deke!* 136–37.

17. Slayton, *Deke!* 136–37.

18. Charles A. Berry, interview, April 29, 1999, NASA Johnson Space Center Oral History Collection, and Shepard and Slayton, *Moon Shot*, 168–69. Shepard cemented his reputation as the "icy commander" during his early days as head of the astronaut office, and his grounding did not sit well with the Mercury veteran. Shepard's secretary, Gaye Alford, warned astronauts of her boss's mood by hanging up one of two different photos of Shepard, one of him smiling and the other of him scowling. Shepard and Slayton, *Moon Shot*, 177–78.

19. Frank Borman, *Countdown: An Autobiography* (New York: Silver Arrow Books, 1988), 102; Eugene Cernan and Don Davis, *The Last Man on the Moon: Astronaut Eugene Cernan and America's Race in Space* (New York: St. Martin's Press, 1999), 66; and Slayton, *Deke!*, 138.

20. Hacker and Grimwood, *On the Shoulders of Titans*, 219; "Grissom, Rookie Picked for Gemini Hop," *Indianapolis Star*, April 14, 1964; and "Gus Is Gemini Pilot," *Mitchell Tribune*, April 16, 1964.

21. Stafford, *We Have Capture*, 52; Grissom, *Gemini*, 74, 79; and Hacker and Grimwood, *On the Shoulders of Titans*, 222–23.

22. John Young, "When I Came Aboard I Felt Like a Rookie," *Life*, June 5, 1964; Michael Collins, *Liftoff: The Story of America's Adventure in Space* (New York: Grove Press, 1988), 83; and Fred Kelly, *America's Astronauts and Their Indestructible Spirit* (Blue Ridge Summit, Pa.: Aero, 1986), 72–77.

23. Grissom, *Gemini*, 93–94; Slayton, *Deke!* 148; and Shayler, *Gemini*, 141. According to Chris Kraft, Gilruth refused orders from George E. Mueller, associate administrator for manned spaceflight at NASA headquarters in Washington, D.C., to get Grissom to change the name *Molly Brown*. See Kraft, *Flight: My Life in Mission Control* (New York: Dutton, 2001), 212.

24. Frank Macomber, "Grissom, Young to Orbit Thrice," *Indianapolis*

Star, January 17, 1965; Hacker and Grimwood, *On the Shoulders of Titans*, 227–31; Young, "When I Came Aboard I Felt Like a Rookie;" and Grissom, *Gemini*, 97–98.

25. Grissom, *Gemini*, 99–100, and Kraft, *Flight*, 214.

26. Kraft, *Flight*, 214; "Gemini 3 Flight," National Aeronautics and Space Administration Fact Sheet #291-A, April 1965, Kennedy Space Center Archives, and Grissom, *Gemini*, 101–2.

27. Shayler, *Gemini*, 185; Stafford, *We Have Capture*, 57; and Walter M. Schirra Jr., *Schirra's Space* (Boston: Quinlan Press, 1988), 148–49. Schirra noted that the corned beef sandwich was not the first time astronauts had received special rations. Gordon Cooper, who served as backup on Schirra's *Sigma 7* mission, had stocked the spacecraft with a steak sandwich, a small bottle of Scotch, and five cigarettes. "My restraint harness prevented me from reaching the goodies, or I might have eaten the sandwich," said Schirra. "Smoking and drinking, of course, were forbidden." Schirra, *Schirra's Space*, 149.

28. Grissom, *Gemini*, 104, 106, and Guenter Wendt and Russell Still, *The Unbroken Chain* (Burlington, Ontario: Apogee Books, 2001), 75.

29. Wendt and Still, *Unbroken Chain*, 75; "Gemini III Mission Final Report," Mission Operation Report, No. M-913-66-03, Kennedy Space Center Archives; and Grissom, *Gemini*, 107.

30. Gus Grissom and John Young, "Molly Brown Was OK from the First Time We Met Her," *Life*, April 2, 1965, p. 41; Evert Clark, "Astronauts Call Flight Almost Perfect," *New York Times*, March 26, 1965; and "Gemini 3 Flight."

31. Grissom, *Gemini*, 110, and "Gemini III Mission Final Report."

32. Grissom and Young, "Molly Brown Was OK from the First Time We Met Her," 42; "Gemini III Mission Final Report"; Transcript of Grissom and Young press conference, *New York Times*, March 26, 1965; Grissom, *Gemini*, 110–11; and Wendt and Still, *Unbroken Chain*, 76.

33. "Gemini 3 Flight"; Hacker and Grimwood, *On the Shoulders of Titans*, 235; and Grissom and Young, "Molly Brown Was OK from the First Time We Met Her," 42.

34. Grissom and Young, "Molly Brown Was OK from the First Time We Met Her," 42; Grissom, *Gemini*, 112–13; and "Gemini III Mission Final Report."

35. "Gemini III Mission Final Report," and Grissom, *Gemini*, 113.

36. "Gemini III Mission Final Report"; Grissom and Young, "Molly Brown Was OK from the First Time We Met Her," 42; and Grissom, *Gemini*, 113–14.

37. Grissom, *Gemini*, 114; "Johnson to Grissom: 'Gus? How Are You?'"; and "Astronauts' Total Pay for 3 Orbits Was $70," *New York Times*, March 24, 1965. The Associated Press noted that Grissom made $1,191.33 per month and Young $1,084.83. Using those figures, the AP came up with the $70 pay for the two astronauts based on each working a forty-hour week and the flight lasting five hours. See "Astronauts' Total Pay for 3 Orbits Was, $70."

38. "'Anxiously Awaiting Lift-Off,' Hoosier Astronaut Tells Parents," *Mitchell Tribune*, March 18, 1965; "Mitchell Applauds Gus' Space Success," ibid., March 25, 1965; and "Mitchell Proud of Achievement by Favorite Son," *Bedford Daily Times-Mail*, March 23, 1965.

39. "Mitchell Proud of Achievements by Favorite Son," and "Parents of 'Gus' are Proud, Happy, Relieved," *Bedford Daily Times-Mail*, March 24, 1965.

40. "During Shot, Gus's Wife to Paste Trading Stamps"; Grissom and Still, *Starfall*, 151; and Rick Boos, "Life without Dad: An Interview with Scott Grissom," *Quest: The Magazine of Spaceflight* 5, no. 2 (1996): 57.

41. "Astronauts Call Flight Almost Perfect."

42. "'Gus,' Young Are Praised in Capital," *Bedford Daily Times-Mail*, March 26, 1965; "Tickertape Parade Next Tribute to Space Twins," ibid., March 27, 1965; "'Gus,' Young Honored with New York Parade," ibid., March 29, 1965; "Windy City in Orbit Over Twin Astronauts," ibid., March 30, 1965; and Grissom, *Gemini*, 115–16.

43. Shepard and Slayton, *Moon Shot*, 180; Kraft, *Flight*, 216; and Slayton, *Deke!* 149.

44. Slayton, *Deke!* 164.

45. Jim Rathmann, interview with the author, February 18, 2003, Melbourne, Florida, and Grissom and Still, *Starfall*, 163, 166, 172.

Chapter 7

1. Wernher von Braun, "Saturn the Giant," in *Apollo Expeditions to the Moon*, Edgar M. Cortright, ed. (Washington, D.C.: National Aeronautics and Space Administration, 1975), 46, and Saturn 5 press kit,

"The Saturn V," Marshall Space Flight Center Web site, http://history. msfc.nasa.gov/saturnV/Saturn_V.pdf.

2. Roger D. Launius, *NASA: A History of the U.S. Civil Space Program* (Malabar, Fla.: Krieger Publishing Company, 1994), 70–73; Courtney G. Brooks, James M. Grimwood, and Loyd S. Swenson Jr., *Chariots for Apollo: A History of Manned Lunar Spacecraft* (Washington, D.C.: National Aeronautics and Space Administration, 1979), 42–44; William E. Burrows, *This New Ocean: The Story of the First Space Age* (New York: Random House, 1998), 372.

3. Walter M. Schirra Jr., *Schirra's Space* (Boston: Quinlan Press, 1988), 178, and Mike Gray, *Angle of Attack: Harrison Storms and the Race to the Moon* (New York: W. W. Norton and Company, 1992), 117–19.

4. Gray, *Angle of Attack*, 250, and W. Henry Lambright, *Powering Apollo: James E. Webb of NASA* (Baltimore: Johns Hopkins University Press, 1995), 107–8.

5. Michael Collins, *Liftoff: The Story of America's Adventure in Space* (New York: Grove Press, 1988), 128–34, and Dick Lattimer, *"All We Did Was Fly to the Moon"* (Gainesville, Fla.: Whispering Eagle Press, 1985), 42–43.

6. John Noble Wilford, "Crew of 3 Named for Apollo Orbit," *New York Times*, March 22, 1966, and Donald K. "Deke" Slayton, *Deke! U.S. Manned Space: From Mercury to the Shuttle* (New York: Tom Doherty Associates, 1994), 165.

7. "Gus to Make Third Space Flight," *Mitchell Tribune*, March 24, 1966; "'It's His Work' Grissoms Say," *Bedford Daily Times-Mail*, March 22, 1966; and "Grissom Apollo Ship Pilot," *Indianapolis Star*, March 22, 1966.

8. Betty Grissom and Henry Still, *Starfall* (New York: Thomas Y. Crowell Company, 1974), 161–62, and "Grissom Hints Interest in Career in Politics," *Indianapolis Star*, February 20, 1966. In pursuing a political career, Grissom would have traveled a path blazed by his brother, Norman, who served as a Republican member of the Mitchell City Council.

9. John Noble Wilford, *We Reach the Moon: The* New York Times *Story of Man's Greatest Adventure* (New York: Bantam Books, 1969), 94; Joseph F. Shea, interview, August 26, 1998, NASA Johnson Space Center Oral History Collection, University of Houston–Clear Lake, Houston, Texas; Collins, *Liftoff*, 135; Thomas P. Stafford, *We Have Capture: Tom Stafford and the Space Race* (Washington, D.C.: Smithsonian Institution

Press, 2002), 98–99; and Slayton, *Deke!* 181.

10. Betty Grissom, interview with the author, April 20, 2002, Houston, Texas; Grissom and Still, *Starfall*, 179–82; Slayton, *Deke!* 186; Guenter Wendt and Russell Still, *The Unbroken Chain* (Burlington, Ontario: Apogee Books, 2001), 97; and Brooks, Grimwood, and Swenson, *Chariots for Apollo*, 209.

11. Gray, *Angle of Attack*, 139–41, and Max Faget, interview, June 18–19, 1997, NASA Johnson Space Center Oral History Collection.

12. Walter Cunningham, *The All-American Boys* (New York: Macmillan Publishing Company, 1977), 77–80; Slayton, *Deke!* 182–83; Walter M. Schirra Jr., interview, December 1, 1998, NASA Johnson Space Center Oral History Collection; and Schirra, *Schirra's Space*, 181–82.

13. Grissom and Still, *Starfall*, 179, and Betty Grissom interview.

14. "Fire in the Spacecraft," *Newsweek*, February 6, 1967, p. 26; Daniel R. Champagne, "'We've Got a Fire in the Cockpit!' The Tragic Story of *Apollo 1*," *Quest: The History of Spaceflight Quarterly* 9, no. 5 (2002): 21; and "Entire Crew of Mission Set for Feb. 21 Is Lost: Grissom, White, Chaffee," *Washington Post*, January 28, 1967.

15. Brooks, Grimwood, and Swenson, *Chariots for Apollo*, 209, 211; Walter Cunningham, interview, May 24, 1999, NASA Johnson Space Center Oral History Collection; *Moon Shot: The Inside Story of the Apollo Project*, directed by Kirk Wolfinger, VHS, 192 min., Turner Home Video, 1994; and Eugene Cernan and Don Davis, *The Last Man on the Moon: Astronaut Eugene Cernan and America's Race in Space* (New York: St. Martin's Press, 1999), 1–2.

16. *Moon Shot*, and Schirra, *Schirra's Space*, 182–83.

17. Joseph F. Shea, interview with Robert Sherrod, May 16, 1971, Johnson Space Center Collection; Slayton, *Deke!* 188–89; Deke Slayton, interview with Robert Sherrod, July 26, 1972, Johnson Space Center Collection; and "Apollo Tragedy Almost Claimed a Fourth," *Washington Post*, February 12, 1967.

18. Brooks, Grimwood, and Swenson, *Chariots for Apollo*, 214, and David J. Shayler, *Disasters and Accidents in Manned Spaceflight* (Chichester, England: Springer-Praxis Books in Astronomy and Space Sciences, 2000), 100.

19. Charles D. Benson and William Barnaby Faherty, *Moonport: A History of Apollo Launch Facilities and Operations* (Washington, D.C.:

National Aeronautics and Space Administration, 1978), 390–91; Slayton interview; and *Report of Apollo 204 Review Board*, NASA Historical Reference Collection, NASA History Office, NASA Headquarters, Washington, D.C., http://www.hq.nasa.gov/office/pao/History/Apollo204/as204report.html.

20. Collins, *Liftoff*, 135; Benson and Faherty, *Moonport*, 391; and *Witness Statements and Releases: Appendix B to Final Report of Apollo 204 Review Board*, Johnson Space Center Collection.

21. Shayler, *Disasters and Accidents in Manned Spaceflight*, 105; "3 Astronauts Death Laid to Asphyxia," *Baltimore Sun*, February 4, 1967; and Benson and Faherty, *Moonport*, 391.

22. *Witness Statements and Releases*, and "The Ten Desperate Minutes," *Life*, April 21, 1967.

23. *Witness Statements and Releases*. See also Charles Murray and Catherine Bly Cox, *Apollo: Race to the Moon* (New York: Simon and Schuster, 1989), 198; "A/S 204 Release #2," John F. Kennedy Space Center, January 27, 1967, Johnson Space Center Collection; and "Fire in the Spacecraft."

24. Sam Beddingfield, interview with the author, February 19, 2003, Titusville, Florida. See also Murray and Cox, *Apollo*, 208–9, and William E. Burrows, *The Infinite Journey: Eyewitness Accounts of NASA and the Age of Space* (New York: Discovery Books, 2000), 77.

25. Slayton, *Deke!* 189–90, and Fred Kelly, *America's Astronauts and Their Indestructible Spirit* (Blue Ridge Summit, Pa.: Aero, 1986), 123–24.

26. Betty Grissom interview; Rick Boos, "Life without Dad: An Interview with Scott Grissom," *Quest: The Magazine of Spaceflight* 5, no. 2 (1996): 58; and Grissom and Still, *Starfall*, 188–89.

27. Grissom and Still, *Starfall*, 189; Jackie Shecklere, "One of the First in Space," *Bloomington Herald-Times*, July 21, 1991; "Tour Cape Kennedy," *Mitchell Tribune*, January 26, 1967; Norman Grissom, interview with the author, August 30, 2001, Mitchell, Indiana; "Hoosier Hometown Not Forgetting Grissom," *Elkhart Truth*, January 27, 1997; and "Grissom's Home Town Stunned by News of Death," *Bedford Daily Times-Mail*, January 28, 1967.

28. Rick Johnson, "Grissom's Kin, All of Mitchell Shaken," *Indianapolis Star*, January 29, 1967, and "Grissom's Home Town Stunned by News of Death."

29. Shayler, *Disasters and Accidents in Manned Spaceflight*, 106–7; autopsy report, enclosure to *Report of Apollo 204 Review Board*; and Kelly, *America's Astronauts and Their Indestructible Spirit*, 126–27.

30. Autopsy report.

31. Lambright, *Powering Apollo*, 145–47; Robert C. Seamans Jr., *Aiming at Targets: The Autobiography of Robert C. Seamans Jr.* (Washington, D.C.: NASA History Office, 1996), n.p.; "LBJ Leads Nation in Mourning," *Bedford Daily Times-Mail*, January 28, 1967; and "Entire Crew of Mission Set for Feb. 21 Is Lost."

32. Frank Murray, "Reporters Off, Tight Security Held on Apollo Tragedy," *Editor & Publisher*, February 4, 1967; "Reproduction of the Pool Report of the White Room at Complex 34 by George Alexander," January 29, 1967, Johnson Space Center Collection; and Shayler, *Disasters and Accidents in Manned Spaceflight*, 112.

33. "Services for the Apollo 204 Crew," NASA Press Release, Johnson Space Center Collection; "Families Attend Texas Services," *Washington Star*, January 30, 1967; "2 Astronauts' Bodies Brought Here for Burial," *Washington Post*, January 31, 1967; and Phil Casey, "Grissom and Chaffee Are Buried in Arlington, White at West Point," *Washington Post*, February 1, 1967.

34. Ben Cole, "LBJ Leads Mourning at Grissom Burial," *Indianapolis Star*, February 1, 1967; Casey, "Grissom and Chaffee are Buried in Arlington"; "Johnson Leads Mourners at Military Services for 'Gus,'" *Bedford Daily Times-Mail*, January 31, 1967; and Grissom and Still, *Starfall*, 191.

35. "Mitchell High School Honors Astronaut at Memorial Service," *Mitchell Tribune*, February 2, 1967, and "Memorial at Park May Honor 'Gus,'" *Bedford Daily Times-Mail*, January 28, 1967.

36. Seamans, *Aiming at Targets*, n.p.; Walter M. Schirra Jr., interview, December 1, 1998, NASA Johnson Space Center Oral History Collection; and Frank Borman, *Countdown: An Autobiography* (New York: Silver Arrow Books, 1988), 173–75.

37. Shea interview with Sherrod.

38. "Part V: Investigation and Analysis, Inspection and Disassembly," *Report of Apollo 204 Review Board*, Johnson Space Center Collection, and Brooks, Grimwood, and Swenson, *Chariots for Apollo*, 220–21.

39. "Excerpts from *Report of Apollo 204 Review Board*," Johnson

Space Center Collection; Borman, *Countdown*, 175; John Noble Wilford, "Apollo Fire Review Board Finds 'Many Deficiencies': Calls for Safety Moves," *New York Times*, April 10, 1967; and Brooks, Grimwood, and Swenson, *Chariots for Apollo*, 221.

40. "Report Called a NASA Indictment," *Houston Post*, April 10, 1967; "The Phillips Report," NASA Historical Reference Collection, NASA History Office Web site, http://www.hq.nasa.gov/office/pao/History/Apollo204/phillip1.html; Mark Damohn, "An Interview with Walter F. Mondale," *Quest: The History of Spaceflight Quarterly* 8, no. 2 (2000): 64.

41. William Hines, "Space Firm Defends Its Work in Apollo Project at Hearing," *Washington Evening-Star*, April 11, 1967; Brooks, Grimwood, and Swenson, *Chariots for Apollo*, 224–25; Thomas O'Toole, "Oxygen Fire Kills 2 at Space School," *Washington Post*, February 1, 1967; John Noble Wilford, "Apollo's Maker Concedes Error," *New York Times*, April 12, 1967; J. Leland Atwood, interview, January 12, 1990, Oral History Project, National Air and Space Museum Web site, http://www.nasm.si/edu/nasm/dsh/TRANSCPT/ATWOOD6.HTM; and Schirra, *Schirra's Space*, 185. Thomas Baron, a quality inspector for North American at Cape Kennedy, had been very critical of his employer and had written reports indicating his displeasure and negative comments supposedly from other employees. He passed along these reports to his supervisors. Baron testified before Congress, but his allegations were refuted by some of the sources he had cited as being critical of North American. Baron and his family were killed in a crash shortly after his testimony. See Brooks, Grimwood, and Swenson, *Chariots for Apollo*, 222–23, and Gray, *Angle of Attack*, 244.

42. William Hines, "Scratch One Hypothesis," *Washington Evening-Star*, April 12, 1967; Slayton, *Deke!* 195; and Gray, *Angle of Attack*, 248–49.

43. Benson and Faherty, *Moonport*, 400; Wendt and Still, *Unbroken Chain*, 98–99; George Low, "The Spaceships," in *Apollo Expeditions to the Moon*, 73; and Collins, *Liftoff*, 137.

44. Petrone and Kraft quoted in *Nova: To the Moon*, DVD, 120 min., WGBH Boston, 2000.

45. Collins, *Liftoff*, 138; *Moon Shot;* and Schirra, *Schirra's Space*, 189, 204–5. The tense exchanges between the *Apollo 7* astronauts and ground controllers in Houston prompted Kraft to tell Slayton the crew should not

be allowed to fly in space again. This proved to be no problem for Schirra, who retired from the program, but it meant that Cunningham and Eisele were cut off from future missions. "I still believe the entire Apollo 7 crew was tarred and feathered due to the actions of Wally Schirra during those eleven days in October," Cunningham said. See Chris Kraft, *Flight: My Life in Mission Control* (New York: Dutton, 2001), 291, and Cunningham, *All-American Boys*, 183.

Epilogue

1. John Noble Wilford, *We Reach the Moon: The* New York Times *Story of Man's Greatest Adventure* (New York: Bantam Books, 1969), 267–68, and Michael Collins, *Liftoff: The Story of America's Adventure in Space* (New York: Grove Press, 1988), 8.

2. Betty Grissom and Henry Still, *Starfall* (New York: Thomas Y. Crowell Company, 1974), 219–20; Valerie Neal, Cathleen S. Lewis, and Frank H. Winter, *Spaceflight: A Smithsonian Guide* (New York: Macmillan, 1995), 149; and Rick Boos, "Life without Dad: An Interview with Scott Grissom," *Quest: The Magazine of Spaceflight* 5, no. 2 (1996): 59.

3. "Young: Gus Rare Individual," *Bedford Daily Times-Mail*, July 21, 1971; "Gus Made Important Space Contributions," *Mitchell Tribune*, July 22, 1971; and Jean Hawkins, "Tributes Paid to Grissom," *Indianapolis Star*, July 21, 1971.

4. "Mrs. Grissom Sues for $10 Million," *Indianapolis Star*, January 19, 1971; Grissom and Still, *Starfall*, 237–48; and Donna Knight, "Astronaut's Widow Calmly Enjoys Quiet Life," *Indianapolis Star*, December 10, 1974.

5. Mary Beth Schneider, "Grissom Feels America Forgot 1st NASA Tragedy," *Indianapolis Star*, February 2, 2003; Steve Herz, "My Astronaut Dad Was Murdered!," *The Star*, February 16, 1999; and John Zarrella, "NASA, Grissom Widow Spar Over Spacesuit," CNN.com Web site, http://www.cnn.com/2002/TECH/space/11/25/grissom.spacesuit/index.html.

6. "Grissom's Widow Protests Mission to Recover Capsule," *Indianapolis Star*, April 17, 1999, and Guenter Wendt and Russell Still, *The Unbroken Chain* (Burlington, Ontario: Apogee Books, 2001), 203. For a complete detailing of the recovery of the *Liberty Bell 7* spacecraft, see Curt Newport, *Lost Spacecraft: The Search for* Liberty Bell 7 (Burlington,

Ontario: Apogee Books, 2002).

7. "Liberty Bell 7 Capsule Raised from Ocean Floor," CNN.com Web site, http://www.cnn.com/TECH/space/9907/20/grissom.capsule.01/; Newport, *Lost Spacecraft*, 173; and Wendt and Still, *Unbroken Chain*, 209.

8. Dan McCue, *The Stuart News*, March 13, 2000, and Marcia Dunn, "Space Capsule May Unlock Mystery," MSNBC Web site, http://www.msnbc.com/news/343255.asp.

9. John Masson, "A Capsule Look at Space: Liberty Bell 7 Exhibit Opens at Children's Museum Today," *Indianapolis Star*, October 7, 2000.

Books

Adams, Sherman. *Firsthand Report: The Story of the Eisenhower Administration*. New York: Harper and Brothers, 1961.

Atkinson, Joseph D. Jr., and Jay M. Shafritz. *The Real Stuff: A History of NASA's Astronaut Recruitment Program*. New York: Praeger Publishers, 1985.

Benson, Charles D., and William Barnaby Faherty. *Moonport: A History of Apollo Launch Facilities and Operations*. Washington, D.C.: National Aeronautics and Space Administration, 1978.

Borman, Frank. *Countdown: An Autobiography*. New York: Silver Arrow Books, 1988.

Boyne, Walter J. *Beyond the Wild Blue: A History of the United States Air Force, 1947–1997*. New York: St. Martin's Press, 1997.

Breuer, William B. *Race to the Moon: America's Duel with the Soviets*. Westport, Conn.: Praeger Publishers, 1993.

Brooks, Courtney G., James M. Grimwood, and Loyd S. Swenson Jr. *Chariots for Apollo: A History of Manned Lunar Spacecraft*. Washington, D.C.: National Aeronautics and Space Administration, 1979.

Burrows, William E. *The Infinite Journey: Eyewitness Accounts of NASA and the Age of Space*. New York: Discovery Books, 2000.
———. *This New Ocean: The Story of the First Space Age*. New York: Random House, 1998.

Caidin, Martin. *The Astronauts: The Story of Project Mercury, America's Man-in-Space Program*. New York: E. P. Dutton and Company, 1960.

Carpenter, Scott, and Kris Stoever. *For Spacious Skies: The Uncommon Journey of a Mercury Astronaut*. Orlando, Fla.: Harcourt, 2002.

———, Gordon Cooper, John Glenn, Virgil Grissom, Walter Schirra Jr., Alan Shepard, and Donald Slayton. *We Seven*. New York: Simon and Schuster, 1962.

Catchpole, John. *Project Mercury: NASA's First Manned Space Programme*. Chichester, England: Springer-Praxis Books in Astronomy and Space Sciences, 2001.

Cernan, Eugene, and Don Davis. *The Last Man on the Moon: Astronaut Eugene Cernan and America's Race in Space*. New York: St. Martin's Press, 1999.

Chaikin, Andrew. *A Man on the Moon: The Voyages of the Apollo Astronauts*. New York: Viking, 1994.

Chancel, Jennie Ethell, and William R. Forstchen, eds. *Hot Shots: An Oral History of the Air Force Combat Pilots of the Korean War*. New York: William Morrow, 2000.

Chappell, Carl L. *Seven Minus One: The Story of Gus Grissom*. Madison, Ind.: New Frontier Publishing, 1968.

Collins, Michael. *Liftoff: The Story of America's Adventure in Space*. New York: Grove Press, 1988.

Cooper, Gordon. *Leap of Faith: An Astronaut's Journey into the Unknown*. New York: HarperCollins, 2000.

Cortright, Edgar M., ed. *Apollo Expeditions to the Moon*. Washington, D.C.: National Aeronautics and Space Administration, 1975.

Cunningham, Walter. *The All-American Boys*. New York: Macmillan Publishing Company, 1977.

Dethloff, Henry C. *Suddenly, Tomorrow Came—: A History of the Johnson Space Center*. [Houston, Tex.]: Lyndon B. Johnson

Space Center; [Washington, D.C.]: National Aeronautics and Space Administration, 1993.

Dickson, Paul. *Sputnik: The Shock of the Century*. New York: Walker and Company, 2001.

Edwards, James W. *History of Mitchell and Marion Township, Indiana*. Mitchell, Ind.: Mitchell Tribune, 1916.

Endicott, Judy C., ed. *The U.S. Air Force in Korea: Campaigns, Units, and Stations, 1950–1953*. Washington, D.C.: Air Force History and Museums Program, 2001.

Faherty, William Barnaby. *Florida's Space Coast: The Impact of NASA on the Sunshine State*. Gainesville: University Press of Florida, 2002.

Gainor, Chris. *Arrows to the Moon: Avro's Engineers and the Space Race*. Burlington, Ontario: Apogee Books, 2001.

Glenn, John. *John Glenn: A Memoir*. New York: Bantam Books, 1999.

Goldman, William. *Adventures in the Screen Trade: A Personal View of Hollywood and Screenwriting*. New York: Warner Books, 1983.

Gray, Mike. *Angle of Attack: Harrison Storms and the Race to the Moon*. New York: W. W. Norton and Company, 1992.

Grissom, Betty, and Henry Still. *Starfall*. New York: Thomas Y. Crowell Company, 1974.

Grissom, Virgil. *Gemini: A Personal Account of Man's Venture into Space*. New York: Macmillan Company, 1968.

Hall, Rex, and David J. Shayler. *The Rocket Men: Vostok and Voskhod, The First Soviet Manned Spaceflights*. London and New York: Springer; Chichester [England]: Published in association with Praxis, 2001.

Hacker, Barton C., and James M. Grimwood. *On the Shoulders of Titans: A History of Project Gemini*. Washington, D.C.: National Aeronautics and Space Administration, 1977.

Heppenheimer, T. A. *Countdown: A History of Space Flight*. New York: John Wiley and Sons, 1997.

Hirsch, Richard, and Joseph John Trento. *The National Aeronautics and Space Administration.* New York: Praeger Publishers, 1973.

Ingells, Douglas J. *The McDonnell Douglas Story*. Fallbrook, Calif.: Aero Publishers, 1979.

Kauffman, James L. *Selling Outer Space: Kennedy, the Media, and Funding for Project Apollo, 1961–1963*. Tuscaloosa: University of Alabama Press, 1994.

Kelly, Fred. *America's Astronauts and Their Indestructible Spirit*. Blue Ridge Summit, Pa.: Aero, 1986.

Kraft, Chris. *Flight: My Life in Mission Control*. New York: Dutton, 2001.

Kranz, Eugene. *Failure Is Not an Option: Mission Control from Mercury to Apollo 13 and Beyond*. New York: Simon and Schuster, 2000.

Lambright, W. Henry. *Powering Apollo: James E. Webb of NASA*. Baltimore: Johns Hopkins University Press, 1995.

Landwirth, Henri; *Gift of Life*. N.p., 1996.

Lattimer, Dick. *"All We Did Was Fly to the Moon."* Gainesville, Fla.: Whispering Eagle Press, 1985.

Launius, Roger D. *Frontiers of Space Exploration*. Westport, Conn.: Greenwood Press, 1998.

———. *NASA: A History of the U.S. Civil Space Program*. Malabar, Fla.: Krieger Publishing Company, 1994.

Lehman, Milton. *This High Man: The Life of Robert H. Goddard*. New York: Farrar, Straus and Company, 1963.

Logsdon, John M. *The Decision to Go to the Moon: Project Apollo and the National Interest*. Cambridge, Mass.: Massachusetts Institute of Technology Press, 1970.

Manchester, William. *The Glory and the Dream: A Narrative History of America, 1932–1972*. New York: Bantam Books, 1990.

McCurdy, Howard E. *Space and the American Imagination*. Washington, D.C.: Smithsonian Institution Press, 1997.

Murray, Charles, and Catherine Bly Cox. *Apollo: Race to the Moon*. New York: Simon and Schuster, 1989.

Neal, Valerie, Cathleen S. Lewis, and Frank H. Winter. *Spaceflight: A Smithsonian Guide*. New York: Macmillan, 1995.

Newport, Curt. *Lost Spacecraft: The Search for* Liberty Bell 7. Burlington, Ontario: Apogee Books, 2002.

Santy, Patricia A. *Choosing the Right Stuff: The Psychological Selection of Astronauts and Cosmonauts*. Westport, Conn.: Praeger Publishing, 1994.

Schefter, James. *The Race: The Complete True Story of How America Beat Russia to the Moon*. New York: Anchor Books, 1999.

Schirra, Walter M. Jr. *Schirra's Space*. Boston: Quinlan Press, 1988.

Shayler, David J. *Disasters and Accidents in Manned Spaceflight*. Chichester, England: Springer-Praxis Books in Astronomy and Space Sciences, 2000.

———. *Gemini: Steps to the Moon*. Chichester, England: Springer-Praxis Books in Astronomy and Space Sciences, 2001.

Shepard, Alan, and Deke Slayton. *Moon Shot: The Inside Story of America's Race to the Moon*. Atlanta: Turner Publishing, 1994.

Sherwood, John Darrell. *Officers in Flight Suits: The Story of American Air Force Fighter Pilots in the Korean War*. New York: New York University Press, 1996.

Sidey, Hugh F. *John F. Kennedy, President*. New York: Atheneum, 1964.

Slayton, Donald K. "Deke." *Deke! U.S. Manned Space: From Mercury to the Shuttle*. New York: Tom Doherty Associates, 1994.

Stafford, Thomas P. *We Have Capture: Tom Stafford and the Space Race*. Washington, D.C.: Smithsonian Institution Press, 2002.

Swenson, Loyd S. Jr., James M. Grimwood, and Charles C. Alexander. *This New Ocean: A History of Project Mercury*. Washington, D.C.: National Aeronautics and Space Administration, 1966.

Taylor, Robert M. Jr., Errol Wayne Stevens, Mary Ann Ponder, and Paul Brockman, eds. *Indiana: A New Historical Guide*. Indianapolis: Indiana Historical Society, 1989.

Thompson, Wayne, and Bernard C. Nalty. *Within Limits: The U.S. Air Force and the Korean War*. Washington, D.C.: Air Force History and Museums Program, 1996.

Topping, Robert W. *A Century and Beyond: The History of Purdue University*. West Lafayette, Ind.: Purdue University Press, 1988.

Wainwright, Loudon. *The Great American Magazine: An Inside History of* Life. New York: Alfred A. Knopf, 1986.

Walker, Lois E., and Shelby E. Wickam, *From Huffman Prairie to the Moon: The History of Wright-Patterson Air Force Base*. Washington, D.C.: Air Force Logistics Command, 1986.

Wendt, Guenter, and Russell Still. *The Unbroken Chain*. Burlington,

Ontario: Apogee Books, 2001.

Wilford, John Noble. *We Reach the Moon: The* New York Times *Story of Man's Greatest Adventure*. New York: Bantam Books, 1969.

Wolfe, Tom. *The Right Stuff*. New York: Farrar, Straus, and Giroux, 1979.

Yeager, Chuck. *Yeager: An Autobiography*. New York: Bantam Books, 1985.

————, Bob Cardenas, Bob Hoover, Jack Russell, and James Young. *The Quest for Mach One: A First-Person Account of Breaking the Sound Barrier*. New York: Penguin Studio, 1997.

Periodicals, reports, media, and interviews

Agle, D. C. "Flying the Gusmobile," *Air & Space Magazine* (August/September 1998).

Beddingfield, Sam. Interview with the author. February 19, 2003. Titusville, Florida.

Berry, Charles A. Interview. April 29, 1999. NASA Johnson Space Center Oral History Collection. University of Houston–Clear Lake, Houston, Texas.

Boos, Rick. "Life without Dad: An Interview with Scott Grissom." *Quest: The Magazine of Spaceflight* 5, no. 2 (1996).

Champagne, Daniel R. "'We've Got a Fire in the Cockpit!' The Tragic Story of *Apollo 1*." *Quest: The History of Spaceflight Quarterly* 9, no. 5 (2002).

Cunningham, Walter. Interview. May 24, 1999. NASA Johnson Space Center Oral History Collection. University of Houston–Clear Lake, Houston, Texas.

Donlan, Charles J. Interview. April 27, 1998. NASA Johnson Space Center Oral History Collection. University of Houston–Clear Lake, Houston, Texas.

Douglas, William K. Interview. February 13, 1986. NASA Johnson Space Center Oral History Collection. University of Houston–Clear Lake, Houston, Texas.

Faget, Max. Interview. June 18–19, 1997. NASA Johnson Space Center Oral History Collection. University of Houston–Clear

Lake, Houston, Texas.

Final Report of Apollo 204 Review Board. Johnson Space Center Collection. University of Houston–Clear Lake, Houston, Texas.

"Fire in the Spacecraft." *Newsweek*, February 6, 1967.

Gamble, Allen O. "Personal Recollections of the Selection of the First Seven Astronauts." Speech given March 10, 1971, to the Men's Club of the Bethesda United Methodist Church, Bethesda, Maryland. http://geocities.com/mingomae/index.html.

Garber, Stephen J. "Multiple Means to an End: A Reexamination of President Kennedy's Decision to Go to the Moon." *Quest: The History of Spaceflight Quarterly* 7 (Summer 1999).

"Gemini 3 Flight." National Aeronautics and Space Administration Fact Sheet #291-A, April 1965. Kennedy Space Center Archives. John F. Kennedy Space Center, Florida.

"Gemini III Mission Final Report." Mission Operation Report, No. M-913-66-03. Kennedy Space Center Archives. John F. Kennedy Space Center, Florida.

Grissom, Betty. Interview with the author. April 20, 2002, Houston, Texas.

———. "I Guess I Will Worry." *Life*, Sept. 21, 1959.

Grissom, Norman. Interview with author. August 30, 2001, Mitchell, Indiana.

Grissom, Virgil. "If it Goes Wrong, I'll Be Responsible." *Life*, June 5, 1964.

———. "You Just Don't Have Time to Get Frightened." *Life*, September 14, 1959.

———, and John Young. "Molly Brown Was OK from the First Time We Met Her." *Life*, April 2, 1965.

Head, Bill. Interview with the author. May 14, 2003, Mitchell, Indiana.

In Search of the Liberty Bell 7. VHS, 104 min. Discovery Communications, 1999.

Mathews, Charles W. Interview. February 25, 1999. NASA Johnson Space Center Oral History Collection. University of Houston–Clear Lake, Houston, Texas.

Mills, Randy K. "Unexpected Journey: Evansville's Marine Corps Reserve and the Korean War." *Traces of Indiana and*

Midwestern History 12, no. 3 (Summer 2000).

Moon Shot: The Inside Story of the Apollo Project. Directed by Kirk Wolfinger. VHS, 192 min. Turner Home Video, 1994.

Rathmann, Jim. Interview with the author. February 18, 2003, Melbourne, Florida.

Results of the Second U.S. Manned Suborbital Space Flight, July 21, 1961. Washington, D.C.: National Aeronautics and Space Administration, 1961.

The Right Stuff. Directed by Phil Kaufman. VHS, 193 min. Warner Brothers, 1983.

Schirra, Walter M. Jr. Interview. December 1, 1998. NASA Johnson Space Center Oral History Collection. University of Houston–Clear Lake, Houston, Texas.

Schmitt, Joe W. Interview. July 1997. NASA Johnson Space Center Oral History Collection. University of Houston–Clear Lake, Houston, Texas.

Shea, Joseph F. Interview. August 26, 1998. NASA Johnson Space Center Oral History Collection. University of Houston–Clear Lake, Houston, Texas.

———. Interview with Robert Sherrod. May 16, 1971. Johnson Space Center Collection. University of Houston–Clear Lake, Houston, Texas.

Shepard, Alan. Interview. February 20, 1998. NASA Johnson Space Center Oral History Collection. University of Houston–Clear Lake, Houston, Texas.

Sherrod, Robert. "The Selling of the Astronauts." *Columbia Journalism Review* (May/June 1973).

Slayton, Donald K. "Deke." Interview. October 15, 1984. Apollo Spacecraft History Interviews. Johnson Space Center History Collection. University of Houston–Clear Lake, Houston, Texas.

Swanson, Glen E. "*Liberty Bell 7* This is *Hunt Club 1*," *Quest: The History of Spaceflight Quarterly* 7 (Spring 2000).

Thompson, Robert F. Interview. August 29, 2000. NASA Johnson Space Center Oral History Collection. University of Houston–Clear Lake, Houston, Texas.

Voas, Dr. Robert B. Interview. May 19, 2002. NASA Johnson Space Center Oral History Collection. University of Houston–Clear

Lake, Houston, Texas.

White, Ron. "The Right Stuff, The Wrong Story: A 'Hollywood History'
Blurs the Truth Behind America's Second Manned Spaceflight."
Quest: The History of Spaceflight Magazine 2 (Fall 1993).

"World Spaceflight News Special Report: Gemini Program Material."
National Aeronautics and Space Administration Fact Sheet
#291, February 1965. Kennedy Space Center Archives. John F.
Kennedy Space Center, Florida

Young John. "When I Came Aboard I Felt Like a Rookie." *Life*, June
5, 1964.

00403 7704